A
GOOD
START

Register This New Book

Benefits of Registering*

- ✓ FREE **replacements** of lost or damaged books

- ✓ FREE **audiobook** – *Pilgrim's Progress,* audiobook edition

- ✓ FREE information about new titles and other **freebies**

www.anekopress.com/new-book-registration

*See our website for requirements and limitations.

A GOOD START

A Book FOR Young Men AND Women

CHARLES H. SPURGEON

**WITH AN INTRODUCTION BY
SIR GEORGE WILLIAMS,**
Founder and President of the Young
Men's Christian Association

ANEKO
PRESS

We enjoy hearing from our readers. Please contact us at www.anekopress.com/questions-comments with any questions, comments, or suggestions.

Cover Designer: Jonathan Lewis

Editor: Paul Miller

Aneko Press

www.anekopress.com

Aneko Press, Life Sentence Publishing, and our logos are trademarks of

Life Sentence Publishing, Inc.

203 E. Birch Street

P.O. Box 652

Abbotsford, WI 54405

JUVENILE NONFICTION / Religious / Christian / Values & Virtues

Paperback ISBN: 978-1-62245-870-7

eBook ISBN: 978-1-62245-871-4

10   9   8   7   6   5   4   3   2   1

Available where books are sold

CONTENTS

INTRODUCTION

This book is intended especially for those who are in the springtime of life. It is during this character-forming time of life that wise counsel, faithful warning, and sympathetic admonition are especially valuable.

Many young men and young women fail in life from the lack of a friendly guiding word at the beginning of their career, while many who now occupy good and honorable positions, owe and attribute their success to the early timely counsel of some friend who was practically interested in their welfare.

Mr. Spurgeon was emphatically the friend of the young. During the course of his successful and God-honored ministry, his supreme aim was to lead them to Christ and to encourage and stimulate them in their aspirations after true nobility. Now that his voice is hushed, his powerful pen still speaks. In this book, with persuasive earnestness and characteristic force, he shows those who are standing upon the threshold of life how to make *A Good Start*.

It is impossible to overestimate the importance of the start we make in the journey of life since it necessarily affects and largely determines all that follows.

By personal experience, I can bear my absolute testimony to the wisdom and perceptiveness of the teaching of my friend C. H. Spurgeon. No life can be truly successful unless lived along the lines of Christian principles. The first step must be surrendering the heart to Christ, and all of life's journey must be lived in conscious fellowship with Him. In this way, we form true perceptions of life and duty, and are enabled to give practical embodiment to God's idea concerning us.

I hope that this book is widely circulated, and I pray that it may be used by God to help thousands of young men and young women not only make a good start, but also to help them build up and live useful, righteous, and God-glorifying lives.

– George Williams

CHAPTER 1

A YOUNG MAN IN CHRIST

Someone who is called a Christian simply because he happens to live in a Christian nation is a very different person from an actual Christian, for unfortunately, the Christianity of Christian nations is something like the gold that is spread over many of our household ornaments: it is very thin indeed. A little Christian gold leaf goes a very long way and makes things look respectable, but the gold-plated articles are not solid gold. National Christianity is no more the real thing than a gold-plated penny is a golden coin of the kingdom.

It is a sad fact that many who are called Christians because they belong to a Christian nation are a grievous dishonor to the name of Christ. The heathen, judging Christianity by them, have often been heard to say, "We are better off remaining as we are than to become as drunken, or swear as profanely, or act as cruelly as these so-called Christian people do." Our missionaries have found this to be a terrible hindrance to the success of their work. I have nothing to do now with merely nominal Christianity. Do what you want with it. Use it as a football if you want to.

Neither do I at all identify a person in Christ with one who is well versed with all the externals of the Christian religion and who gives himself up devotedly to them, but never looks into the center – into the heart and kernel of the matter. It has been well said that when a man possesses nothing but the externals of religion, he is generally very dogmatic about them because he has nothing else, while a man who has passed beyond the externals into the very soul and essence of our holy faith can allow a thousand differences of opinion in his fellow Christians as to outward forms without feeling that these differences constitute any barrier whatsoever to the warmest fellowship. A person may go as far as he pleases in the observance of religious rites, and he can become a stickler for even the tithing of the mint, anise, and cumin of ceremonials, sacraments, and the like (Matthew 23:23), yet for all that, he may not be a man in Christ.

I am also bound to confess that there are members of evangelical churches, not devotees of ceremonialism, but advocates for the barest simplicity of worship, who make a very high profession of being real Christians and who talk a great deal about vital godliness, yet nevertheless they are not men in Christ. The church of Christ has been plagued by hypocrites from the first day even until now. There was a Judas among the apostles themselves. Are you surprised at this? I confess I am not. Because Christianity is in itself so valuable, therefore there are many worthless imitations. People counterfeit money because it is worth having. If the money ever becomes worthless, the trade of the counterfeiter would be gone.

It is because the possession of true godliness is such a valuable thing that there are so many who pretend to have it who know nothing about it. I quite often distrust those who are so loud in their professions. I know that the cart that rings the loudest bell when it goes through the street only carries dust, but I never hear a bell rung when they are carrying diamonds or gold bullion through the city.

The best actions that are worked in this world are for the most part done in secret by those who desire no eye to observe them except the eye of the Almighty God. Some people, though, under the pretense of doing that, are really standing up for themselves rather than for Christ. They are not quite as anxious to cry, *Behold the Lamb of God* (John 1:29) as to say, "Come, see my zeal for the Lord of hosts! Admire me and see what a wonderful honor I am to the religion of Jesus Christ." I give up these religious pretenders to the world's utmost scorn. I have nothing to say in their defense, but very much to say by way of disgust at their untruthfulness. I am now going to speak about men who are really in Christ – men who have Christ in their heart of hearts and are in Christ themselves.

A man in Christ is a man, and being a man, he is therefore imperfect. I have heard a great deal of talk about perfect men, but I believe that a little examination with the microscope, or even without it, would have discovered a great many flaws in them, and probably more in those who thought themselves perfect than in others who have honestly confessed their imperfections. There is not a Christian man whose entire life might be read instead of the Bible whose life would not need notes, additions, and corrections before it would exactly correspond with the perfect law of the Lord.

Ask him, "May I learn Christian principles entirely from your conduct?" He would say, "I wish I could answer yes. I am striving to make my conduct so, but even though I try to copy my Master in every detail, I am afraid that I have still failed in some respects to reproduce the full spirit of the grand original. I wish you could read me and see the spirit of the New Testament in every little act as well as in every great transaction of my life. However, I make mistakes, and what is more, I sometimes drop my guard and allow the old nature that remains in me to come to the front. I am not what I should be, nor what I want to be, nor, blessed be God, what I will be. I hope you will see something of Christ in me, but I am just a man, and being in this body, I have many weaknesses."

When you are judging Christian men, should not you who may not happen to be Christians remember this? Be fair! Be honest! If a man does not receive the gospel himself, at least let him treat those who do receive it with the honesty that he would desire to be exercised toward himself. A man in Christ is a man; do not expect him to be an angel.

When I say that a man in Christ is a man, I mean that if he is truly in Christ, he is therefore manly. Somehow there is an idea that if you become a Christian, you must sink your manliness and become soft and weak. It is supposed that you allow your liberty to be curtailed by a set of negations that you do not have the courage to break through, although you would if you tried. Some people think that you must not do this, and you must not do that, but you are to take out your backbone and become like a mollusk. You are to be as sweet as honey toward everybody, and every atom of spirit is to be evaporated from you. You are to ask permission from ministers and church authorities to breathe, and you are to become a sort of living martyr who lives a miserable life in the hope of dying in the aroma of sanctity.

I do not believe in such Christianity at all. The Christian man, it seems to me, is the noblest style of man, He is the freest, bravest, most heroic, and most fearless of men. If he is what he should be, he is, in the best sense of the word, a man all over, from the crown of his head to the sole of his foot.

He is such a man because he has realized his own personal responsibility to God. He knows that to his own Master he stands or falls – that he will have to give an account in the day of judgment for his thoughts, words, and actions, and therefore he does not pin himself to any man's sleeve, no matter if he is a priest, minister, or anything else. He thinks for himself, takes the Bible and reads for himself, and comes to God in Christ Jesus personally and on his own account. He is not content to do business with subordinates, but goes to the Head of the great firm.

Being accustomed also to try to do that which is right at all times, if he is a man in Christ, he is bold. I heard a story of a man who was so continually in debt, and was so often arrested for it, that one day, catching his sleeve on a fence, he turned around and begged to be let alone this time. There are many people who go through life much like that. They know that they have done wrong, and that they are doing wrong, and therefore "conscience doth make cowards" of them.[1] However, when the conscience has been quieted, and the heart knows itself to be set upon integrity and established in the right, the Christian man is not afraid to go anywhere.

Moreover, a man in Christ is accustomed to wait upon his Lord and Master to know what he should do, and he recognizes Christ's law as being his sole rule. For this reason, he is the freest man under heaven because he does not recognize the slavish rules that make most men tremble lest they should lose their social status or forfeit the favor of the society in which they move. He obeys the laws of his country because Christ has commanded him to do so, and all things that are right and true are happy bonds to him that he does not want to break. As for the foolish customs and frivolous formalities that fashion ordains, he delights to put his foot through them and trample them under his

---

1 "Conscience doth make cowards" is from Act 3, Scene 1, of Shakespeare's play *Hamlet*.

feet, for he says, "I am Your servant, O Lord. You have loosed my bonds" (Psalm 116:16). When he has anything to say, he considers whether his Master would approve. As to whether the world would approve or not, it does not enter into his mind to consider. He has passed beyond that. He knows the liberty wherewith Christ makes us free (Galatians 5:1).

When we become servants of Christ, we cease to be servants of men. When Christ's yoke is upon you, then you are free to do what is right, no matter who may forbid it. From that time forth, you would not say anything that is not true even in order to win the acclamation of a nation, nor would you suppress the truth even if the universe itself would disapprove. A man in Christ bowing the knee before the King Himself is too noble to submit to error or to sin, even if it is robed in all the pomp of power. He stands up for what is right and true, and if the heavens would fall, he would still be found standing tall.

A man in Christ is manly because he is trusting in Providence. If he is what I mean by a man in Christ, he believes that whatever happens here below is ordered and arranged by his great Lord and Master. Therefore, when anything occurs that surprises and maybe perplexes him for the moment, he feels that it is still not an accident nor an unforeseen calamity beyond divine control. He believes that his Lord has a bit in the mouth of the tempest and reins up the storm. He is sure that Jesus, as King of kings, sits in the cabinets of princes and rules all the affairs of mankind.

Therefore, he is *not afraid of evil tidings: his heart is fixed, trusting in the LORD* (Psalm 112:7). If he lives as a Christian should live, he can wait when others are seized with sudden panic, for he knows that there is no panic in heaven, and that all things are rightly arranged and ordered by the powers above. Committing his present situation into the hands of his Lord Jesus, he both patiently waits and quietly hopes. He is thus enabled to become master of the situation, for he is cool and calm when others are confused. He is a match for any man in the hour of perplexity, for he has flung his burden off his shoulder and left it with his Lord. Now he can go forward with a clear and peaceful mind to do his work, or to leave it undone, as the peril of the moment demands. A Christian man, because he trusts in the God of providence, stands tall like a man (1 Samuel 4:9) and is not afraid.

He is manly because as a Christian, he does not retreat when he is opposed, for he expects opposition. That man who, being in Christ, never meets with any opposition, must either be in very happy and unique circumstances, or he must somewhat hide his religion; for from the first day until now, it has been found that those who will live godly in Christ Jesus must suffer persecution (2 Timothy 3:12). The man in Christ, being a true man, does not worry about that. If a joke is told at his expense, he knows that it does not break any bones. There is a little laughter over a story that is more clever than true, and perhaps a smirk or two caused by some very nasty sarcasm, but he expected that and brushed it aside when he became a Christian. Little by little, he has become so used to it that if it pleases other people, it does not annoy him. Now and then, when a sting does go rather near the heart, he is inclined to sing to himself very quietly:

> If on my face for thy dear name
> Shame and reproaches be
> All hail reproach and welcome shame
> If thou remember me.[2]

So he gets to be an all-around man, and it frequently happens that, as he pursues the even tenor of his way, those who at first despised him come to respect him. Men trust him, and finding him honorable, they honor him. Yes, they honor him for his faithfulness to his convictions; for even with those who do not care for Christianity, there is something that makes them reverence the man who is truly what he professes to be. We have seen this to be true in others, and may each one of us live long enough to experience it in ourselves. Simply let the Christian live on and live well, and he will live down opposition; or, if the opposition continues, he will live above it and flourish all the more.

I have said that a man in Christ is truly a man, and I will give one more meaning to my words. **He is a man in this sense, that he is human. It gives a better meaning if we lengthen out that last syllable: he is humane.** Of all who live, the man in Christ is the most human,

---

2   This is from a hymn by Thomas Haweis (1734-1820) that begins with "O Thou from whom all goodness flows."

or really the most humane, man. In this he follows the Lord Christ Himself. Ah, what a man He was! There is no one you could not point to and say, "He is an Englishman," or "He is a German," or "He is a Jew," or "He is a philosopher," or "He is a clergyman," or something else that is special and distinguishing. However, of Jesus of Nazareth, as a human being, you could never say more than that He was a Man – the noblest, purest specimen of man who ever adorned this world. He was a Man who belonged to all nations, to all ranks, and to all times. Do you not notice in His life how everything that had to do with man lay near His heart? I take it that He was more completely a man than John the Baptist, although there are many who consider that type of manhood to be the very highest.

John the Baptist came neither eating nor drinking, but Jesus came both eating and drinking; and although the rough crowd said, "He is a drunken man and a winebibber," yet He was all the more a perfect Man because He was a Man among men (Matthew 11:18-19). He did not dwell in the wilderness, but among the people. He did not eat locusts and wild honey, but went to a marriage and ate bread at the tables of those who invited Him. He entered into all that men did except their sins. He was in all things to man a true brother and friend. He was not merely a preacher, but He became a physician and healed bodily sicknesses.

The Christian man should always be the helper of everything that promotes the health and welfare of the people. Christ was not only the bread from heaven (John 6:51), but He gave the bread of this life to the poor and needy. He fed thousands of the weak with loaves and fishes (Matthew 14:13-21; Matthew 15:32-39). Even if all other hands are tightly closed, the hand of the Christian man should always be open to relieve human necessity. Being a man, the believer is a brother to all men – rich and poor, sick and healthy – and he should seek their good in every possible way, aiming still at the highest good – namely, the saving of their souls.

The man in Christ also is in the best sense human in that he lives in a real world and not in an ideal castle of sanctity. He has learned how to spiritualize the secular. He elevates the things of a man until they become the things of God. It is very easy to secularize the spiritual. There are many who have desecrated the pulpit and have brought it down to the lowest conceivable level, but there are others who have elevated the carpenter's bench and have made it *holiness unto the LORD* (Exodus 39:30).

The man in Christ does exactly that. He does not draw a line and say, "My life in Christ goes this far, but no further. My religion is a thing for Sundays, but not for the stock exchange. 'Do unto others as you would like them to do unto you' [Matthew 7:12] is a golden rule for the family, but it will not do for our workplace at all. We could not make a living on any such principle." No, he considers that no religion can be true that disqualifies a man for a lawful calling. His religion is part and parcel of himself. He does not carry it *with* him, but it is *in* him. It has come to be himself.

A man in Christ lives his life and does his work as sacredly as he reads his Bible. He does not pray only upon his knees when he is alone, but he speaks with God in all places. His service of God is not confined to his closet and his pew, but even when diligent in business, he is still *fervent in spirit, serving the Lord* (Romans 12:11). All that Christians do should be done as unto the Lord – *whether ye eat, or drink, or whatsoever ye do* (1 Corinthians 10:31). If there is anything in this world that you cannot do to the glory of God, you must not do it at all; but all things that you do, if you are Christian men, are to be done in the spirit of faith, in the presence of God, and for the glory of God Most High. Such is the man in Christ Jesus.

It is also his trait as a man, and a humane one – that he does not seek his own gain in selfishness. Of course, going into the world, he does not tell a lie and say, "I am not going to try and make money. I will not try to succeed in business." He is going to try to make a profit, and he would be a great fool for going into business at all if he had no such goal. Does he go into business with the intent of losing his capital? Nobody would believe him if he said so. No, but he goes to his office with this determination: "I am not going to rob someone to enrich myself. It will not be said of one single grain of gold that I have that I squeezed it from the widow or the orphan, or that I gained it by driving a man hard who needed it more than I, or that I took it by force from someone who, whether he needed it or not, had a better right to it than I."

The doctrine of the worlding in Horace, when he said, "Get money, fairly if you can, but by all means get it," is not a Christian doctrine. It is worthy of heathenism in its worst form. The man in Christ, although active, earnest, intelligent, and by no means a fool (if you think he is, deal with him and see), is considered to be a fool by some people when he makes a promise to his own loss and keeps his word (Psalm 15:4), and when he sees a fine opportunity at which some would leap, but he stands back and says, "I do not do so because of the fear of the Lord." He cannot and will not bring a curse upon himself by an unjust action, and this, it seems to me, makes him all the more truly a man, although it demonstrates one of the characteristics of his being a man in Christ Jesus.

Young men, I would honestly say to you that I would be ashamed to speak of a religion that would make you soft, cowardly, effeminate, and spiritless – one that would make you unrefined in business, having no souls of your own, the prey of every shrewd crook. Young men, I have tried the faith of Jesus Christ, and I have found that it gave me "pluck" – that is an old Saxon word, but it is exactly what I mean. It puts soul into a man – firmness, resolution, courage. If he is in the habit of talking with his own conscience, and his Bible, and his God, he can look the whole universe in the face – and a universe of devils, too – and never feel the slightest fear.

Why should he? Is not the Eternal One on the Christian man's side? Is not the risen and reigning Christ on his side? Is not the blessed Spirit his friend? Yes, the angels of God, and providence, and time, and eternity, and all the forces that exist, are his allies, with the only exception of death and hell – and his Lord has conquered these and has trampled them underfoot. I wish that every young man would enlist in the army of Christ fairly early, for none make such good soldiers as those who begin while they are still young.

CHAPTER 2

SOME ADVANTAGES OF A YOUNG MAN IN CHRIST

First, a young man in Christ has the advantage that the greatest burden of this mortal life is off his shoulders. He is less weighted in the race of life than most men, for the main load of life is sin – the consciousness of having broken the law of God, the consciousness that all is not right – and this is gone from him. A man in Christ has confessed his sin to his Lord, and there is a promise that he who confesses and forsakes his sin will find mercy (Proverbs 28:13). He has looked to Jesus, the great Sin-Bearer, and he has seen his sin transferred to the great Substitute and put away. Now, being justified by faith, he has peace with God through Jesus Christ his Lord (Romans 5:1). That great burden has gone.

When a man sits quietly in his room at night and begins to think over his past life, it will make him tremble unless he is able to see Christ on the cross putting away sin, and unless he knows by the assuring witness of the Holy Spirit that his transgressions were thus put away. Then the nightmare of a half-awakened conscience is gone. The dreadful burden from his spirit is lifted, and he is another man – a man with this wonderful advantage that no matter what burdens he has to bear, the intolerable weight of sin is gone – forever gone.

Better still, he has the further advantage that all his major matters are perfectly safe. He goes into business knowing that he may lose a fortune with the turn of the market, but his best capital is settled upon him forever. It might be that everything goes against him week after week, but he is like Little Faith, of whom John Bunyan says that the thieves robbed him of all his spending money, but they could not find his jewels, for they were hidden away where no one could reach them.[3] The Christian man feels the same way: "I may lose everything I possess of worldly substance, but I will never lose my God; and while I possess my God and my hope, I can still 'take arms against a sea of troubles, and, by opposing, end them.'"[4]

I heard of someone who walked down the Borough with unpardonable carelessness, carrying a considerable sum of money in his coat pocket. As he stopped to look in a window, a thief stole his handkerchief from that very pocket. He was not at all distressed about that loss when he reached home, for thrusting his hand to the bottom of his pocket, he found that the parcel that contained his money was still there. He said, "I have not lost the money. I care little for the handkerchief!" In fact, he seemed so happy that his money was safe that he forgot the other loss. In the same way, a man in Christ considers all that he has on earth to be inconsiderable compared with the treasure of salvation that he knows to be secure in the keeping of his Redeemer. His sorrow at any present loss is swallowed up in the joy that his eternal interests are safe.

As for his minor burdens, this is another point of advantage to a Christian man, for by faith he leaves them with God, and he expects good to come from them. He believes that any evil that happens to him is robbed of its sting and is made to benefit him. He bears the misfortunes of life, not merely with patience, but with submission in the will that appointed them, because he has the promise that *all things work together for good to them that love God, to them who are the called according to His purpose* (Romans 8:28). So the great load of sin is gone, and now the little loads are transformed and the great future is all secure. Is not such a man placed at a wonderful advantage in the race of life?

In addition to all this, the fear of death is removed from him. Is there anything more desirable than to have the dread of the grave, and of that "something after death," effectually taken away? This body does not love death, nor is it right that it should, for the law of self-preservation

---

3   Little Faith is a character in John Bunyan's *Pilgrim's Progress*, which is available from Aneko Press.

4   This quote is from Act III of William Shakespeare's play *Hamlet*.

is stamped upon us, and a natural fear of the stroke of death hangs over us, lest in some evil hour we should be tempted to end our own lives. Still, however, the Christian frequently looks forward to the time of his departure with intense expectancy and joy, and he awaits the inevitable hour with perfect peace, for he knows that his Redeemer lives, and that though the worms devour his body, yet in the latter day he shall in his flesh behold his God (Job 19:25-26); and so he looks serenely forward to the dreadful thing of death. Is he not placed at an advantage compared with all the rest of mankind?

Let me also say about the man in Christ that he has other advantages. **First, in the troubles of life, he always has a Friend.** You know how it is in business: if you have a good, substantial friend at your back, you feel very confident. Many young men starting out in life would have made a failure of it if they had not had wise and wealthy friends to support them. Sometimes they step out of the business or out of the warehouse and consult such a friend, and they feel that this advice is worth anything to them.

A man in Christ has a Friend. It is his own living, loving Lord, who condescends to speak with him, to hear his troubles, and to provide him with assistance. Many Christian men here know what it is to seek that Friend and to speak with Him. Would not your heart have broken sometimes if you could not have poured your sorrows into that fraternal heart and tell them to One who, having been tempted in all points like as you are (Hebrews 4:15), is able to meet your cares?

It is a great thing to a man, too, in the voyage of life, to have a good map, and the Christian man has that. He has the Bible to tell him exactly what to do under all circumstances. You say to me, "No, that is not so. That Book gives general principles, but not specific directions." However, these general principles are applicable under all circumstances. I also claim that the Bible does more than supply principles, for its words are often as particularly appropriate to the individual situation as if it alone had been in the writer's eye. I have often met with texts that seemed written for that very hour, and which met my situation to the very letter. Every believer knows that this has happened to himself.

After all, the general principle of the Bible – to always do what is right – is the best guide a man can have. When ambassadors meet in the council chamber, the man who amazes all the rest with his policy is he who has no policy at all except that of speaking the truth. He puzzles rivals, and they suspect him of some deep-laid scheme. All over the world, the man whom nobody can match or defeat is the man who has no policy except that of believing that a straight line is the shortest distance between any two places, and that he intends to follow that straight line, leaving the twisting and the indirectness to those who prefer them. The Word of God makes the simplest mind wise and discreet because it sets forth the path of right and truth.

Moreover, remember that a Christian man has a mighty Spirit dwelling within him. Every Christian has had a miracle worked upon him. The human nature has been outdone by a divine work. The Holy Spirit has come to dwell in the believer, and He, in addition to enlightening him as to his way, enlivens him that he may follow it. He admonishes him when he goes astray, and inspires him with passion and zeal to press forward in his lifework. Our own spirits weaken and falter, but the Divine Spirit is free from all imperfections. Where He dwells, there is a power, a light, and a joy unknown to all the rest of the world.

A man in Christ also has the high privilege of being under the special care of God. He and his brethren are like an army marching through a foreign country, having at its back a good and steady source of supplies. Many commanders have been beaten because they have advanced too far while forgetting the necessity of having to be supplied, but the Christian knows that it is written, *My God shall supply all your need according to His riches in glory by Christ Jesus* (Philippians 4:19). His firm conviction is that those who seek the Lord and wait upon Him will not lack *any good thing* (Psalm 34:10). Then, being free from care, he has in his heart a wellspring of content. Moreover, he has constant communication with headquarters where his supplies are stored, for prayer communicates to heaven, and the promise is, *Before they call, I will answer; and while they are yet speaking, I will hear* (Isaiah 65:24).

A man in Christ is a man upon an extraordinary vantage ground. The world cannot understand him, nor can it withstand him. He lives in it, yet lives above it. He glides through it, not without trial, *for in the world ye shall have tribulation*, but certainly without defeat, for Christ has said, *Be of good cheer; I have overcome the world* (John 16:33). If I did not look for immortality, but expected to die like a dog, I would still want to be a Christian.

If there were no hereafter, if there were no heaven or hell, if I only had to meet the sorrows, the strifes, and the cares and burdens of this mortal life, I would ask our great Master, Jesus, to let me enlist beneath His banner, for He gives peace and rest to all who come under His command.

How did a man in Christ get to be such a man? It began when he became uneasy at finding himself where he was. He had many pleasures, but they decreased. He used to enjoy many sweets of the world, but suddenly he found them distasteful. The world grew stale. The dry and yellow leaf was on all its trees. Its flowers were faded and its lights burned low. The man began to look around him. He looked upward and downward, within and around. Things looked as he did not like to see them. He began to think more about these things, and the more he thought, the more unrestful his heart was.

Do you dare to think? I know some men who dare not. If they were to attempt to think for two hours about their own condition, they would almost rather be flogged. Well, that is how it came about. The man considered himself and his ways, and as he considered, he discovered that he was without God, without Christ, and without hope. He knew that he would die. He trembled as to what his destiny must be, and a voice within him warned him to expect the worst. The good Spirit was working on him, and this was the beginning of a blessed change.

Then there came across his path the good news that Jesus Christ was able to save him, and to save him at once – that He could blot out all his past sins and rescue him from the present power of evil. Only one thing must be done: Christ must be trusted – and he did trust Him.

It took him some time to see that this simple trust in Jesus could do such wonders, but he at last saw it. He trusted Jesus Christ for everything, and he found his sin pardoned and also conquered. He had always trusted himself before, but now he gave himself up to be saved by the merit of the Redeemer's blood and by the power of the Holy Spirit. Then he became indeed a man in Christ.

What else happened to him when he was saved? He was given a new life. A miracle was worked upon him. A life that he had never before possessed was bestowed upon him, and this elevated him as much above other men as other men are elevated above the beasts that perish. He was body and soul before, but the Spirit of God came upon him and gave him a spirit – a third and higher principle that lifted him up into a spiritual region in which he lived as a spiritual man. He found himself completely changed from his former self: the things he loved before, he now hated; and the things he hated before, he now loved. He could see what he never saw before, and what once seemed very attractive to him had lost all its attractiveness. He would not have known his former self if he had met him in the street. In fact, he and his old self disagreed once for all. They have never made up the quarrel, and never will. He is a new creature in Christ Jesus; old things have passed away; *behold all things are become new* (2 Corinthians 5:17).

Since he has received that life, he has entered farther into Christ, for he has consecrated himself to Christ. If he is a man in Christ of the type I mean, he has given himself up, and all that he has, to serve his Savior. Some Christians remind me of the little boys who go to bathe; frightened and shivering, they enter the water just a little. They wade up to their ankles, and they shiver again. However, the man who is really in Christ is like the experienced swimmer who plunges into the stream headfirst and finds waters to swim in. He never shivers. It strengthens him. He rejoices in it.

See how at home the man of God is in the river of grace. It has become his element. For him *to live is Christ* (Philippians 1:21). He has devoted himself, his substance, and all that he has to the glory of God. This is the man who understands the happiness of the Christian religion in a manner far beyond the conception of the half-hearted professing Christian who has only enough religion to make him miserable.

An American gentleman said to a friend, "I wish you would come down to my garden and taste my apples." He asked him about a dozen times, but the friend never came. At last the fruit-grower said, "I suppose you think my apples are good for nothing, so you won't come and taste them."

"Well, to tell you the truth," said the friend, "I have tasted them. As I went along the road, I picked up one that fell over the wall, and I never tasted anything so sour in all my life. I do not particularly want to have any more of your fruit."

"Oh," said the owner of the garden, "I thought it must be so. Those apples around the outside are for the special benefit of the boys. I went fifty miles to select the sourest sorts to plant all around the orchard so that the boys might give them up as not worth stealing; but if you come inside, you will find that we grow a very different quality there that are as sweet as honey."

You will find that on the outskirts of religion, there are a number of *Thou shalt nots* and *Thou shalts* and convictions and terrors and alarms, but these are only the bitter fruits with which this wondrous Eden is guarded from thieving hypocrites. If you can pass by the bitterness on the exterior, and give yourself completely up to Christ and live for Him, your peace will be like a river, your righteousness will be like the waves of the sea (Isaiah 48:18), and you will find that the fruits of this *apple tree among the trees of the wood* (Song of Solomon 2:3) are the most pleasing that can be enjoyed this side of our eternal home.

To all who are men in Christ, I recommend the fullest consecration to His service. May this lead to your being in Christ in the sense of being devoted to Him. The flower and crown of true Christianity is devotion. Until the name of Jesus stirs our blood, as the sound of the trumpet stirs the soldier in the day of battle; until we feel that we could die for Jesus; until we count all things but loss that we may win Christ and be found in Him (Philippians 3:8-9); until we grow so passionate and fervent that we want all others to know what we know, to feel what we feel, and to enjoy what we enjoy; and until we become so intense that our religion becomes bold and seeks to conquer the world, we have not known the full elevating power of the gospel of Jesus Christ.

CHAPTER 3

RUTH'S FAITH AND REWARD

Many young converts deserve encouragement because they have left all their old associates. Ruth, no doubt, had many friends in her native country, but she tore herself away to cling to Naomi and her God. Perhaps she parted from a mother and a father; if they were alive, she certainly left them to go to the Israelites' country. Possibly she said good-bye to brothers and sisters. She certainly left old friends and neighbors. She resolved to go with Naomi and share her fate. She said:

> *Intreat me not to leave thee, or to return from following after thee: for whither thou goest, I will go: and where thou lodgest, I will lodge: thy people shall be my people, and thy God my God: where thou diest, will I die, and there will I be buried: the LORD do so to me, and more also, if ought but death part thee and me.* (Ruth 1:16-17)

A young convert to Christianity is an emigrant from the world, and has become, for Christ's sake, a stranger. He might have had many companions, friends who made him happy after their own way, men of fascinating manners who could easily provoke his laughter and make the hours fly by; but because he found in them no savor of Christ, he has forsaken them – and for Christ's sake, they have forsaken him. He has become as a speckled bird among his old associates, and they are all against him. Maybe you have seen a canary that has flown from its home, where it enjoyed the kindness of its owner. You have seen it out among the sparrows. They pursue it as though they would tear it into pieces, and they give it no rest anywhere.

In the same way, the young convert, being no longer of the same feather as his associates, is the subject of their persecution. He endures trials of *cruel mockings* (Hebrews 11:36), and these are as hot irons to the soul. He is now to them a hypocrite and a fanatic. They honor him with ridiculous names by which they express their scorn. In their hearts, they crown him with a fool's cap, and consider him both a fool and a fiend. He will need to exhibit years of holy living before they will be forced into respect for him, and all because he is quitting their Moab to join with Israel.

Why should he leave them? Has he grown better than they? Does he pretend to be a saint? Can he not drink with them as he once did? His life is now a protest against their excesses, and men don't care for such protests. Can he not sing an amusing song as they do? They know he has turned saint, and what is a saint to them but a hypocrite? He is much too strict and puritanical for them, and is not to be endured in their free society.

According to the rank in life, this opposition takes one form or another, but in no case does Moab admire the Ruth who deserts her idols to worship the God of Israel. It is not natural that the Prince of Darkness would want to lose his subjects, or that the men of the world would love those who shame them.

When Ruth had left her former connections, it was wise and kind for Boaz to address her in words of comfort: *The LORD recompense thy work, and a full reward be given thee of the LORD God of Israel, under whose wings thou art come to trust* (Ruth 2:12).

After Ruth had left her old companions, she went among strangers. She was not yet at home in the land of Israel, but confessed herself *a stranger* (Ruth 2:10). She knew Naomi, but she knew no one else in the entire town of Bethlehem. When she went into the harvest field, the neighbors were there gleaning, but they were not her neighbors. They offered her no glance of sympathy. Perhaps they looked at her with cold curiosity. They may have thought, "What business has this Moabitess to come here to take away a part of the gleaning that belongs to the poor of Israel?"

I know that such feelings do arise among country people when a stranger from another parish comes gleaning in the field. Ruth was a foreigner, and of course, in their eyes, she was an intruder. She felt herself to be alone, although under the wings of Israel's God. Boaz very properly felt that she should not think that courtesy and kindness had died out of Israel. He made a point, although he was by far her superior in position, to go to her and speak a word of encouragement to her.

A new convert is like Ruth in another respect: he is very lowly in his own eyes. Ruth said to Boaz, *Why have I found grace in thine eyes, that thou shouldest take knowledge of me, seeing I am a stranger?* (Ruth 2:10). She said again, *Let me find favor in thy sight, my lord; for that thou hast comforted me, and for that thou hast spoken friendly unto thine handmaid, though I be not like unto one of thine handmaidens* (Ruth 2:13). She had little self-esteem, and therefore she won the esteem of others. She felt herself to be a very insignificant person to whom any kindness was a great favor.

Young converts also feel this way if they are real and true. We meet with a certain class of them who are rather brash and forward, as the fashion of the day is in certain places, and then we do not think as much of them as they do of themselves. The genuine ones, though, who are truly renewed and who really hold out and continue to the end, are always humble, and are frequently very trembling, timid, and lacking confidence. They feel that they are not worthy to be put among the children, and they come to the Lord's Table with holy wonder.

I remember when I first went to the house of God as a Christian youth. I had recently come to know the Lord, that I looked with veneration on every officer and member of the church. I thought they were all, if not quite angels, yet very nearly as good. At any rate, I had no heart to criticize them, for I felt myself to be so undeserving.

A young convert is like Ruth because he has come to trust under the wings of Jehovah, the God of Israel. This is a beautiful metaphor. You know that the wing of a strong bird especially, and of any bird relatively, is strong. It makes a kind of arch, and from the outer side you have the architectural idea of strength. Under the wings, even of such a feeble creature as a hen, there is a complete and perfect refuge for her little chicks, judging from without. The inside of the wing is lined

21

with soft feathers for the comfort of the young. The interior of the wing is arranged as though it would prevent any friction from the strength of the wing to the weakness of the little bird. I do not know of a more snug place than under the wing feathers of the hen.

Have you never thought of this? In times of trouble, would not the Lord want us to come and take refuge under the great wing of His omnipotent love, just as the chicks do under the mother? Here is the Scripture: *He shall cover thee with His feathers, and under His wings shalt thou trust: His truth shall be thy shield and buckler* (Psalm 91:4). What a warm defense! When I have seen the little birds poke their heads out from under the feathers of their mother's breast, it has looked like the perfection of happiness. When they have chirped their little notes, they have seemed to tell how warm and safe they were, even though there may have been a rough wind blowing around the hen. They could not be happier than they are. If they run a little way, they are soon back again to the wing, for it is house and home to them; it is their shield and refuge, their defense and delight.

This is what our young converts have done. They have come, not to trust themselves, but to trust in Jesus. They have come to find a righteousness in Christ – yes, to find everything in Him – and so they are trusting, trusting under the wings of God. Is not this what you are doing?

There is no rest, no peace, no calm, no perfect quiet like that of giving up all care because you cast your care on God, of renouncing all fear because your only fear is a fear of offending God. Oh, the joy of knowing that the universe will sooner be dissolved than the great heart that beats above you cease to be full of tenderness and love to all those who shelter beneath it! Faith, however little, is a precious plant of the Lord's right-hand planting. Do not trample on it, but tend it with care and water it with love.

What is the full reward of those who come to trust under the wings of God? I would answer that a full reward will come to us in that day when we lay down these bodies of flesh and blood so that they may sleep in Jesus, while our unclothed spirits are absent from the body and present with the Lord (2 Corinthians 5:8). In this bodiless state, we will enjoy perfect happiness of spirit, but a fuller reward will be ours when the Lord will come a second time and our bodies will rise from the grave to share in the glorious reign of the descended King. Then we will behold the face of Him whom we love, and we will be like Him (1 John 3:2). Then will come the adoption – that is, *the redemption of our body* (Romans 8:23), and we, as body, soul, and spirit, a trinity in unity, will be forever with Father, Son, and Holy Spirit, our triune God (1 Thessalonians 4:17). This unspeakable joy is the full reward of trusting beneath the wings of Jehovah.

There is also a present reward, and Boaz referred to it. There is in this world a present reward for the godly, despite the fact that *many are the afflictions of the righteous* (Psalm 34:19). Years ago, a brother minister printed a book entitled *How to Make the Best of Both Worlds*. It contained much wisdom, but at the same time, many of us objected to the title as it seemed to divide the pursuit of the believer and put the two worlds too much on the same level. Certainly it would be wrong for any godly man to make it his goal in life to make the best of both worlds in the way in which the title is likely to suggest. This present world must be subordinate to the world to come, and is to be cheerfully sacrificed to it, if necessary.

Yet let it never be forgotten that if any man will live unto God, he will make the best of both worlds, for godliness has the promise of the life that now is, as well as of that which is to come (1 Timothy 4:8). Even in losing the present life for Christ's sake, we are saving it (Matthew 10:39), and self-denial and taking up the cross are simply forms of blessedness. If we seek first the kingdom of God and His righteousness, all other things will be added to us (Matthew 6:33).

Do you ask, "How will we be rewarded for trusting in the Lord?" I answer, first, by the deep peace of conscience that He will give you. Can any reward be better than this? When a man can say, "I have sinned, but I am forgiven," is not that forgiveness an unspeakable blessing? My sins were laid on Jesus, and He took them away as my scapegoat. They are gone forever, and I am consciously absolved. Is not this a glorious assurance? Is it not worth worlds? A calmness settles down upon the heart that is under the power of *the blood of sprinkling* (Hebrews 12:24). A voice within proclaims the peace of God, and the Holy Spirit seals that peace by His own witness. Thus, all is rest.

If you were to offer all that you have to buy this peace, you could not purchase it; but if it were able to be purchased, it would be worthwhile to forego the inheritance of a thousand worlds to win it. Even if you had all riches and power and honor, you could not reach the price of the pearl of peace. The revenues of kingdoms could not purchase as much as a glance at this jewel. A guilty conscience is the undying worm of hell. The torture of remorse is the fire that can never be quenched (Mark 9:48). He who has that worm gnawing at his heart and that fire burning in his heart is lost already.

On the other hand, he who trusts in God through Christ Jesus is delivered from inward pangs of hell. The burning fever of unrest is cured. He may well sing for joy of soul, for heaven is born within him and lies in his heart like the Christ in the manger. The harps of glory ring out no sweeter note than that of transgression put away by the atoning sacrifice!

What was the full reward that Ruth obtained? I do not think that Boaz knew the full meaning of what he said. He could not foresee all that was appointed by the Lord. In the light of Ruth's history, we will read the good man's blessing. This poor stranger, Ruth, in putting her trust in the God of Israel, was giving up everything – but she was also gaining everything. If she could have looked behind the veil that hides the future, she could not have conducted herself more to her own advantage than she did.

She had no likelihood of gain. She followed Naomi expecting poverty and obscurity, but in doing that which was right, she found the blessing that makes rich. She lost her Moabite kindred, but she found a noble kinsman in Israel. She gave up the home of her fathers in the other land and found a heritage among the chosen tribes, a heritage redeemed by one who loved her.

When you come to trust in Christ, you find in the Lord Jesus Christ one who is next of kin to you, who redeems your heritage, and who unites you to Himself. You thought that He was a stranger. You were afraid to approach Him, but He comes near to you, and you find yourself near to His heart and one with Him forever.

Yes, this is a good illustration of each convert's reward. Ruth found what she did not look for – she found a husband. It was exactly what was for her comfort and her joy, for she found rest in the house of her husband, and she became a possessor of his large estate by virtue of her marriage union with him. When a poor sinner trusts in God, he does not expect such a great blessing, but to his surprise, his heart finds a Husband, a home, and an inheritance that is priceless beyond any dream – and all this is found in Christ Jesus our Lord. Then is the soul brought into loving, living, lasting, indissoluble union with the Well-beloved, the unrivalled Lord of love. We are one with Jesus. What a glorious mystery this is!

Ruth obtained an inheritance among the chosen people of Jehovah. She could not have obtained it except through Boaz, who redeemed it for her, but thus she came into indisputable possession of it. When a poor soul comes to God, he thinks that he is running to Him only for a refuge, but he is indeed coming for much more. He is coming for an *inheritance incorruptible, and undefiled, and that fadeth not away* (1 Peter 1:4). He becomes an heir of God and a joint-heir with Jesus Christ (Romans 8:17).

CHAPTER 4

PARENTS' GOOD PRINCIPLES TO BE FOLLOWED

My son, keep thy father's commandment, and forsake not the law of thy mother: bind them continually upon thine heart, and tie them about thy neck. When thou goest, it shall lead thee; when thou sleepest, it shall keep thee; and when thou awakest, it shall talk with thee. For the commandment is a lamp; and the law is light; and reproofs of instruction are the way of life. (Proverbs 6:20-23)

You have here the advice of King Solomon, rightly considered to be one of the wisest men who ever lived. Truly, he must be wise indeed who could excel the son of David, the king of Israel, in wisdom. It is worthwhile to listen to what Solomon has to say. It is good for the most intelligent young person to listen, and to listen carefully, to what so experienced a man as Solomon has to say to young men. I must remind you, though, that a greater than Solomon –the Spirit of God – inspired the Proverbs. They are not merely jewels from earthly mines, but they are also precious treasures from the heavenly hills. The advice we have here is not only the counsel of a wise man, but it is also the advice of that Incarnate Wisdom who speaks to us out of the Word of God. Do you want to become the sons of wisdom? Then come and sit at the feet of Solomon. Do you want to become spiritually wise? Then come and hear what the Spirit of God has to say by the mouth of the wise man. I want to show that true Christianity comes to many when it is recommended by parental example.

Unhappily, it is not so with all. There are some people who had a bad example in their childhood and never learned anything that was good from their parents. I adore the sovereignty of divine grace that there are many who are the first in their families who ever made a profession of faith in Christ. They were born and brought up in the midst of everything that was opposed to godliness, yet they are (although they can hardly tell you how) brought out from the world as Abraham was brought out from Ur of the Chaldees. If this is true of you, then you have special cause for thankfulness, but it should be a note to be entered in your diary that your children will not be subjected to the same disadvantages that you suffered. Since the Lord has looked in love upon you, let your households be holiness to the Lord, and bring up your children in such a way that they will have every advantage that Christian instruction can give, and every opportunity to serve the living God.

There are many people, though, who have had the immense privilege of godly training. It seems to my mind that a father's experience is the best evidence that a young man can have of the truth of anything. My father would not say anything false anywhere to anyone, but I am sure that he would not say it to his son. Even if, after serving God for fifty years, he had found Christianity to be a failure, even if he did not have the courage to communicate it to the whole world, I am certain that he would have whispered in my ear, "My son, I have misled you. I was mistaken, and I have found it out." However, when I saw him the other day, he had no such information to convey to me. Our conversation was concerning the faithfulness of God, and he delights to tell of the faithfulness of God to him and to his father, my dear grandfather, who has now gone up above. They have often told me that in a long lifetime of testing and proving the promises, they have found them all true, and they could say, in the language of the hymn:

> 'Tis religion that can give
>   Sweetest pleasures while we live;
> 'Tis religion must supply
>   Solid comfort when we die.[5]

As for myself, if I had found out that I was mistaken, I would not have

---

5   This is a stanza from "Let Us Walk in the Light," a hymn written by Mary Masters (1694?- 1771?).

been so foolish as to rejoice that my sons would follow the same way of life and would devote themselves with all their might to preaching the same truth that I delight to proclaim. Dear son, if you have a godly father, believe that the religion upon which he has fixed his faith is true. He tells you that it is so. He is a sincere and honest witness to you. Therefore, I urge you not to forsake your father's God.

I think that one of the most tender bonds that can ever bind man or woman is the affection of a mother. It may be true that many people might possibly break away from the law of the father, but who among us can break away from the love of the mother? Next to the godly example of a father, a mother's affection is the best of arguments. You remember how she prayed for you. Among your earliest memories is when she sat you on her knees and taught you to say:

> Gentle Jesus, meek and mild,
> Look upon a little child.[6]

Maybe you have tried to disbelieve, but your mother's firm faith prevents it. I have heard of someone who said that he could easily have been an atheist if it had not been for his mother's life and his mother's death. Yes, these are hard arguments to get over, and I hope that you will not get over them. You remember well her quiet patience in the house when there was much that might have ruffled her. You remember her gentleness with you when you were going a little wild. You hardly know, perhaps, how you cut her to the heart and how her nights were sleepless because her boy did not love his mother's God.

I do ask you, by the love you bear for her, that if you have received any impressions that are good, cherish them and do not cast them aside. If you have received no such impressions, at least let the sincerity of your mother (for whom it was impossible to have been untrue) and the deep affection of your mother (who could not and would not betray you into a lie) persuade you that there is truth in this religion that now some of your companions might be trying to teach you to ridicule. *My son, keep thy father's commandment, and forsake not the law of thy mother* (Proverbs 6:20).

I think that to any young man or woman who has had a godly father

---

6   This is from the first stanza of "Gentle Jesus," a hymn written by Charles Wesley (1707-1788).

and mother, the best way of life that they can mark out for themselves is to follow the road in which their parents' principles would conduct them. Of course, we make great advances on the old folks, do we not? The young men are wonderfully bright and intelligent, and the old people are a good deal behind them. Yes – that is the way we talk before our beards have grown. Possibly, when we have more sense, we will not be quite so conceited about it. At any rate, I, who am not very old, but who dare not any longer call myself young, venture to say that, for myself, I desire nothing as much as to continue the traditions of my household. I do not want to find any course except that which will run parallel with that of those who have gone before me.

I think, dear friends, that you who have seen the holy and happy lives of Christian ancestors will be wise to pause a good deal before you begin to make a deviation, either to the right or to the left, from the course of those godly ones. I do not believe that he begins life in a way that God is likely to bless, and which he himself will, in the long run, judge to be wise, who begins with the notion that he will upset everything and that all that belonged to his godly family will be cast aside. I do not seek to have heirlooms of gold or silver, but even if I die a thousand deaths, I can never give up my father's God, my grandfather's God, his father's God, and his father's God. I must hold this to be the most important possession that I have, and I ask all young men and women to think the same.

Do not stain the glorious traditions of noble lives that have been handed down to you. Do not disgrace your father's shield. Do not blemish the coat of arms of your honored predecessors by any sins and transgressions on your part. May God help you to feel that the best way of leading a noble life will be to do as they did who trained you in the fear of God!

Solomon tells us to do two things with the teachings that we have learned from our parents. First he says, *Bind them continually upon thine heart* (Proverbs 6:21), for they are worthy of loving obedience. Show that you love these things by binding them upon your heart. The heart is the vital point. Let godliness lie there. Love the things of God. If we could take young men and women and make them professedly religious without them truly loving godliness, we would be simply making them hypocrites, which is not what we desire. We do not want you to say that you believe what you do not believe, or that you rejoice in what you do not rejoice in.

But our prayer, and we desire it to be your prayer, too, is that you may be helped to bind these things about your heart. They are worth living for, and they are worth dying for. These immortal principles of the divine life that come from the death of Christ are worth more than all the world. *Bind them continually upon thine heart.*

Then Solomon, because he does not want us to keep these things secret as if we were ashamed of them, adds, *and tie them about thy neck* – for they are worthy of boldest display. Did you ever see the Lord Mayor wearing his chain of office? He is not at all ashamed to wear it. The sheriffs proudly wear their badges too. I have a vivid recollection of how large some of those displays were, and they make sure to wear them. Now then, you who have any love for God, tie your religion around your neck. Do not be ashamed of it. Put it on as an ornament. Wear it as the mayor does his chain. When you go into company, never be ashamed to say that you are a Christian. If there is any company where you cannot go as a Christian, well, do not go there at all. Say to yourself, "I will not be where I could not introduce my Master. I will not go where He could not go with me." You will find that resolve to be a great help to you in the choice of where you will go and where you will not go. Therefore, bind it upon your heart and tie it around your neck. May God help you to do this, and so to follow those godly ones who have gone before you!

I hope that I am not weak in wishing that some of you may be touched by affection to their parents. I have sometimes had very sorrowful sights in the course of my ministry. A dear father, an honest, upright, godly man – what lines of grief I saw upon his face when he came to me and said, "Oh, sir, my boy is in prison!" I am sure that if his boy could have seen his father's face as I saw it, it would have been worse than prison to him. I have known young men – they were nice boys too – who have gone into situations in the city where they have been tempted to steal, and they have yielded to the tempter and lost their character. Sometimes the deficiency has been met and they have been rescued from a criminal's career, but sadly, sometimes they have fallen into the hands of a wicked woman, and then tragedy has befallen them!

Occasionally, it has seemed to be utter unrestraint and wickedness that has made them act unrighteously. I wish I could let them see, not merely the misery they will bring upon themselves, but I wish I could also show them their mother at home when news came that John had lost his position because he had been acting dishonestly, or that I could give them a glimpse of their father's face when the unpleasant news reached him. The poor man stood stunned. He said, "There was never a stain upon the character of anyone in my family before." If the earth had opened under the godly man's feet, or if the good mother could have gone down straight into the grave, they would have preferred it to the lifelong tribulation that has come upon them.

Therefore, I urge you, young man or young woman, do not kill the parents who gave you life. Do not disgrace those who brought you up. Instead, I plead with you to seek the God of your father and the God of your mother, and give yourselves to the Lord Jesus Christ and live wholly for Him.

Solomon also tells us that true religion guides us under all circumstances. He says that when we are active, there is nothing like true godliness to help us: *When thou goest, it shall lead thee* (Proverbs 6:22). In the same verse, he tells us that when we are resting, there is nothing better than this for our preservation: *When thou sleepest, it shall keep thee.* And when we are just waking up, there is nothing better than this with which to delight the mind: *When thou awakest, it shall talk with thee.*

I do not intend to expand those three thoughts except just to say that when you are busiest, Christianity will be your best help. When your hands are full of toil and your head is full of thought, nothing can do you more service than to have a God to go to, a Savior to trust in, and a heaven to look forward to. When you go to your bed to sleep or when you are sick, you can have nothing better to smooth your pillow and to give you rest than to know that you are forgiven through the precious blood of Christ, and saved in the Lord with an everlasting salvation.

CHAPTER 5

WHY THE YOUNG NEED CONVERSION

I want to say something to you who are unconverted. Our great concern is for you to know the Lord at once, and our reason is that it will prepare you for the world to come. Whatever that world may be, and no matter how full of vast mysteries it is, no one is as prepared to launch upon the unknown sea as the one who is reconciled to God, who believes in the Lord Jesus Christ, who trusts Him and rejoices in the pardon of his sin through the great atoning sacrifice, and who experiences in his own heart the marvelous change that has made him a new creature in Christ Jesus.

I think that is a very good reason for seeking the Lord – that you may be prepared for eternity. I saw an elderly friend who was eighty-six years old and on the decline. She said, "I have no fear. I have no fear of death. I am on the Rock. I am on the Rock Christ Jesus. I know whom I have believed, and I know where I am going." It was delightful to hear the elderly saint speak like that, and we are always hearing such talk from our dear friends when they are going home. They never seem to have any doubts. I have known some who had many doubts while they were well, but when they came to die, they seemed to have none at all, but were joyously confident in Christ.

There is another reason why we want our friends converted, and that is so that they may be prepared for this life. I do not know what kind of life you have set before yourself. Perhaps some young men hope to have lives consecrated to learning and crowned with honor. Possibly some have no prospect except that of working hard to earn their bread by the sweat of their brow. Some have begun to lay bricks or build houses or work in a warehouse. There are all sorts of ways of mortal life, but there is no better provision and preparation for any kind of life on earth than to know the Lord and to have a new heart and a right spirit. He who rules millions of men will do it better with the grace of God in his heart. He who is a servant would be happier in his situation if he had the grace of God in his heart. You who are young, you who are employers, and you who are employees – true Christianity cannot disqualify you from playing your part here in the great drama of life, but the best preparation for that part, if it is a part that should be played, is to know the Lord and to feel the power of divine grace upon your soul.

Let me just show you how this is the case. **The man who lives before God, who calls God his Father and feels the Spirit of God working a hatred of sin and a love of righteousness within him, is the man who will be conscientious in carrying out his duties.** That is the kind of man, and the kind of woman too, whom we need nowadays. We have so many people who need to be looked after. If you give them anything to do, they will do it quickly enough if you stand and look on, but the moment you turn your back, they will do it as carelessly or as slowly and as badly as can be. They are the kind of workers who only do their jobs well when they are being watched.

A truly Christian man, a man who is really converted, sees that he serves God in doing his duty to his fellow men. *Thou God seest me* (Genesis 16:13) is the power that always influences him. He desires to be conscientious in the discharge of his duties, no matter what those duties may be. I once told the story of the servant girl who said that she hoped she was converted. Her minister asked her, "What evidence can you give of your conversion?" Among many other reasons, she gave this good one: "Now sir," she said, "I always sweep under the mats." It was a small matter, but that principle of sweeping under the mats is the kind of thing we need to carry out in daily life. Many people have a little corner where they pile up all the fluff and the dust, and the room looks as if it was nicely swept, but it is not. There is a way of doing everything so that nothing is really done, but that is not the case where there is grace in the heart. Grace in the heart makes a person feel that he wants to live wholly for God, and he serves God in serving man. If you get that grace, you will have great preparation for life as well as for death.

A man who has a new heart has received a purity that preserves him in the midst of temptation. Oh, this dreadful city of London! I am amazed that God endures the filth of it. I frequently converse with good young men who come up from the country to their first job in London, and the first week they live in London is a revelation to them that makes their hair almost stand on end. They see things they never dreamed of. Well now, you young fellows who have just come to London, give yourselves to the Lord at once, I urge you. Yield yourselves to Jesus Christ, for another week in London may be your damnation. Only a week in London may have led you into acts of impurity that will ruin you forever.

Before you have gone into those things, devote yourselves to God and to His Christ so that with pure hearts and right spirits you may be preserved from *the pestilence that walketh in darkness* and *the destruction that wasteth at noonday* (Psalm 91:6) in this terribly wicked city. There is no hope for you young men and young women in this great world of wickedness unless your hearts are right toward God. If you give yourselves completely to follow the Lamb wherever He goes, He will keep and preserve you even to the end; but if you do not give yourselves to the Lord, no matter what good resolutions you may have formed, you are doomed, I am sure you are, to be carried away with the rivers of iniquity that run down our streets today. Therefore, purity of heart, which comes from faith in Christ, is an excellent preparation for life.

So also is truthfulness of speech. What a wretched thing it is when people tell lies! The heart that is purified by the grace of God hates the thought of a lie. The man changed by God speaks the truth, the whole truth, and nothing but the truth, and he is the man who will pass through life unscathed, will be honored, and will be successful in the long run. He may have to suffer for a time through his truthfulness, but in the end, nothing will clear a way for him so well as being true in thought and word and deed.

If you love the Lord with all your heart, you will also learn honesty in business and in all of your dealings with others, and that is a great help in life. I know that a dishonest person sometimes seems to succeed for a time, but what is his success? It is a success that is only another name for ruin. If all people could be made honest, how much more happiness there would be in the world! The way to be upright among men is to be sincere toward God and to have the Spirit of God dwelling within you.

True Christianity is also of great value because it comforts a man under great troubles. You do not expect many troubles, my young friend, but you will have them. You expect that you will be married and then your troubles will be over; some say that they begin then. I do not endorse that statement, but I am sure that they are not over, for there is another set of trials that begin then.

Maybe you think that after you complete your apprenticeship it will be all right; will it? Journeymen do not always find it so. Maybe you do not intend to always be a journeyman, but you want to own your own business. Ask the business owners whether everything is pleasant with them in these times. If you want to escape trouble completely, you had better go up in a hot-air balloon – and then I am sure that you would be in trouble for fear of going up too high or coming down too fast.

Troubles will come, and what is there that can preserve a man in the midst of trouble like feeling that things are safe in his Father's hands? If you can say, "I am His child, and all things are working together for my good. I have committed myself entirely into the hands of Him who cannot err and who will never do me an unkindness," then you have on a breastplate that the darts of care cannot pierce, you are shod with the preparation of the gospel of peace (Ephesians 6:11-17), and you may tread on the briars of the wilderness with an unwounded foot.

True Christianity will also build firmness of character in you. That is another quality that I want to see in our young people today. We have some splendid men, and some splendid women too. Even if the devil himself were to preach to them, I would not be afraid that he would cause them to turn from the faith. If all the new heresies that can rise were to be proclaimed in their presence, they know too well what the truth is to ever be led astray. On the other hand, we have a number of people who are led by their ears. If I pull their ear one way, they follow me. If they happen to go somewhere else and somebody pulls their ear the other way, they follow him.

There are lots of people who never do their own thinking, but let other people do it for them, just as some people have others do their laundry and never think of doing it at home. These people are just like the chaff on the threshing floor. When the wind begins to blow, away they go. Do not be like that. Dear young sons and daughters of church members, know the Lord. May He reveal Himself to you at once, and when you do know Him and get an understanding of the gospel, bind it to your heart, tie it around your neck (Proverbs 6:21), and say, "Yes. I am going to follow in the footsteps of those I love, and especially in the footsteps of the Lord Jesus Christ."

> Through floods and flames, if Jesus lead,
> I'll follow where He goes.[7]

May God help you to do it! First believe in the Lord Jesus Christ. Trust yourselves completely to Him, and He will give you grace to stand fast, even to the end.

---

7   These lines are from a hymn by John Ryland (1753-1825) that begins with "In all my Lord's appointed ways."

CHAPTER 6

A DESIRABLE SERVICE

*O LORD, truly I am thy servant; I am thy servant, and
the son of thine handmaid: thou hast loosed my bonds.*
(Psalm 116:8)

When a young man starts out in life, he is apt to inquire of an older person in this manner: "I would like to get into such a business, but is it a good one? You have been in it for years. How do you like it?" He seeks the advice of a friend who will tell him all about it. Someone will warn him that their trade is declining and that there is nothing to be done in it. Others will say that their business is very demanding and they would get out of it if they could. Someone else will answer, "Well, I have found it all right. I must speak well of the bridge that has carried me over. I have been able to earn a living, and I recommend you try it." I give my own experience, and therefore I want to say concerning the service of the Lord that I have never regretted that I entered it.

Certainly at some time or other since I put on Christ's uniform and became His servant, I should have found out the evil if there had been anything wrong in the religion of Jesus. At some time or other, I should have discovered that there was a mistake and that I was under a delusion. But it has never been so. I have regretted many things that I have done, but I have never regretted that I gave my heart to Christ and became a servant of the Lord. In times of deep depression – and I have had plenty of them – I have feared this and feared the other, but I have never had any suspicion of the goodness of my Master, the truth of His teaching, or the excellence of His service; neither have I ever wanted to go back to the service of Satan and sin. If we have been paying attention to the country from which we came out, we know that it has offered us many opportunities to return.

All sorts of enticements have assailed me, and siren voices have often tried to lure me upon the rocks, but never, never since the day in which I enlisted in Christ's service have I said to myself, "I am sorry that I am a Christian. I am dissatisfied that I serve the Lord." Therefore, from my own experience, I think that I may honestly and wholeheartedly recommend to you the service that I have found so good. I have been a bad enough servant, but never has a servant had such a loving Master or such a blessed time in serving.

I would add this personal testimony: the service of God is so delightful that I would like to die in it! When I have been unable to preach because of physical pain, I have taken my pen to write, and I have found much joy in making books for Jesus. When my hand has been unable to grasp the pen, I have wanted to talk about my Master to somebody, and I have tried to do so. I remember that David Brainerd, when he was very ill and could not preach to the Indians, was found sitting up in bed teaching a little Indian boy his letters so that he could learn to read the Bible. Brainerd said, "If I cannot serve God one way, I will serve Him another. I will never leave off this blessed service." This is my personal resolve, and truly, there is no virtue in saying this, for my Lord's service is a delight. It is a great pleasure to have anything to do for our great Father and Friend. Therefore, most affectionately and for your own good, I recommend the service of God to you.

To serve God is the most reasonable thing in the world. It was He who made you; should not your Creator have your service? It is He who supports you in being; should not that being be spent for His glory? If you had a cow or a dog, how long would you keep either of them if it were of no service to you? Suppose it were a dog, and it never showed affection toward you, but followed at everybody else's heel and never took notice of you – it never acknowledged you as its master at all. Would you not soon tire of such a creature? Which of you would make an engine, or devise any piece of machinery, if you did not hope that it would be of some service to you? God has made you, and the human body is a wonderful mechanism. The soul is also a wondrous thing. Will you not obey Him with the body or think of Him with the mind? This is Jehovah's own lament: *Hear, O heavens, and give ear, O earth: for the* LORD *hath spoken, I have nourished and brought up children, and they have rebelled against Me. The ox knoweth his owner, and the donkey his master's crib: but Israel doth not know, my people doth not consider* (Isaiah 1:2-3).

To have lived to the age of twenty-one without God is a terrible robbery. How have you managed it? To have lived to be thirty or forty, and never to have paid any reverence to Him who has kept the breath in your nostrils, without which you would have been a foul carcass in the grave long ago, is a base injustice. How do you dare to continue in it? To have lived so long, and, in addition to that, to have often insulted God, to have spoken against Him, to have profaned His day, to have neglected His Book, and to have turned your back on the Son of His love – is not this enough? Will you not cease from such an evil course?

There are some men who cannot bear provocation for five minutes, or even five seconds. It is "a word and a blow" with them;[8] only the blow frequently comes first. But God has been provoked for twenty years at a time – or thirty, forty, or fifty years or more, yet He bears patiently with us. Is it not time that we give to Him our reasonable service? If He has made us, if He has redeemed us, if He has preserved us in being, it is only what we owe to Him to be His servants.

This is the most honorable service that can ever be. Did you say, "Lord, I am Your servant"? I see a bright spirit coming like a flash of light from heaven, and my imagination realizes his presence. There he stands, a living flame. It is a seraph fresh from the throne, and what does he say? "O Lord, I am Your servant." Are you not glad to enter into such company as this? When cherubim and seraphim count it their glory to be the servants of God, what man among us will think it to be a low office? A prince or an emperor, if he is a sinner against God, is but a servant in the kitchen compared with the true nobleman who

---

8   "A word and a blow" is found in William Shakespeare's *Romeo and Juliet*, as well as in John Bunyan's *Pilgrim's Progress*.

serves the Lord in poverty and toil. This is the highest style of service under heaven. No honor of anyone who waits upon any earthly king can rival it. The prestigious British Knights of the Garter, or any other honorable distinction you like, loses its glory in comparison with the man whom God will call servant in the day of the appearing of our Lord and Savior Jesus Christ. You are in great company, young friend, if you are a servant of God.

Let me note that this service is full of goodness. If I had to engage in a trade, I would like to spend my time and strength in a pursuit that did no harm to anybody, and did good to many. Somehow, I do not think that I would like to deal in deadly weapons, and certainly not in the accursed alcohol business. I would rather starve than earn my bread by selling alcohol or anything else that would debase my fellowmen and degrade them below the level of brute beasts.

It is a wonderful thing, I think, if a young man can follow a calling in which he may do well for himself, and be doing well to others at the same time. It is a fine thing to act as some have done who have not grown rich by grinding the faces of poor needlewomen (Isaiah 3:15), or by withholding the wage of the servant behind the counter, but have lifted others up with them, and as they have advanced, those in their employment have advanced also. That is something worth living for in the lower sphere of things, but he who becomes a servant of God is doing good all along, for there is no part of the service of God that can do any harm to anybody.

The service of the Lord is all goodness. It is good for yourself, and it is good for your fellowmen, for what does God ask in His service but that we would love Him with all our heart, and that we love our neighbour as ourselves (Matthew 22:37-39)? He who does this is truly serving God by the help of His Spirit, and he is also greatly blessing others. It is a most kindhearted work to engage in, and that is why I recommend it to you – for its reasonableness, its honorableness, and its goodness.

It is the most beneficial work under heaven. "Not always today," someone may say. Yet I presume to say, "Always today." To serve God is beneficial now. How so? Certainly not in hard cash, as misers rightly call their gold, but in better material. A quiet conscience is better than gold, and to know that you are doing good is something more sweet in life than to know that you are getting rich or famous. Have not some of us lived long enough to know that most of the things of this world are simply foam upon the top of the cup that is far better blown away than preserved? The main joy of life is to be right with yourself, your neighbor, and your God. He who gets right with God – what more does he need? He is paid for anything that he may suffer in the cause of God by his own peace of mind.

There was a martyr once in Switzerland standing barefooted on the pile of wood, and he was about to be burned to death. There was no pleasant prospect for him. He called to the magistrate who was in charge of his execution and asked him to come near him. He said, "Please place your hand upon my heart. I am about to die by fire. Place your hand on my heart. If it beats any faster than it ordinarily beats, do not believe my religion." The magistrate, with palpitating heart himself and all in a tremble, laid his hand upon the martyr's chest and found that he was just as calm as if he were going to his bed rather than to the flames. That is a glorious thing! To wear in your buttonhole that little flower called heart's ease, and to have the jewel of contentment in your heart – this is heaven begun below. Godliness is great gain to him who has it (1 Timothy 6:6).

I think that all that we can get in this world is inconsequential, because we must leave it, or it must leave us, in a very short time. Young men – if you live, your hair will very soon be powdered with the grey of age! How short life is! How swift time is! The older we get, the faster years fly. Only that which I can have forever is worth having. Only that which death cannot tear out of my hand is worth grasping. The supreme reward of being a servant of God is hereafter.

If, young man, you would serve God and meet with losses here for Christ's sake, you may consider these to be light afflictions that are only for a moment (2 Corinthians 4:17), and you may think them to be quite unworthy to be compared with the glory that will be revealed (Romans 8:18). This is true because there is a resurrection of the dead. There is a judgment to come. There is a life eternal. There is a heaven of unspeakable splendor, and there is a place in that heaven for every one of us who become true servants of the living God.

I think that I hear somebody saying, "Well, I do not want to be a servant." You cannot help it, my friend; you cannot help it. You must be a servant of somebody. "Then I will serve myself," someone says. Pardon me, brave sir, if I whisper in your ear that if you serve yourself, you will serve a fool. The man who is the servant of himself – listen to this sentence – the man who is the servant of himself is the slave of a slave. I cannot imagine a more degrading position for a man to be in than to be the slave of a slave. You will certainly serve somebody. You will wear shackles, too, if you serve the master that most men choose.

Oh, simply look at this city – this city full of free men; do most of them know real liberty? Look at this city full of "freethinkers." Is there any man who thinks in chains like the man who calls himself a freethinker? Is there any man as misguided as the man who will not believe in the Bible? He swallows a ton of difficulties, yet complains that we have swallowed an ounce of them. He has much more need of faith of a certain type than we have, for skepticism has far harder problems than faith.

Then look at the one who claims to live free – one who lives to gratify the desires of the flesh – what a bondage is his life! *Who hath woe? . . . Who hath redness of eyes* but the slave of strong drink (Proverbs 23:29-30)? Who has rottenness in the bones but the slave of his passions (Proverbs 14:30)? Is there any wretch who ever rowed in the Spanish galley, or any bondsman beneath the sun, who is half as much of a slave as he who will be led tonight of his lusts like a bullock to the slaughter, going to his own damnation, and even to the ruin of his body, while he makes himself the victim of his own passions?

If I must be a slave, I will be a slave to Turk or savage, but never to myself, for that would be the lowest pit of degradation. You must be a servant to somebody. There is no getting through the world without it, but if you are the servant to yourself, your bondage will be terrible. *Choose you this day whom ye will serve* (Joshua 24:15), for you must serve. Every man must get to his task, whether he is a prince or a pauper, a millionaire or a beggar. Kings and queens are usually the most wearied servants of all. The higher men climb, the more they have to serve their fellowmen. You must serve. Oh, that you would enter the service of your God!

There is room in it. Other places are crowded. Hundreds of young men go from shop to shop and beg for the opportunity to earn a livelihood. I lament that in many instances they beg in vain. Some of you wear the boots off your feet in trying to get some work to do. How sincerely I desire that you may find the employment you seek! But there is room in the service of God, and He is willing to receive you. Let me tell you that if you enter His service, it will help you in everything that you have to do in this life.

They say that a Christian man is a fool. Oh, proud opposers, though we do not say the same to you, we can, perhaps, truthfully think the same about you. I have seen many believers in Jesus whom it would have been very dangerous to deal with as with fools, for very soon he who dealt with them in that way would have found that he made a great mistake. They are not always fools who are called so; they are such sometimes who use those names about others.

I like a Christian man to be all the better in every way for being a Christian. He should be a better employee and a better employer. He should be a better tradesman and a better artisan. Certainly there is no poet whose poetry excels that of the poet of the sanctuary. John Milton still sits alone above the rest. There is no painter who should paint as well as he who tries to make immortal the memorable scenes in which great deeds were done. That which you can now do well, you could do better by becoming a servant of God.

CHAPTER 7

OVERCOMING THE EVIL ONE

There are men who have overcome the devil, and they have overcome him in many shapes. There are many pictures of the devil around, but I am afraid that none of them are accurate, for he assumes different shapes in different places. He is a chameleon, always affected by the light in which he happens to be. He is a Proteus, assuming every shape so that it may serve his purpose.

Some young men have overcome that blue devil that keeps men despairing, doubting, trembling, and fearing. You once were subject to him. You said that you could not believe in Christ. You were afraid you would never be saved. You wrote bitter things against yourself. But now you have cast him out by a simple faith in Jesus, for you know whom you have believed, and you are persuaded that He is able to keep that which you have committed unto Him (2 Timothy 1:12). You have overcome that devil, and although he does try to come back, and when your business is a little troublesome or your liver may not be acting properly, he tries to sneak his way in, yet by God's grace he will never fasten the old chains on you again.

Then there is that dust-eating devil of whom we can never speak too badly – the yellow devil of *the mammon of unrighteousness* (Luke 16:9), the love of gold and silver. This is the dreadful god of London that rolls over this city as if it were all its own. I think I see him as a dragon on the top of the church steeple, laughing at the inscription of Psalm 24:1 over the Royal Exchange: *The earth is the LORD's and the fullness thereof.* He is laughing because he knows better, for he believes that it all belongs to him, just as he said to Christ long ago: *All these things will I give Thee, if Thou wilt fall down and worship me* (Matthew 4:9).

What deceit is done nowadays in business for the love of gold! In fact, some of us who are not businessmen, but who, nevertheless, are not blind, know that dishonest marks and dishonest measures have become so systematic that their effect is lost, and the thing itself is almost as honest as if it were honest. It is the fact that men have become so accustomed to say that three times two makes seven that their neighbors all say, "Exactly so, and we will pay you for the goods using the same kind of calculation," so that the thing has to align itself.

However, the genuine Christian, the man who is strong and has the Word of God abiding in him, rejects all this. He hears others say, "We must live," but he replies, "Yes, but we must die." He determines that he will not throw away his soul in order to grasp wealth, and that if it is not possible to become a wealthy merchant without violating the code of honor and Christ's law, then he will be content to be poor. Young man, if you have reached this conclusion, you have overcome the Wicked One indeed! I am afraid there are some people with gray heads who have hardly tried to fight this. It is sad for them.

Another form of the Wicked One we must speak of softly, but oh, how difficult she is to be overcome by the young man! I am referring to Madame Wanton – lust, immorality, promiscuity – that fair but foul, that smiling but murderous, monster of hell by whom so many are deluded. Solomon spoke of the *strange woman* (Proverbs 2:16; 5:3; 7:5), but the strong Christian in whom the Word of God abides passes by her door and shuts his ear to her siren song. He flees youthful lusts that war against the soul (1 Peter 2:11). He reserves both his body and his soul for his Lord, who has redeemed him by His precious blood.

Young man, if you are strong and have overcome the Wicked One, you have overcome, I believe, that Lucifer of pride, and it is your work to walk humbly with your God (Micah 6:8)! You have given up all idea of merit. You cannot boast or exalt yourself, but you bow humbly at the foot of the cross and adore Him who has saved you from the wrath to come.

I trust, young man, that you have also given up all subjection to the great red dragon of fashion, who draws with his tail even the very stars of heaven (Revelation 12:4). There are some people who would think it is far worse to be considered unfashionable than to be thought unchristian. To be unchristian would be such a common accusation that they could submit to it, but to be unfashionable would be horrible indeed! Young men in London get to be influenced by this. If the young men in the house are going to a certain entertainment, if they all read a certain kind of book, if they are immoral and corrupt and unbelieving, then the temptation is to join in with them. Only the man who is strong and has the Word of God abiding in him will overcome the Wicked One by doing only what is right: "Faithful among the faithless found."[9]

Of course, certain talents are necessary for certain positions, but it is a rule without exception that every child of God may be useful in the family of God. God does not have one single servant for whom He has not appointed a service. You are now strong. This very strength that you now have will enable you to do mission work for God, and the graces that have been worked in you through Christ Jesus – faith, love, courage, patience – are your preparations for sacred labor.

If you are to be a minister, you may need to acquire a measure of learning; if you are to be a missionary, you will need a special kind of training – but you can get these. God will give you strength to obtain them, and the spiritual strength will go very far to help you. Meanwhile, for other work, all the strength you require is that which you already possess. There are people in the world who will not let us speak a word to the unconverted because they say, and say very truly, that unconverted people are dead in sin, and therefore we are not to tell them to live because they have no power to live. They forget that we have the power in the vitalizing Word and Spirit of God, and that as we speak the Word for God, power goes with it.

There is among us too much forgetfulness of the fact that we actually have power from on high. We are always praying for the outpouring of the Holy Spirit, which is very appropriate, but remember that we have the Holy Spirit; the Spirit is here. He is not always outwardly observable, but He is given to His church to abide in every one of His people, and if we would only believe in His presence, we would feel this more.

---

9   This comes from Book 5 of John Milton's *Paradise Lost*, which says "So spake the Seraph Abdiel faithful found, among the faithless, faithful only he."

Those who preach most successfully will tell you that one cause of it is that they expect to be successful. They do not preach hoping that one or two may be saved, but they know that they will be because the Word of God is the power of God unto salvation (Romans 1:16). They believe in the Holy Spirit, and those who do believe see the Holy Spirit, but those who only hesitantly hope in the Holy Spirit do not discern Him. According to their faith, so is it unto them (Matthew 9:29).

Believe, my brother, that as a believer you have within you the power that is necessary for reforming that house of business of yours, which is now so godless, into a house of prayer. Believe it, and begin to work like those who do believe it. Believe that those who pass you in the morning, my young artisan friend, may be and will be converted by you and by God if you speak to them out of your heart. Go up to them as one who knows that God is working with him. They will be awed by your manner, and if they reject your message, their consciences will feel the effect.

If the young man inquires for tools and weapons with which to serve his Master, know that *the Word of God abideth in you* (1 John 2:14). If you desire to teach others, you do not have to ask what the lesson will be, for it abides in you. Do you want a text that will make an impression on the careless? What made an impression on you? You cannot have a better text. You desire to speak a word in season from the Word of God that will be likely to comfort the downhearted. What has comforted your own soul? You cannot have a better guide.

You have within your own experience a tutor that cannot fail you, and you also have an encouragement that cannot be taken from you. The Word of God within you will well up like a spring, and truth and grace will pour forth from you in rivers. I have heard our Lord compared to a man carrying a waterpot, and as he carried it upon his shoulder, the water fell dropping, dropping, dropping, so that everyone could track the water bearer.

All God's people should be like this, carrying such a fullness of grace that everyone should know where they have been by that which they have left behind. He who had lain in the beds of spices will perfume the air through which he walks. One who, like Asher, has dipped his foot in oil (Deuteronomy 33:24), will leave his footprints behind him. When the living and incorruptible seed remains within (1 Peter 1:23), the divine instincts of the new nature will guide you to the wisest methods of activity. You will do the right thing under the inward impulse rather than the written law, and your personal salvation will be your prime qualification for seeking out others of your Master's flock.

You have overcome the wicked one (1 John 2:13). Once a man has given Satan a slap in the face, he does not need to be afraid of men. If you have often stood toe-to-toe with a violent temptation, and after wrestling have overcome it, you can laugh to scorn all the puny adversaries who assail you. Being experienced in inward conflicts will breed manliness within the young man and will make him a truly muscular Christian. You have overcome Satan by the power of grace – *you*. Then there is hope that in the Sunday school class that you teach, that Satan may again be conquered in the hearts of those boys and girls. There is hope for that drunken man you have been talking with lately; why should he not overcome the Wicked One? You were once weak enough, but grace has made you strong. What grace has done for you, it can do for another. Someone said, "After I was saved myself, I never despaired of anyone else."

The fact that you have been enabled to achieve a conquest in a very terrible strife should comfort you with regard to all other cases. Go into the back slums. They are not far off. Penetrate the dark lanes and alleys. You *have overcome the wicked one*. You cannot meet with anything worse than him whom you have already conquered. Let the majesty of grace in your souls be comfort and motivation to you, and never say that anything is too hard for you to do when you have already met Apollyon face to face and saw him retreat in defeat.

In the French wars, certain young men unhappily found their names written down in the conscription and were marched to the wars. In a war from which none of us desire to escape, I hope there are young men whose names are written down – heavenly conscripts – who are summoned more fully than ever before in their lives to go forth to the battle of the Lord of Hosts.

I invite every young man who is already converted to God to dedicate himself to the Lord Jesus Christ. It is not a matter that I can talk you into, nor indeed would I try it, but I would ask you to sit still a moment and consider with yourselves in this way: "I am a believer in Christ. I have recently been to the sacramental table. I profess to have been chosen by God, to have been redeemed with His precious blood, to have been separated from the rest of mankind, and to be destined for a most magnificent immortality. Am I living as a redeemed one should live?"

Passing your hand over your brow thoughtfully, you will probably conclude, "I am not. I am serving God, I hope, in some way, but not with all my heart, soul, and strength as I should be doing. What about my time? Do I devote as much of that as I can to sacred work? What about my talent? Does that display itself most in the literary association or in the Sunday school? Are my oratorical abilities most developed in the debating room or in preaching at the street corner? Am I giving to Christ the prime, the best, and the strength of my life? If I am not, I should do so. I should be entirely Christ's. It is not that I should leave my business, but I must make my business Christ's business. I should so conduct it and distribute its results as to prove that I am Christ's steward working in the world for Him and not for self."

If today you will not simply vow, but will pray that from this time forward there will not be a drop of blood in your body, nor a hair of your head, nor a penny in your pocket, nor a word on your tongue, nor a thought in your heart that will not be completely the Lord's, I will be glad enough.

It will be good if you take a step further as recruits. You "holy work folk," as they used to call those who lived around the cathedral at Durham and were exempt from all service to the baron because they served the church, think of some specific walk and area in which as young men you can devote yourselves wholly to Christ. Generalities in religion are always to be avoided, and more especially generalities in service. A man might come to you for a job, and you might ask him, "What do you do?" If he replies, "I am a painter" or "I am a carpenter," you might be able to find him work; but if he says, "Oh, I can do anything," you understand that he can do nothing. So it is with a sort of spiritual laborers who profess to be able to do anything in the church, but who really do nothing.

What can you do? What is your calling? Schools for the poor children? Sunday schools? Street preaching? Tract distribution? Here is a choice for you; which do you select? Do not waste time, but say, "This is my calling, and by God's grace I will give myself up to it. I intend to do it as well as, or if possible, better than, anyone ever did it. If I teach in the school, I will be a thoroughly good teacher of those little children. If I teach in the Sunday school, I intend to make myself as efficient in the class as ever a teacher could be." It will be no small blessing to the churches that you represent if such a decision is made, and if the workers are of such a type.

There are many men who should be employed in Christian work who avoid it or abstain from participating in it. You do not need to think that you will gain earthly wealth by it. If you have any idea of that kind, I must ask you to keep breaking stones or continue in whatever work you are doing, for that will pay you better. If you have any idea that you will find the ministry an easy life, I entreat you to try treading grain in a mill, for that would be an amusement compared with the life of the genuine Christian minister – in London, at least.

However, if you feel an intense earnestness, if you have succeeded in speaking on other subjects and have had some influence, think whether you can devote yourself to the work of God. Oh, young man, if I cast an ambitious thought into your mind, I mean it only for my Master's glory. If the Lord should say, *Separate Me Saul and Barnabas to this work* (Acts 13:2), if He should call out some fine, noble young fellow who might have given himself up, perhaps, to the pursuits of business, but who now will dedicate himself to the service of the Christian ministry, it would be well. Be careful that you do not keep back whom God would have.

May there not also be some young man who will enlist for missionary service abroad? *I write unto you, young men, because ye are strong, and the Word of God abideth in you, and ye have overcome the wicked one* (1 John 2:14). You are the men we need: "Wanted: young men who are strong, in whom the Word of God abides, and who have overcome the Wicked One."

You who are weak had better stop at home in the Christian nursery a little while. You, in whom the Word of God does not yet abide, have need to stay until you are taught the elements of the faith. You who have not overcome the Wicked One had better flash your unproven swords in home fields of conflict first. You are not the men who are now needed.

However, you who are strong enough to do and to dare for Jesus, you who are spiritually minded enough to have overcome the monster of evil within yourselves, you are the men to fight Satan abroad in his strongholds of heathenism, Roman Catholicism, and Islam. You, the finest men of the church, are the men whom the missionary society requires. Think of it before you go to sleep, and if the Lord prompts you, come forward and say, *Here am I; send me* (Isaiah 6:8).

It is good to be zealous always in a good thing (Galatians 4:8). We should forget the things that are behind, and press forward to that which is before (Philippians 3:13). It will be a great thing when all Christian businessmen do what some are doing – giving of their substance to the cause of Christ in due proportion. It is a blessed thing for a young man to begin business with the rule that he will give the Lord at least his tenth. That habit of weekly setting it aside for Christ, and then giving to Christ out of His own bag instead of giving from your own purse, is a most blessed one.

Cultivate it, you young tradesmen who have just set up in business for yourselves. You good wives, help your husbands to do it. You young men who are clerks and have regular incomes, make that a regular part of your weekly business, and let some portion of the consecrated treasure go to the Lord's foreign field. At the same time, never let your donations to this or that cause be used as an attempt to excuse you from personal service. Give yourselves to Christ. Give your whole selves in the highest state of strength. Give your whole selves constantly, intelligently, and without adding any selfish or ulterior motives.

CHAPTER 8

ESTHER DEFEATS HER ENEMIES

By the narrative of Esther's history, the Lord intended to set before us a wonderful example of His providence so that when we had viewed it with interest and pleasure, we might praise His name, and then go on to acquire the habit of observing His hand in other histories, and especially in our own lives. John Flavel says well that he who observes providence will never be long without a providence to observe.[10] The man who can walk through the world and see no God is said upon inspired authority to be a fool (Psalm 14:1; 53:1; Romans 1:20-22). The wise man's eyes, though, are in his head; he sees with an inner sight and discovers God everywhere at work. It is his joy to perceive that the Lord is working according to His will in heaven, and on earth, and in all deep places. It has been well said that the book of Esther is a record of wonders without a miracle, and therefore, though equally revealing the glory of the Lord, it sets it forth in another manner from that which is displayed in the overthrow of Pharaoh by miraculous power.

Let us now get to the story. There were two races, one of which God had blessed and promised to preserve, and another of which He had said that He would utterly put out the remembrance of it from under heaven. Israel was to be blessed and made a blessing, but the Lord had sworn in regard to Amalek that *the LORD will have war with Amalek from generation to generation* (Exodus 17:16). These two peoples were

---

10   John Flavel (c. 1628-1691) was an English Puritan minister and author. Some of his writings, including *Preparations for Sufferings*, *Biblical Mourning*, and *Keeping the Heart*, are available from Aneko Press.

therefore in deadly hostility, like the seed of the woman and the seed of the serpent, between whom the Lord Himself has put an enmity (Genesis 3:15).

Many years had rolled by. The chosen people were in great distress, and at this far-off time there still existed upon the face of the earth some relics of the race of Amalek. Among them was one descended of the royal line of Agag, whose name was Haman, and he was in supreme power at the court of Ahasuerus, the Persian monarch. It was God's intent that one last conflict should take place between Israel and Amalek. The conflict that began with Joshua in the desert was to be finished by Mordecai in the king's palace.

This last struggle began with great disadvantage to God's people. Haman was the prime minister of the far-extending empire of Persia, the favorite of a despotic monarch, who was compliant to his will. Mordecai, a Jew in the employment of the king, sat in the king's gate, and when he saw proud Haman go to and fro, he refused to pay him the homage that others so subserviently gave to him. Mordecai would not bow his head or bend his knee to Haman, and this aggravated Haman exceedingly.

It came into his mind that Mordecai was of the seed of the Jews, and with that remembrance came the costly determination to avenge the quarrel of his race. He thought it repulsive to involve only one man, so he resolved to incarnate all the hate of generations, and at one blow sweep the accursed Jews, as he thought them, from off the face of the earth. He went in to the king, with whom his word was power, and told him that there was a certain people scattered up and down the Persian empire who were different from all others and were opposed to the king's laws. He explained that it was not to the king's benefit to tolerate them.

Haman asked that they might all be destroyed, stating that he would pay an enormous sum of money into the king's treasury to compensate for any loss of revenue by their destruction. He intended that the spoil that would be taken from the Jews would tempt their neighbors to kill them, and that the portion allotted to himself would repay the amount that he advanced. Thus, he intended to make the Jews pay for their own murder. He had no sooner asked for this horrible grant than the monarch allowed it. He took his signet ring off his finger and told Haman to do with the Jews whatever seemed good to him.

Thus the chosen seed are in the hands of the Agagite, who thirsts to annihilate them. Only one thing stands in the way: the Lord has said, *No weapon that is formed against thee shall prosper, and every tongue that riseth against thee in judgment thou shalt condemn* (Isaiah 54:17). We will see what happens, and learn from it.

We will learn from the narrative that God places His agents in the right places for doing His work. The Lord was not taken by surprise by this plot of Haman. He had foreseen it and forestalled it. In order to match Haman's deceptive, malicious plan, it was necessary for someone of Jewish race to have great influence with the king. How was this to be brought about? If a Jewess were to become the queen of Persia, the power she would possess would be useful in counteracting the enemy's design. This had been all arranged years before Haman had dreamed up in his wicked heart the scheme of murdering the Jews.

Esther, whose sweet name signifies myrtle, had been elevated to the position of the queen of Persia by a remarkable course of events. It happened that Ahasuerus, at a certain drinking session, was so far gone with wine as to forget all the proprieties of Eastern life, and he sent for his queen, Vashti, to display herself to the people and the princes. No one dreamed in those days of disobeying the tyrant's word, and therefore all stood shocked when Vashti, evidently a woman of proper royal spirit, refused to degrade herself by being made a spectacle before that crude crowd of drinking princes, and she refused to come.

For her courage, Vashti was divorced, and a new queen was sought for. We cannot commend Mordecai for putting his adopted daughter in competition for the monarch's choice. It was contrary to the law of God, and it was dangerous to her soul in the highest degree. It would have been better for Esther to have been the wife of the poorest man of the house of Israel than to have gone into the den of the Persian despot.

The Bible does not excuse, much less commend, the wrongdoing of Esther and Mordecai for acting in this way, but simply tells us how divine wisdom brought good out of evil, even as the chemist draws out healing drugs from poisonous plants. The high position of Esther, though gained contrary to the wisest of laws, was overruled for the best interests of her people. Esther in the king's house was the means of defeating the malicious adversary. But Esther alone was not enough.

She was closed up in the harem, surrounded by her attendants and her maids of honor, but quite secluded from the outside world.

A watchman is needed outside the palace to guard the people of the Lord and to urge Esther to action when help is needed. Mordecai, her cousin and foster father, obtained a job that placed him at the palace gate. Where could he be better posted? Much of the royal business will come under his eye here, and he is quick, courageous, and unflinching. Israel never had a better sentinel than Mordecai, the son of Kish, a Benjamite. He was a very different man from that other son of Kish who had allowed Amalek to escape in former times (1 Samuel 15). Mordecai's relationship to the queen allowed him to communicate with her through Hatach, one of the king's attendants, and when Haman's evil decree was published, it was not long before intelligence of it reached her ear and she felt the danger to which Mordecai and all her people were exposed.

By remarkable providences, the Lord placed those two most efficient instruments in their places. Mordecai would have been of little use without Esther, and Esther could have rendered no aid if it had not been for Mordecai. Meanwhile, a conspiracy was hatched against the king, which Mordecai discovered and communicated to the highest authority. This put the king under obligation to him, which was a necessary part of the Lord's plan.

Now whatever trouble may be brewing against the cause of God and truth (and I dare say there is very much going on at this moment, for neither the devil, the Jesuits, nor the atheists are quiet for very long), we can be sure that the Lord knows all about it, and He has His Esther and His Mordecai ready at their posts to frustrate their plans. The Lord has His men well placed, and He has His ambushes hidden, ready to surprise His foes. We never need to be afraid that the Lord has not forestalled His enemies and provided against their evil.

Every child of God is where God has placed him for some purpose, and the practical use of this first point is to lead you to inquire for what practical purpose God has placed each one of you where you now are. You have been hoping for another position where you could do something for Jesus. Do not wish for anything of the kind, but serve Him where you are. If you are sitting at the king's gate, there is something for you to do there, and if you were on the queen's throne, there would be something for you to do there. Do not ask to be either gatekeeper or queen, but whichever you are, serve God in that position.

Are you rich? God has made you a steward; take care that you are a good steward. Are you poor? God has thrown you into a position where you will be better able to give a word of sympathy to poor saints. Are you doing your allotted work? Do you live in a godly family? God has a motive for placing you in such a happy position. Are you in an ungodly house? You are a lamp hung up in a dark place; make sure you shine there. Esther did well because she acted as Esther should, and Mordecai did well because he acted as Mordecai should.

I like to think that God has put each one of us in the right place, even as a good captain well arranges the different parts of his army. Although we do not know the captain's plan of battle, it will be seen during the conflict that he has placed each soldier where he should be. Our wisdom is not to desire another place, nor to judge those who are in another position, but each one who has been redeemed with the precious blood of Jesus should say, "Lord, what do You want me to do, for here I am, and by Your grace I am ready to do it." Do not forget the fact that God in His providence places His servants in positions where He can make use of them.

The Lord not only arranges His servants, but He restrains His enemies. I want to call your attention particularly to the fact that Haman, having gained a decree for the destruction of all the Jews upon a certain day, was very anxious to have his cruel work done thoroughly, and therefore, being very superstitious and believing in astrology, he told his magicians to cast lots so that he might find a lucky day for his great undertaking. The lots were cast for the various months, but not a single fortunate day could be found until near the end of the year. The chosen day was the thirteenth day of the twelfth month. The magicians told gullible Haman that on that day, the heavens would be propitious and the star of Haman would be ascending. Truly the lot was cast into the lap, but the disposal of it was of the Lord (Proverbs 16:33). There were eleven months left before the Jews would be put to death, and that would give Mordecai and Esther time to turn around, and if anything could be done to reverse the cruel decree, they had time to do it in.

If the lot had fallen on the second or third month, the swift dromedaries and camels and messengers would hardly have been able to reach the far borders of the Persian dominions. Certainly a second set of messengers to counteract the decree could not have done so, and, humanly speaking, the Jews would have been destroyed. But in that secret council chamber where the sorcerers and the man who asks counsel at the hands of the devilish powers sit, the Lord Himself is present, frustrating the signs of the liars and making fortune-tellers mad. Their enchantments and their many sorceries were in vain. The astrologers, the stargazers, and the monthly diviners were all fools together, and they led the superstitious Haman to destruction. *Surely there is no enchantment against Jacob, neither is there any divination against Israel* (Numbers 23:23). You who are righteous, trust in the Lord, and in patience possess your souls (Luke 21:19). Leave your adversaries in the hands of God, for He can make them fall into the snare that they have secretly laid for you.

Notice well that Haman selected a method of destroying the Jews that was wonderfully overruled for their preservation. They were to be slain by any of the people among whom they lived who chose to do so, and their plunder was to reward their slayers. This was a very shrewd plan, for greed would naturally incite the lower sort of men to murder the thrifty Jews, and no doubt there were debtors who would also be glad to see their creditors disposed of. But notice the loophole for escape that this provided! If the decree had stated that the Jews should be slain by the soldiers of the Persian empire, it would have been done, and it is not easy to see how the Jews could have escaped. However, since the matter was left in private hands, the subsequent decree that they could defend themselves was sufficient to counteract the first edict. Thus, the Lord arranged that the wisdom of Haman would turn out to be foolishness after all.

In another point, we notice the restraining hand of God. Although Mordecai had provoked Haman to the utmost, he was not immediately put to death. *Haman refrained himself* (Esther 5:10). Why did he do so? Proud men are usually in a mighty uproar if they consider themselves insulted, and they are ready at once to take revenge; but *Haman refrained himself.* Until that day in which his anger burned furiously and he set up the gallows, he smothered his passion. I marvel at this. It shows how God makes the wrath of man to praise Him, and He restrains the rest. Mordecai will not die a violent death by Haman's hand.

The enemies of the church of God, and of His people, can never do more than the Lord permits. They cannot go a hair's breadth beyond the divine permission, and when they are permitted to do their worst, there is always some weak point about all that they do, some extreme folly that renders their fury vain. The wicked carry about them the weapons of their own destruction, and when they rage most against the Most High, the Lord of all brings out of it good for His people and glory to Himself. Do not judge providence in little pieces, for it is a magnificent mosaic and must be seen as a whole. Do not say of any one hour, "This is dark." It may be so, but that darkness will minister to the light, even as the dark gloom of midnight makes the stars appear more bright. *Trust ye in the LORD forever, for in the LORD JEHOVAH is everlasting strength* (Isaiah 26:4). His wisdom will undermine the mines of deceit, and His skill will reach above the climbing of guile. *He taketh the wise in their own craftiness, and the counsel of the froward is carried headlong* (Job 5:13).

God, in His providence, tests His people. God tested Mordecai. I have no doubt that he was a quiet old man, and it must have been a daily trial to him to stand upright, or to sit in his place when Haman, that proud peer of the realm, went strutting by. His fellow servants told him that the king had commanded all men to pay homage to Haman, but he held his own, knowing what it might cost him to be so sternly independent. Haman was an Amalekite, and Mordecai the Jew would not bow before him. What trouble it must have been to the heart of Mordecai when he saw the proclamation that all the Jews must die! The good man must have bitterly lamented his unhappy fate in being the innocent cause of the destruction of his nation. Even if you know you have done right, yet if you bring down trouble, and especially destruction, upon the heads of others, it cuts you to the quick. You could bear martyrdom for yourself, but it is sad to see others suffer through your firmness.

CHAPTER 9

PRAYER AND PROVIDENCE – ESTHER'S ACTION

Esther had to be tested. Amid the glitter of the Persian court, she might have grown forgetful of her God, but the sad news came to her that her cousin and her nation were to be destroyed. Sorrow and dread filled her heart. There was no hope for her people unless she would go in unto the king – that despot from whom one angry look would be death. She must risk all and go unrequested into his presence and plead for her nation.

Do you wonder that she trembled? Do you marvel that she asked for the prayers of the faithful? Are you surprised to see both herself and her attendants fasting and lamenting before God? Do not think, my prosperous friend, that the Lord has given you a high place so that you may escape the trials that belong to all His people. Yours is not a position of ease, but it is one of the fiercest parts of the battle. Neither the lowest and most quiet position, nor the most public and exposed condition, will enable you to escape the *much tribulation* through which the church militant must fight its way to glory (Acts 14:22). Why should we want to escape the trial? Should not the gold be tested in the crucible? Should not the strong pillar sustain great weight?

When the Menai Bridge was first flung across the straits from Bangor, Wales, to the Isle of Anglesey, the engineer did not stipulate that his bridge should never be tested with great weights. On the contrary, I can imagine him saying, "Bring up your heaviest trains and load the bridge as much as you can, for it will bear every strain." *The LORD trieth the righteous* (Psalm 11:5) because He has made them of metal that will endure the test. He knows that by the sustaining power of His Holy Spirit, they will be held up and made *more than conquerors* (Romans 8:37). Therefore, it is a part of the operation of Providence to try the saints. Let that comfort those of you who are having trouble at this time.

The Lord's wisdom is seen in arranging the smallest events so as to produce great results. We frequently hear people say of a pleasant or a great event, "What a providence!" They are silent, though, as to anything that appears less important or has an unpleasant quality. But the place of the grass upon the prairie is as fixed as the station of a king, and the dust that is raised by a chariot wheel is as surely steered by providence as the planet in its orbit. There is as much providence in the creeping of an aphid upon a rose leaf as in the marching of an army to ravage a continent. Everything, the most insignificant as well as the most magnificent, is ordered by the Lord who has prepared His throne in the heavens, whose kingdom rules over all. The history before us furnishes proof of this.

We have reached the point where Esther is to go in unto the king and plead for her people. Strengthened by prayer, but doubtless still trembling, Esther entered the inner court, and the king's affection led him to hold out the golden scepter instantly. Being told to ask what she wanted, she invited the king to come to a banquet, and she asked him to bring Haman with him. He came, and for the second time invited her to ask what she wanted up to half of his kingdom.

Why, when the king was in such a kind spirit, did not Esther speak? He was charmed with her beauty, and his royal word was given to deny her nothing, so why not speak out? But no, she merely asked that he and Haman would come to another banquet of wine tomorrow. Daughter of Abraham, what an opportunity you have lost! Why did you not plead for your people? Their very existence depends upon your request, and the king has asked you what you wanted, yet you are hesitant? Was it timidity? It is possible. Did she think that Haman stood too high in the king's favor for her to prevail? It would be hard to say.

Some of us are very mysterious, but far more was depending on that woman's unexplainable silence than appears at first sight. She undoubtedly desired to bring out her secret, but the words did not come out. God was in it; it was not the right time for her to speak, and therefore she was led to put off her disclosure. I dare say she regretted it and wondered when she would be able to get to the point, but the Lord knew best. After that banquet, Haman went out joyfully at the palace gate, but being mortified beyond measure by Mordecai's uncompromising posture, he called for his wife and his friends and told them that his riches and honors availed him nothing as long as Mordecai, the Jew, sat in the king's gate. They could have told him, "You will destroy Mordecai and all his people in a few months, and the man is already worrying himself over the decree. Let him live, and be content to watch his miseries and gloat over his despair!"

But no, they counsel speedy revenge. Let Mordecai be hanged on a rope on the top of the house, and let the gallows be set up at once. Early in the morning, let Haman ask for the Jew's life, and let his disrespect be punished. Go, call the workmen, and let the gallows be set up at a great height that very night. It seemed a small matter that Haman would be so enraged just at that hour, but it was a very important item in the whole transaction, for if he had not been so hasty, he would not have gone so early in the morning to the palace, and would not have been at hand when the king asked, *Who is in the court?* (Esther 6:4).

What happened? That very night, when Haman was devising to hang Mordecai, the king could not sleep. What caused the monarch's restlessness? Why did this happen on this night among all others? Ahasuerus is master of 127 provinces, but not master of ten minutes' sleep. What should he do? Will he call for soothing instruments of music? Will he be entertained with a tale that is told or with a merry ballad of the minstrel? No, he calls for a book. Who would have thought that this luxurious prince would listen to a reader at the dead of night. He wanted a book. What book? A volume perfumed with roses, musical with songs, and sweet as the notes of the nightingale? No. *He commanded to bring the book of records of the chronicles* (Esther 6:1). That sounds like dull reading. However, there are 127 provinces; which volume will the page bring from the recorder's shelves? He chose the record of Shushan, the royal city. That is the center of the empire, and its record is lengthy.

In which section will the reader begin to read? He may begin where he pleases, but before he closes the book, the story of the discovery of a conspiracy by Mordecai has been read in the king's hearing. Was not this a remarkable accident? Remarkable if you like, but it was no accident. Out of ten thousand other records, the reader finds that one of all others. The Jews tell us that he began at another place, but that the book closed and fell open at the chapter about Mordecai. Be that as it may, it is certain that the Lord knew where the record was, and He guided the reader to the right page.

Speaking after the manner of men, there were a million chances against one that the king of Persia would, in the dead of the night, be reading the chronicle of his own kingdom, and that this specific part of it would happen to be read to him. But that was not all; the king is interested. He had wanted to go to sleep, but that desire is gone, and he is in a hurry to act. *The king said, What honour and dignity hath been done to Mordecai for this? Then said the king's servants that ministered unto him, There is nothing done for him* (Esther 6:3). Then the impulsive monarch said, "He shall be rewarded at once. Who is in the court?" It was the most unlikely thing in the world for the indulgent Ahasuerus to be in a hurry to do justice, for he had done injustice thousands of times without remorse, and especially on that day when he recklessly signed the death warrant of that very Mordecai and his people.

For once, the king is intent on being just. Haman stands at the door – but you know the rest of the story. He had to lead Mordecai in public through the streets (Esther 6:8-11). It seems a very small matter whether you or I will sleep tonight or toss restlessly on our beds, but God will be in our rest or in our wakefulness. We do not know what His purpose may be, but His hand will be in it. No one sleeps or wakes except according to the decree of the Lord.

Observe well how this matter prepared the way for the queen at the next banquet, for when she unfolded her sorrow and told of the threatened destruction of the Jews, and then pointed to that wicked Haman, the king must have been even more interested and ready to grant her request when he learned that the man who had saved his life was a Jew and that he had already awarded the highest honors to a man in every way suited to supersede his worthless favorite. All was well. The plotter was unmasked, the noose was made ready, and he who ordered it was made to try his own arrangements.

In His providence, the Lord calls His own servants to be active. This business was done, and well done, by divine providence, but those concerned had to pray about it. Mordecai and all the Jews outside in Shushan fasted and cried unto the Lord. Unbelievers inquire, "What difference could prayer make?" Prayer is an essential part of the providence of God. It is so essential that you will always find that when God delivers His people, His people have been praying for that deliverance. They tell us that prayer does not affect the Most High and cannot alter His purposes. We never thought it did, but prayer is a part of the purpose and plan, and it is a most effective wheel in the machinery of providence. The Lord sets His people praying, and then He blesses them.

Moreover, Mordecai was quite sure that the Lord would deliver His people. He expressed that confidence, but he did not therefore sit still. Rather, he stirred up Esther, and when she seemed a little slack, he put it very strongly: *If thou altogether holdest thy peace at this time, then enlargement and deliverance will arise from another place; but thou and thy father's house shall be destroyed* (Esther 4:14). Invigorated by this message, Esther braced herself to the effort. She did not sit still and say, "The Lord will arrange this business. There is nothing for me to do." Instead, she pleaded with God and risked her life and her all for her people's sake, and then she acted very wisely and discreetly in her meetings with the king.

We rest confidently in providence, but we are not idle. We believe that God has an elect people, and therefore we preach in the hope that we may be the means, in the hands of His Spirit, of bringing this elect people to Christ.

We believe that God has appointed for His people both holiness here and heaven hereafter. Therefore, we strive against sin and press forward to the rest that remains for the people of God (Hebrews 4:9). Instead of repressing our energies, faith in God's providence moves us to diligence. We labor as if all depended upon us, and then we fall back upon the Lord with the calm faith that knows that all depends upon Him.

Never was a man so completely defeated as Haman. Never was a project so entirely turned aside. He was taken in his own trap, and he and his sons were hanged upon the gallows set up for Mordecai. As for the Jews, they were in a special kind of danger. They were to be destroyed on a certain day, and although Esther pleaded with the king for their lives, he was not able to alter his decree, though willing to do so, for it was a rule of the constitution that the law of the Medes and Persians could not be changed. The king could decree whatever he pleased, but once he had decreed it, he could not change it. The people thought it was better to submit to the worst established law than to be left entirely to every sudden whim of the king.

Now what was to be done? The decree was given that the Jews could be slain, and it could not be reversed. Here was the door of escape: another decree was issued giving the Jews permission to defend themselves and allowing them to take the property of any who dared to attack them. Thus one decree effectively neutralized the other. With great haste, this mandate was sent all over the kingdom. On the appointed day, the Jews stood up for themselves and slew their enemies.

According to their tradition, nobody attempted to attack them except the Amalekites, and consequently only Amalekites were slain. The race of Amalek was on that day swept off the face of the earth. God thus gave to the Jews a high position in the empire. We are told that many became Jews, or were proselytes to the God of Abraham, because they saw what God had done (Esther 8:17).

As I began by saying that God sometimes darted flashes of light through the thick darkness, you will now see what a flash this must have been. All the people were perplexed when they learned that the Hebrews could be put to death, but they must have been far more astonished when the decree came that they could defend themselves. All the world asked, "Why is this?" The answer was, "The living God, whom the Jews worship, has displayed His wisdom and rescued His people." All nations were compelled to feel that there was a God in Israel, and thus the divine purpose was fully accomplished, His people were secured, and His name was glorified to the world's end.

It is clear that the divine will is accomplished, yet men are perfectly free agents. Haman acted according to his own will, Ahasuerus did whatever he pleased, Mordecai behaved as his heart moved him, and Esther did the same. We see no interference with them. We see no force or coercion. Therefore, the entire sin and responsibility rest with each guilty person, yet acting with perfect freedom, none of them acts otherwise than divine providence had foreseen. "I cannot understand it," someone says. I am compelled to say the same. I do not understand it either. I have known many people who think they understand all things, but I think they have a higher opinion of themselves than truth would support.

Some of my brethren deny free agency, and so try to get out of the difficulty that way. Others assert that there is no predestination, and so cut the knot. Since I do not desire to get out of the difficulty, and have no desire to close my eyes to any part of the truth, I believe both free agency and predestination to be facts. How they can be made to agree, I do not know, or care to know. I am satisfied to know anything that God chooses to reveal to me, and I am equally content not to know what He does not reveal.

There it is. Man is a free agent in what he does. He is responsible for his actions, and he is truly guilty when he does wrong. He will be justly punished, too, and if he is lost, the blame will rest with himself alone. Yet there is One who rules over all, who, without complicity in their sin, makes even the actions of wicked men to serve His holy and righteous purposes. Believe these two truths, and you will see them in practical agreement in daily life, even though you will not be able to devise a theory for harmonizing them on paper.

Wonders can be worked without miracles. When God does a wonderful thing by suspending the laws of nature, people are greatly astonished and say, *This is the finger of God* (Exodus 8:19). Today, though, they say to us, "Where is your God? He never suspends His laws now!" I see God in the history of Pharaoh, but I must confess I see Him just as clearly in the history of Haman, and I think I see Him there in an even brighter light, for (I say it with reverence to His holy name) it is a somewhat rough method of accomplishing a purpose to stop the wheels of nature and reverse wise and admirable laws. Certainly it reveals His power, but it does not so clearly display His immutability.

When, however, the Lord allows everything to go on in the usual way, and gives mind, thought, ambition, and passion their full liberty, yet still achieves His purpose, it is doubly wonderful. In the miracles of Pharaoh, we see the finger of God, but in the wonders of providence, without a miracle, we see the hand of God.

Today, whatever the event may be, the attentive eye will as clearly see the Lord as if by miraculous power the hills had leaped from their place, or the floods had stood upright as a heap. I am sure that God is in the world, and is even at my own fireside and in my room. He manages my affairs and orders all things for me – and for each one of His children. We do not need any miracles to convince us of His working, for the wonders of His providence are just as great marvels as miracles themselves.

Let each child of God rejoice that we have a Protector so near the throne. Every Jew in Shushan must have felt hope when he remembered that the queen was a Jewess. Today let us be glad that Jesus is exalted.

> He is at the Father's side,
> The Man of love, the crucified.[11]

How safe are all His people, for *if any man sin, we have an advocate with the Father, Jesus Christ the righteous* (1 John 2:1)! There is One who remains in the presence of God who will plead for all those who put their trust in Him. Therefore, be not dismayed, but let your souls rest in God and wait patiently for Him. Heaven and earth will sooner pass away than those who trust the Lord will perish.

---

11   This is from a hymn by Josiah Conder (1789-1855) that begins with "The Lord is King! Lift up thy voice."

CHAPTER 10

THE WORD IN THE HEART

The Word of God abideth in you (1 John 2:14).

I labor under the opinion that there was never a time in which the people of God had greater need to understand this passage than now. We have entered upon that part of the pilgrim path that is described by John Bunyan as the Enchanted Ground: the church and the world appear to be similarly enchanted with folly. Half the people of God hardly know their head from their heels at this time. They are staring after wonders, running after a sounding brass and a tinkling cymbal, and waiting for still more astounding inventions.

Everything seems to be spinning. A tornado has set in, and the storm is everywhere. Christians used to believe in Christ as their leader and the Bible as their standard, but some of them are pleased with the kinds of leaders and standards that He never knew! Believe me, there will soon come new messiahs. Men are already pretending to work miracles. We will soon have false Christs, and "Lo! here," and "Lo! there," will be heard on all sides (Matthew 24:23-24). Anchors are up, winds are out, and the whole fleet is getting into confusion. Men in whose sanity and stability I once believed are being carried away with one delusion or another, and I am driven to cry out, "What next, and what next?"

We are only at the beginning of an era of mingled unbelief and fanaticism. Now we will know who are God's elect and who are not, for there are spirits abroad at this hour that would, if it were possible, deceive even the very elect (Matthew 24:24), and those who are not deceived are, nevertheless, severely tried. *Here is the patience of the saints* (Revelation 14:12). Let him look to himself who is not rooted and grounded in Christ, for the hurricane is coming. The signs of the times indicate a celebration of delusions. People have ceased to be guided by the Word, and claim to be prophets themselves. Now we will see what we will see. Blessed is the sheep that knows his Shepherd and will not listen to the voice of strangers. Here is the way to be kept steadfast: *The Word of God abideth in you.*

The Word of God: that is to say, we are to believe in the doctrines of God's Word, and these will make us strong. What strength they impart! Get the Word into you thoroughly, and you will overcome the Wicked One. When the devil tempted Martin Luther, the Reformer's grand grip of justification by faith made him quickly victorious. Keep a firm grasp on the doctrines of grace, and Satan will soon give up attacking you, for they are like plate armor through which no dart can ever force its way.

The promises of God's Word, too, give much power! To get a hold of a "shall" and "will" in the time of trouble is a heavenly safeguard. *My God will hear me* (Micah 7:7). *I will not fail thee nor forsake thee* (Joshua 1:5).[12] These are divine anchors. Oh, how strong a man is for overcoming the Wicked One when he has such a promise at hand! Do not trust yourself out on the street in the morning until you have laid a promise under your tongue.

I see people put respirators on in foggy weather. The respirators do not make them look very lovely, but I believe they are useful. I recommend the best respirator for the harmful atmosphere of this present evil world when I urge you to take a promise to your lips. Did not the Lord conquer the Tempter in the wilderness with that promise, *Man shall not live by bread alone, but by every word that proceedeth out of the mouth of God* (Matthew 4:4)? If you get the promises of God to lodge within you, you will be strong.

Then pay attention to the precepts, for a precept is often a sharp weapon against Satan. Remember how the Lord Jesus Christ struck Satan

---

12   Two books (among others) available from Aneko Press that discuss the promises of God are Charles Spurgeon's *According to Promise* and a daily devotional, *Faith's Checkbook*.

a killing blow by quoting a precept: *It is written, Thou shalt worship the Lord thy God, and Him only shalt thou serve* (Matthew 4:10). If the precept had not been at hand, with what would the Adversary have been rebuked? Nor is a threatening at all a weak weapon. The most terrible threatenings of God's Word against sin are the best helps for Christians when they are tempted to sin: *How can I do this great wickedness, and sin against God?* (Genesis 39:9). How would I escape if I turned away from Him who speaks from heaven? Tell Satan the threatenings, and make him tremble. Every word of God is life to holiness and death to sin. Use the Word as your sword and shield; there is none like it.

Now notice that John not only mentions *the Word of God*, but the Word of God *in you*. The inspired Word must be received into a willing mind. How? The Book that lies there is to be asserted here, in the inmost heart, by the work of the Holy Spirit upon the mind. All of this letter has to be translated into spirit and life. *The Word of God abideth in you* – that is, first to know it, and then to remember it and treasure it up in your heart.

Following this, we must understand it and learn the analogy of faith by *comparing spiritual things with spiritual* (1 Corinthians 2:13) until we have learned the system of divine truth and are able to explain it and promote it. Next, have the Word in your affections. Love it so much that it is as honey or the droppings of the honeycomb to you (Psalm 19:10). When this is the case, you must and will overcome the Wicked One. A man instructed in the Scriptures is like an armed knight who inflicts many wounds when he goes among the mob, but suffers none, for he is sealed up in steel.

But that is not all. It is not simply that the Word of God is in you, but the Word of God *abideth* in you. It is always there. It cannot be removed from you. If a man gets the Bible right into him, he is all right then because he is full and there is no room for evil. When you have filled a container full of wheat, you have effectually gotten the chaff out. Men go after strange and false doctrines because they do not really know the truth, for if the truth had gotten into them and filled them, they would not have room for these daydreams. A man who truly knows the doctrines of grace is never removed from them. I have heard our opponents rant at what they call obstinacy, but being steadfast in the truth is not a fault.

Once the truth really gets into you, it will enter into the texture of your being and nothing will get it out of you. It will also be your strength by causing you to watch against every evil thing. You will be on your guard if the Word abides in you, for it is written, *When thou goest, it shall lead thee; when thou sleepest, it shall keep thee* (Proverbs 6:22). The Word of God will be to you a fortress and a high tower, a castle of defense against the foe. See to it that the Word of God is in you, in your very soul, permeating your thoughts, and so operating upon your outward life so that all people may know that you are a true Bible Christian because they see it in your words and deeds.

This is the sort of army that we need in the church of God – men who are strong by feeding on God's Word. Aim for that, and when you have reached it, then aim for even greater heights so that you may become fathers in Israel. Up to this measure, at any rate, let us endeavor to advance, and advance at once.

CHAPTER 11

THE ATTACK

Ye are strong, . . . and ye have overcome the wicked one.
(1 John 2:14)

Young men who are strong must expect to be attacked. This also follows from a rule of divine management. Whenever God stores up supplies, it is because there will be need of them. When Egypt's granaries were full with the supply of seven years of plenty, one might have been sure that seven years of famine were about to come. Whenever a man is strong, it is because he has rigorous work to do. Just as the Israelites of old never had an ounce of manna left over until the morning except that which *bred worms and stank* (Exodus 16:20), so there never will be a Christian who has a penny's worth of grace left over from his daily requirements.

If you are weak, you will have no trial happen to you except that which is *common to man* (1 Corinthians 10:13); but if you are strong, rest assured that many difficult trials await you. Every muscle in the arm of faith will have to be tested. Every single weapon given out from the armory of God will be called for in the conflict.

Christian soldiering is not just military diversion or a proud parade. It means hard fighting from the day of enlistment to the day of reward. The strong young man may rest assured that he has no force to spend in display, no energy that he may use in boasting and pride. There is a heavy burden for the strong shoulder and a fierce fight for the trained hand.

Why does Satan attack this class most? I suppose that the first reason is because Satan is not always sure that the infants in grace are in grace, and therefore he does not always attack beginners. However, when they are sufficiently developed to make him see who and what they are, then he awakens his wrath. To the utmost of his power, he will weary and worry those who have thoroughly escaped from him.

A friend wrote to me to inquire whether Satan knows our thoughts. I do not believe he does, not as God does. But, he may pretty cleverly guess at them from our actions and our words, and perhaps even from expressions on our faces, yet I firmly believe only the Lord knows the thoughts of men immediately and by themselves.

Satan is an old hand at studying human nature. He has been watching and tempting men and women for about six thousand years, and therefore he is full of subtlety. However, he is not omniscient, and therefore it may be that he thinks a certain person is so little in grace that he might not be in grace at all, so he lets him alone; but as soon as it is certain that the man is of the royal seed, then the devil is at him.

I do not know whether our Lord was ever tempted at Nazareth while He was still in His obscurity, but the moment He was baptized and the Spirit of God came upon Him, He was taken into the wilderness to be tempted of the devil. If you become an avowed servant of God, do not think the conflict is over, for it is then that the battle begins. You will have to go into such a wilderness and such a conflict as you never knew before. Satan knows that young men in grace can do his kingdom great harm, and therefore he would gladly slay them early in the day, just as Pharaoh wanted to kill all the male children in Israel (Exodus 1:16). You are strong to overthrow his kingdom, and therefore you do not need to be amazed that he desires to overthrow you.

It is right that young men should endure hardness and difficulty, or else they might become proud. It is hard to hide pride from people. Full of strength, courage, patience, and zeal, such men are ready enough to believe the Wicked One when he whispers that they are perfect, and therefore trials are sent to keep them out of that grievous snare of the Evil One. The devil tempts the saint, and thus the saint sees his inward depravity and is no longer able to boast. The devil thinks he is going to destroy the man of God, but God is making the temptation work for the believer's eternal good. It is far better to have Beelzebub, the god of flies, pestering you, than to become contaminated and corrupted with ideas of your own excellence.

Besides, not only might this young man be a prey to pride, but he certainly would not bring the glory to God if he is untested that he brings to Him when he overcomes temptation. Read the story of Job up to the time when he is tempted. You might say, "We have no story to read." Just so, there was nothing worthy of record in Job's life – only that his flocks and herds continued to multiply, that another child was born, and so forth. There is no memorable history to a nation when everything goes well, and it is the same with a believer. But when trial comes, and the man plays the man (1 Corinthians 16:13) and is valiant for God against the archenemy, I hear *a voice from heaven saying unto me, Write* (Revelation 14:13).

Now you will have history – history that will glorify God. It is only right that those who are young men in Christ should endure conflicts so that they may bring honor to their Father, their Redeemer, and the Holy Spirit who dwells in them.

Besides, it prepares them for future usefulness, and here I will attempt to include the testimony of my own experience. When I first came to Christ, I often wondered why I had such a hard time of it when I was coming to the Lord, and why I was so long and so wearied in finding the Savior. After that, I wondered why I experienced so many spiritual conflicts while others were in peace. I did not know that I was destined to preach. I did not understand in those days that I would have to minister to hundreds, and even thousands, of distressed spirits who were storm-tossed and ready to perish. But now when the afflicted mention their experience, I can usually reply, "I have been there." I can help them as one who has felt the same way. It is good, therefore, that the young men should bear the yoke in their youth (Lamentations 3:27), and that while they are strong, they should gain experience – not so much for themselves as for others – that in later days, when they come to be fathers, they may be able to help the little ones of the family.

Take your tribulation kindly. Yes, take it gratefully. Thank your King that He puts you in a place where the thick of the battle centers around you. You will never be a warrior if you never enter the dust clouds where garments are rolled in blood. You will never become a veteran if you do not fight through the long campaign. The man who has been at the head of the desperate hope is he who can tell what tough fighting means. May it be so with you. May your Captain save you from the corruption of inglorious ease. You must fight in order to acquire the character that inspires others with confidence in you, and thus equips you to lead your comrades to the fight.

Oh, that we may have an abundance of the young men of the heavenly family who will defend the church against worldliness and error, defend the weaker ones from the wolves that prowl around, and guard the feeble against the many deceivers that attack the church of God! As you love the Lord, I direct you to grow in grace and be strong, for we have need of you right now. Take hold of your sword and shield. Watch and stand fast (1 Corinthians 16:13)! May the Lord teach your hands to war and your fingers to fight (Psalm 144:1). In these evil days, may you be as an army to protect our Israel. The Canaanites, the Hivites, and the Jebusites are upon us just now. War is in all our borders. Therefore, let each valiant man stand about the King's chariot, each man with *his sword upon his thigh because of fear in the night* (Song of Solomon 3:8).

I have written unto you, young men, because ye are strong (1 John 2:14). They have overcome the Wicked One. Then they must be strong, for a man who can overcome the Wicked One is no average man of war – write him down among the first three (2 Samuel 23; 1 Chronicles 11). Wicked ones abound, but there is one devious being who deserves the name of *the* Wicked One. He is the arch-leader of rebellion, the first of sinners, the chief of sinners, the tempter of sinners. He is the Wicked One who leads assaults against the pilgrims to Zion. If any man has ever stood toe-to-toe with him, he will never forget it. It is a fight that once fought will leave its scars, even though the victory is won.

In what sense have these young men overcome the Wicked One? They have broken right away from his power. They were once his slaves, but now they are not. They once slept beneath his roof in perfect peace, but conscience raised an uproar, the Spirit of God troubled them, and they completely escaped his power. There was a time when Satan did not troubled them at all. Why should he? They were good friends together.

Now he tempts them and worries them and assaults them because they have left his service, have committed themselves to a new Master, and have become the enemies of him who was once their god.

I speak to many people who gladly acknowledge that from the crown of their head to the sole of their feet, not a bit of them now belongs to the devil, for Christ has bought them – body, soul, and spirit – with His precious blood, and they have approved of the purchase. They feel that they are not their own, and are certainly not the devil's; for they are bought with a price, and they belong to Him who purchased them (1 Corinthians 6:19-20).

The strong man armed has been turned out by a stronger than he (Luke 11:21-22). Jesus has carried the fortress of the heart by storm and has driven out the foe. Satan is not inside our heart now. He entered into Judas, but he cannot enter into us, for our soul is filled by another who is well able to hold His own. The Wicked One has been expelled by the Holy One, who now lives and reigns within our nature as Lord of all.

Moreover, these young men have overcome the Wicked One, not only in breaking away from his power and in driving him entirely out of control so that he is no longer master, but they have overcome him by the very fact of their opposition to him. When a man resists Satan, he is victorious over Satan in that very resistance. Satan's empire consists in yielding our will to his will, but when our will revolts against him, then we have already overcome him in part. It is true that sometimes we are much better at willing than we are at doing, as the apostle Paul was, for he said, *To will is present with me; but how to perform that which is good I find not* (Romans 7:18). However, if the will is clean from sin, it is a victory over sin – and as that will grows stronger and more determined to resist the temptations of the Evil One, in that degree we have overcome sin and Satan.

What a blessed thing this is! Do not fail to remember that Satan has no weapons of defense, so when we resist him, he must flee. A Christian has both defensive and offensive weapons. He has a shield as well as a sword, but Satan has fiery darts and nothing else. I never read of his having any shield whatsoever, so when we resist him, he is bound to run away. He has no defense for himself, and the fact of our resistance is in itself a victory.

But besides that, brothers and sisters, some of us who are young men in Christ have won many victories over Satan. Have we not been tempted, and fearfully tempted? Yes, but the mighty grace of God has come to the rescue, and we have not given in. Cannot you look back (not with pharisaic boasting, but with gracious exultation) over many evil habits that once had the mastery over you, but which is master of you no longer? It was a hard conflict. You bit your lip sometimes and feared that you would give in! There were times when your steps had almost gone and your feet had nearly slipped (Psalm 73:2), but here you are, still conqueror! Thanks be to God who gives us the victory through our Lord Jesus Christ (1 Corinthians 15:57). Hear what the Spirit says to you when John writes to you: because you have overcome the Wicked One, he says, *Love not the world, neither the things that are in the world* (1 John 2:15).

In Christ Jesus, we have entirely overcome the Wicked One already. The Enemy we have to contend with is a vanquished foe; our Lord and Master met him and destroyed him. He is now destitute of his boasted battle axe, that dreadful weapon that has made the bravest men to tremble when they have seen it in his hand. You ask, "What weapon is that?" That weapon is death. Our Lord overthrew him who had the power of death – the devil – and therefore Satan does not have the power of death any longer. The keys of death and of hell are in the possession of Christ (Revelation 1:18).

Ah, Wicked One, we who believe in Jesus will defeat you, for our Lord defeated you! That bruise upon your head cannot be hidden (Genesis 3:15)! Your crown is dashed in pieces! The Lord has severely wounded you, O Dragon, and your deadly wound can never be healed! We face you with fearless courage, for we believe the promise of our Lord, that He will bruise Satan under our feet shortly (Romans 16:20). As certainly as you were bruised under the feet of our crucified Lord, so you will be bruised under the feet of all His seed, to your complete overthrow and contempt. Let us take courage and abide steadfast in the faith, for we have overcome the Wicked One in our Lord Jesus. *We are more than conquerors through Him that loved us* (Romans 8:37).

CHAPTER 12

SARAH, A WOMAN OF FAITH

Sarah was calm and quiet and was not put in fear by any terror. There were several occasions on which she might have been much concerned and distressed. The first was in the breaking up of her house life. Her husband, Abraham, got a call to leave Ur of the Chaldees (Genesis 12:1). They moved to Haran – a considerable journey. There are some women – unbelieving women – who would not have understood the move. "Why does he want to go away from the land in which he lives, and from all our kindred, away to Haran?" That would have been her question if she had not been a partaker in her husband's faith. An unbelieving woman would have said, "A call from God? Nonsense! Fanaticism! I do not believe it," and when she saw that her husband intended to go, she would have been afraid and bewildered.

Abraham went to Haran with his father Terah, and Terah died in Haran. Then God called him to go further, and they had to cross the Euphrates River and get right away into a land that he knew nothing about. This must have been a more severe trial still. When they packed up their goods on the camels and on the donkeys, and started with their train of servants and sheep and cattle, Sarah might very naturally have said, if she had been an unbelieving woman, "Where are you going?"

"I do not know," answered Abraham.

"What are you going for? What are you going to get?"

"I do not know," Abraham replied. "God has told me to go, but I do not know where I am going to, and I cannot exactly say what I am going for, except that God has said, *Get thee out of thy country, and from thy kindred, and from thy father's house, unto a land that I will shew thee. And I will make of thee a great nation, and I will bless thee, and make thy name great; and thou shalt be a blessing"* (Genesis 12:1-2).

We do not read that Sarah ever asked these questions, or that she was ever troubled at all about them. Their possessions were put on the camels' backs, and away she journeyed, for God had called her husband to go, and she determined to go with him. Through floods or flames, it mattered not to her. She felt safe with her husband's God, and she calmly journeyed on. She was *not afraid with any amazement* (1 Peter 3:6).[13]

Although we do not hear much about her, we know that she had to live in a tent all those years. The man is out abroad attending to his business, and he does not know much about the discomforts of home – not even in such homes as ours. But if you were called to give up your house and go and live in a tent – well, the husband might not mind it, but the wife would. It is a very demanding life for a housewife. Sarah traveled from day to day, and with the constant moving of the tent, as the cattle had to be taken to fresh pastures, it must have been a life of terrible discomfort; yet Sarah never said a word about it.

Wake up tomorrow morning and pull up every tent pin. Get all the canvas rolled away, for you must move to another site. The sun scorches like an oven, but you must ride across the plain. If the night is cold with frost and heavy dews, canvas is still your only wall and roof. Remember, they were dwelling in tents as pilgrims and strangers, not for one day, or two, nor for a few days a year, but for dozens of years at a time. It was bravely done by this good woman that she was *not afraid with any amazement.*

Then there was a special time when Abraham put on his battle gear and went to war (Genesis 14). He heard that Chedorlaomer had come down with tributary kings and swept away the cities of the plain, taking captive his nephew Lot. Abraham said, "I will go and deliver him." Sarah could have said, "My husband, you are an old man. Those grey locks should not be touched with the stains of warfare." She said nothing of the sort, but undoubtedly cheered him on and smiled as he invited

---

13   That is, she did not give in to fear and terror. She stayed calm and in peace during fearful occasions.

some of his neighbors who lived nearby to go with him. Although her husband is gone, and all the herdsmen and servants round about the tents were all gone, she felt no distress from being left alone with her women servants. No; she sits at home as a queen, fearing no robbers, but abiding calmly and confidently in her God. Abraham has gone to battle, and she does not fear for him. She does not need to fear for him, for he defeated the kings. They were given like *driven stubble to his bow* (Isaiah 41:2), and he came back laden with spoil. God was pleased with Sarah's quiet faith, because in troublous times she was *not afraid with any amazement.*

Then a little while later, that great trial of faith came that must have touched Sarah, even though its full force fell on her husband. She observed the sudden disappearance of her husband and his servant. "Where is your master? He has not come in for breakfast."

The servants say, "He was up a great while before day, and he has gone with the servant, and with the donkey, and with Isaac" (Genesis 22:3). Abraham has not told her, for he had struggled enough with himself to take Isaac away to the mountain and offer him, and he could not bear to repeat the struggle in Sarah. He left without telling Sarah of his movements. This was a new state of things for her. He did not return all day. "Where has your master gone? I never knew him to go away before without informing me. And where is Isaac?" Oh, that Isaac! How she feared for her jewel, her delight, the child of promise, the wonder of her old age! He did not come home that night, nor Abraham either – nor the next day, nor the next.

Three days passed, and I can hardly picture the anxiety that would have fallen upon you if you had been Sarah, unless you had enjoyed Sarah's faith, for by faith in this trying case she was *not afraid with any amazement.* I imagine that it took three days for Abraham to come back again, so that it was nearly a week, and no Abraham and no Isaac. One would have thought she would have wandered about, crying, "Where is my husband, and where is my son?" But not so. She calmly waited, and said within herself, "If he has gone, he has gone upon some necessary errand, and he will be under God's protection. God, who promised to bless him and to bless his seed, will not allow any evil to harm him." So Sarah rested quietly when others would have been in dire dismay. She was *not afraid with any amazement.* We hear so little said about Sarah that I am compelled to imagine what I feel she must have been like, because human nature is so like itself, and the effect of events upon us is very much like the effect that would have been produced upon the mind of Sarah.

This is a point in which Christian women should seek to imitate Sarah: we should not let our hearts be troubled, but rest in the Lord and wait patiently for Him. What is this virtue? It is a calm, quiet trusting in God. It is freedom from fear, such as is described in another place in these words: *He shall not be afraid of evil tidings: his heart is fixed, trusting in the LORD* (Psalm 112:7); or as we read in David's words, *Yea, though I walk through the valley of the shadow of death, I will fear no evil: for Thou art with me; Thy rod and Thy staff they comfort me* (Psalm 23:4). It is composure of mind, freedom from anxiety, the absence of irritability, and absolute deliverance from worry – so that whatever happens, trepidation does not seize upon the spirit, but the heart continues at its own quiet pace, delighting itself in a faithful God. This is the virtue that is worth a king's ransom, and Sarah had it – *whose daughters ye are, as long as ye do well, and are not afraid with any amazement* (1 Peter 3:6).

When is this virtue to be exercised by us? Well, it should be exercised at all times. If we are not self-composed when we are happy, we are not likely to be calm when we are sad. I notice that if I am at all pleased with the praise of a friend, I become in that degree open to be grieved by the criticism of an enemy. By however much you are delighted by prosperity, by so much you are likely to be depressed when adversity comes; but if you are calm, quiet, and happy (no more than that) when everything goes well, then you will be calm, quiet, and happy (not less than that) when everything goes wrong. To keep up a calm and steady frame of mind is something to aim at, just as the gardener desires an even temperature for his prized flowers.

Who is to exercise this virtue? We are all to do so, but the text is especially directed to the sisterhood. I suppose women are exhorted to it because some of them are rather excitable, a little hysterical and emotional, and tend to be fearfully depressed and utterly carried away. I am not saying that this fault is general or common among women, nor am I blaming them, but I am only stating the fact that some are thus afflicted, and it is a happy, happy thing if they can master it so that they are *not afraid with any amazement*.

This virtue especially serves in time of trouble, when a very serious trial threatens us. Then the Christian is not to say, "What will I do now? I will never endure it. I cannot live through it. Surely God has forgotten me. This trouble will crush me. I will die of a broken heart." No. Do not talk like that. If you are God's child, do not even think like that. In patience, try to lift up your head and remember Sarah, *whose daughters ye are, as long as ye do well, and are not afraid with any amazement.*

This is how it must be in times of personal sickness. How many are the pains and sufferings that fall to the lot of the sisterhood! But if you have faith, you will not be afraid *with any amazement*. I saw one who was about to suffer from the surgeon's knife. It was a serious operation about which all stood in doubt, but I was happy to see her as composed in the prospect of it as though it had been a pleasure rather than a pain. A Christian should be similarly calmly resigned.

I went to see an elderly sister who was nearly eighty years of age. She was dying with dropsy, or edema, and was unable to lie down in bed. She was forced to always sit up – a posture that allows little or no rest. When I entered her room, she welcomed me most enthusiastically, which, perhaps, was not too surprising, for she was greatly attached to her minister. The wonder lay in the fact that she expressed herself as being full of happiness, full of delight, and full of expectancy of being with Christ.

I went to comfort her, but she comforted me. What could I say? She talked about the goodness of God with an eye as full of pleasure as if she had been a young woman speaking about the young companion of her marriage day. I was pleased to see one with such evident marks of long-continued pain upon her face who had such sweet peacefulness there too – yes, and with even more than peace, but with unspeakable joy in the Lord, such as I fear some who are in good health and strength have not yet learned. A Christian woman should not be afraid with any amazement either in adversity or in sickness, but her holy patience should prove her to be a true daughter of Sarah and Abraham.

Christian women in Peter's day were subject to persecution just as much as their husbands. They were locked up in prison, scourged, tortured, burned, or slain with the sword. One holy woman in the early days of the church was tossed upon the horns of bulls; another was made to sit in a red-hot iron chair. They were tortured, not accepting deliverance. In the early days of martyrdom, the women were brave and courageous as well as the men. They defied the tyrant to do his worst upon their mortal bodies, for their conquering spirits laughed at every torment. If persecuting times should come again, or if they are here already in some measure, do well, O daughters of Sarah, and be *not afraid with any amazement.*

If you are called to some difficult duty, if you are obligated to do what you feel you cannot do, remember that anybody can do that which he can do. It is the believing person who does that which he cannot do. We achieve impossibilities by the power of the Almighty God. Do not be afraid, then, of any duty, but believe that you will be able to do it, for grace will be sufficient for you (2 Corinthians 12:9).

At last, in the expectation of death, may you not be *afraid with any amazement!* Oftentimes a deathbed is vantage ground for a Christian. Where others show their fear, and sometimes their terror, there should the believer show his peacefulness and his happy expectancy, *not afraid with any amazement*, no matter what the form of death may be.

What is the excellence of this virtue? I will answer that question by saying it is due to God that we should not be *afraid with any amazement.* Such a God as we have should be trusted. Under the shadow of such a wing, fear becomes a sin (Psalm 36:7; 57:1; 63:7; 91:4). If God were other than He is, we might be afraid; but while He is such a God, it is due to Him that fear is banished. Peacefulness is true worship. Calmness under alarming conditions is devotion. He worships best who is most calm in difficult times.

Moreover, the excellence of this virtue is that it is most impressive to people. I do not think anything is more likely to impress the ungodly than the quiet peace of mind of a Christian in danger or near to death. If we can be happy then, our friends will ask, "What makes them so calm?" This usefulness is not just confined to others, but it is most useful to ourselves, for he who can be calm in times of trouble will be most likely to make his way through them. Once you become afraid, you cannot judge wisely as to your best course. You generally do wrong when you are frightened out of your confidence in God. When the heart begins palpitating, then the whole system is out of order for the battle of life. Be calm, and watch your opportunity.

Napoleon's victories were to a large extent due to the calmness of that masterly warrior, and you can depend upon it that it is so with you, Christian people. You will win if you can wait. Do not be in a hurry. Consider what you should do. Do not be so alarmed as to make haste. Be patient. Be calm. Wait on God's time, and you wait your own time. Wait upon God to open your mouth. Ask Him to guide your hand and to do everything for you. Calmness of mind is the mother of prudence and discretion. It gives the firm foothold that is needful for the warrior when he is about to deal a victorious blow. Those who cannot be amazed by fear will live to be amazed with mercy.

How can we obtain it? That is the question. Remember that it is an outgrowth of faith. You will have it in proportion as you have faith. Have faith in God, and you will not be afraid with any amazement or dread. Very early in my preaching days, I had faith in God during times of thunderstorm. When I have walked out to preach, it has happened that I have been wet through with the storm, yet I felt no annoyance from the thunder and lightning.

On one occasion I turned aside by reason of the extreme severity of the rain to a little lone cottage, and I found a woman there with a child who seemed somewhat relieved when she had let me in, but previously she had been crying bitterly with sheer alarm and terror. She said, "This is a little round lodge house, and the lightning comes in at every window. There is no place into which I can get to hide it from my eyes." I explained to her that I liked to see the lightning, for it showed me that an explosion was all over, and since I had lived to see the flash, it was clear it could now do me no harm. I told her that to hear the thunder was a splendid thing – that it was only God saying, "It is all over."

If you live to see the lightning flash, there is nothing to be afraid of. You would have been dead and would never have seen it if it had been sent to kill you. I tried to console her on religious grounds, and I remember well praying with her and making her as happy as a bird. It was my being so calm and quiet and praying with her that cheered her up. When I went on my way, I left her in peace.

You may depend upon it that unless our own souls have peace, we cannot communicate it to others. In this way, we must believe in God about everything. It so happened that about that matter of the thunder and lightning, I did believe in God up to the very last degree, and therefore I could not be alarmed because of that. If you believe in God about any other subject, no matter what it is, you will have perfect peace with God about it. If you can believe God when you are in a storm at sea, that He holds the water *in the hollow of His hand* (Isaiah 40:12), you will be at peace about the tempest. It is the thing that troubles you that you must believe about. When faith makes an application of her hand to the particular trial, then peace of mind will come to you.

This holy calm also comes from walking with God. No spot is so peaceful as the secret place of the tabernacles of the Most High. Commune with God, and you will forget fear. Keep up daily fellowship with Christ in prayer, in praise, in service, in searching the Word, and in submitting your heart to the work of the eternal Spirit – and as you walk with God, you will find yourself calm. You know how the poet William Cowper puts it:

> Oh, for a closer walk with God,
> A calm and heavenly frame.

These go together.

If you want to feed upon certain truths that will produce this calm of mind, first remember that God is full of love, and therefore nothing that God sends can harm His child. Take everything from the Lord as a token of love, even if it is a stroke of His rod or a cut of His knife. Everything from that dear hand must mean love, for He has said, *I have graven thee upon the palms of My hands* (Isaiah 49:16). When you accept every affliction as a token of love, then your fear will be ended.

CHAPTER 13

SARAH, A WOMAN WHO DID WELL

Look unto Abraham your father, and unto Sarah that bare you. (Isaiah 51:2)

Even as Sara obeyed Abraham, calling him lord: whose daughters ye are, as long as ye do well, and are not afraid with any amazement. (1 Peter 3:6)

What a happy circumstance it is when a godly, gracious man has an equally godly and gracious wife! It is awful when there is a difference, a radical difference, between husband and wife – when one fears God, and the other has no regard for Him. What a pain it is to a Christian woman to be yoked with an unbelieving husband (2 Corinthians 6:14)! In a case that I remember, the husband lived all his life indifferent to divine things, while the wife was a sincere Christian woman and saw all her children grow up in the ways of the Lord. The father lived unregenerate, and died without giving any testimony of a change of heart. When our sister speaks of him, it is with fearful anguish. She does not know what to say, but leaves the matter in the hands of God, often sighing, "Oh, that by a word or a look, I could have been enabled to enjoy a hope that my poor husband looked to Jesus in the end." The same must be the case of a husband who has an ungodly wife. No matter how much God may bless him in all other respects, there seems to be a great miss there, as if a part of the sun were eclipsed – a part of that life that should be all light is left in thick darkness.

Let those of us who have the happiness of being joined together in the Lord thank and bless God every time we remember each other. Let us appeal to God that, having such a privilege so that our prayers are not hindered by irreligious partners, we may never hinder our prayers ourselves. May God grant that we may give unto His name great glory because of His great blessing to us in this respect! Abraham had cause to praise God for Sarah, and Sarah was grateful for Abraham. I do not have the slightest doubt that Sarah's character owed its excellence very much to Abraham.

I would not wonder, however, if we discover when all things are revealed, that Abraham owed just as much to Sarah. They probably learned from each other. Sometimes the weaker comforted the stronger, and often the stronger sustained the weaker. I would not wonder if a mutual interchange of their various graces tended to make them both rich in the things of God. Perhaps Abraham would not have been all that he was if Sarah had not been all that she was. We thank God if we, like Abraham, are favored with holy spouses whose gracious temperaments and loving characters tend to make us better servants of God.

God does not forget the lesser lights. Abraham shines like a star of the first magnitude, and we do not at first observe that other star, with light so bright and pure, shining with milder radiance but with similar brightness, close at his side. The light of Mamre, which is known under the name of Abraham, resolves itself into a double star when we apply the telescope of reflection and observation. To the common eye, Abraham is the sole character, and ordinary people overlook his faithful spouse – but God does not overlook. Our God never omits the good who are obscure. You may depend upon it that there is no such difference in the love of God toward different people that would make Him fix His eye only upon those who are strong, and omit those who are weak. Our eyes see the great things, but God's eye is such that nothing is great with Him, and nothing is little. He is infinite, and therefore nothing bears any comparison to Him.

You remember how it is written that He who tells the number of the stars and calls them all by name (Psalm 147:4) also heals the broken in heart and binds up all their wounds (Psalm 147:3). He who treasures the names of His apostles also notes the women who followed Him. He who marks the brave confessors and the bold preachers of the gospel also remembers those helpers who labor quietly in the gospel in places of retirement into which the hawk's eye of history seldom pries. God does not forget the less in His care for the greater. Sarah was covered with the shield of the Almighty in her life as well as Abraham, her husband. In death, she rested in the same tomb. In heaven, she has the same joy. In the Book of the Lord, she has the same record.

It would be good for us to imitate God in this – in not forgetting the lesser lights. Important people may not often be good examples. I am sad when people who have been clever and successful are held up to imitation, even though their motives and morals have been questionable. I would rather have people simple and honest than clever and scheming. It is better to act rightly and fail completely than to succeed by falsehood and deceit. I would rather have my son imitate an honest man who has no talent, and whose life is unsuccessful, than to have him imitate the cleverest and greatest person who ever lived, whose life has become a brilliant success, but whose principles are shameful.

Do not learn from the great, but from the good. Do not be dazzled by success, but follow the safer light of truth and right. It is true that people mainly observe only that which is written in big letters, but you know the finest parts of God's Book are printed in small characters. Those who only want to know the basics may spell out the words in large type designed for young children, but those who want to be fully instructed must sit down and read the small print of God, which is given us in lives of saints whom most people neglect. Some of the finest virtues are not so much seen in the great as in the quiet, obscure life.

Many Christian women manifest a glory of character that is to be found in no public man. I am sure that many flowers that are "born to blush unseen," and, as we think, to "waste its fragrance on the desert air,"[14] are fairer than the beauties that reign in the conservatory and are the admiration of all. God has ways of producing very fine things on a small scale. Just as rare pearls and precious stones are never great

---

14   These quotes are from "Elegy Written in a County Courtyard," a poem by Thomas Gray (1716-1771).

masses of rock, but always lie within a narrow compass, so very often the finest and richest virtues are to be found in the humblest individuals. A person may be too great to be good, but he cannot be too little to be gracious. Do not, therefore, be always studying Abraham, the greater character. Does not the text say, *Look unto Abraham, your father, and unto Sarah that bare you* (Isaiah 51:2)? You have not learned the full lesson of patriarchal life until you have been in the tent with Sarah as well as among the flocks with her husband.

God does not by His grace lift us out of our place. A man is made gentle, but he is not made a fool. A woman is made brave, but grace never made her overbearing and domineering. Grace does not make the child so self-willed that he disobeys his father; it is something else that does that. Grace does not take away from the father his authority to command the child. It leaves us where we were, in a certain sense, as to our position, and the fruit it bears is related to that position. Thus Sarah is ornamented with the virtues that adorn a woman, while Abraham is adorned with all the virtues that are proper and good in a godly man.

According as the virtue is required, so is it produced. If the circumstances require courage, God makes His servant heroic. If the circumstances require great modesty and prudence, then modesty and prudence are given. Faith is a wonderful magician's wand: it works marvels, it achieves impossibilities, and it grasps the incomprehensible. Faith can be used anywhere – in the highest heaven touching the ear of God and winning our desire of Him, and in the lowest places of the earth among the poor and fallen, encouraging and elevating them.

Faith will quench the violence of fire, turn the edge of the sword, snatch the prey from the enemy, and turn the alien to flight. There is nothing that it cannot do. It is a principle available for all times, to be used on all occasions, suitable to be used by all people for all holy ends. Those who have been taught the sacred art of believing God are truly knowledgeable. No degree from the most prestigious university can equal in value that which comes with much boldness in the faith. If Abraham walks before God and is perfect (Genesis 17:1), if he smites the kings who carried Lot captive, if he does such daring deeds as are fitting for a man – then the self-same faith makes Sarah walk before God in her perfectness; she performs the actions that are fitting for her womanhood, and she, too, is written among the worthies of faith who magnified the Lord.

There were two fruits of faith in Sarah: she did well, and she was *not afraid with any amazement.*

She did well as a wife. She was all her husband could desire, and when, at the age of 127, she at last fell asleep, it is said that Abraham not only mourned for her, but the old man wept for her most true and genuine tears of sorrow (Genesis 23:2). He wept for the loss of one who had been the life of his house. As a wife, she did well. All the duties that were incumbent upon her as the queen of that traveling company were performed admirably, and we find no fault mentioned concerning her in that respect.

She did well as a hostess. It was her duty, as her husband was given to hospitality, to be willing to entertain his guests. There is no doubt that the one instance recorded is representative of her common mode of procedure. Though she was truly a princess, yet she kneaded the dough and prepared the bread for her husband's guests. They came suddenly, but she had no complaint to make. She was, indeed, always ready to lay herself out to perform that which was one of the highest duties of a God-fearing household in those primitive times.

She did well also as a mother. We are sure she did because we find that her son Isaac was such an excellent man, and say what you will, but in the hand of God, the mother forms the boy's character. Perhaps the father unconsciously influences the girls, but the mother has evidently most influence over the sons. Any of us can bear witness that this is so in our own case. There are exceptions, of course, but for the most part, the mother is the queen of the son, and he looks up to her with infinite respect if she is at all someone who can be respected. Sarah, by faith, did her work with Isaac well, for from the very first, in his yielding to his father when he was to be offered up as a sacrifice, we see in him evidence of a holy obedience and faith in God that were seldom equaled, and never surpassed.

In addition, it is written that God said of Abraham, *I know him, that he will command his children and his household after him* (Genesis 18:19). One trait of Abraham's character was that he set up an altar unto the Lord wherever he went. His rule was a tent and an altar. Do you always make these two things go together – a tent and an altar? Wherever you live, is there sure to be family worship there? I am afraid that many families neglect it, and often it is so because husband and wife are not agreed about it. I feel certain that there would not have been that invariable setting up of the worship of God by Abraham in his tent unless Sarah had been as godly as himself.

She also did well as a believer. That is not a little point. As a believer, when Abraham was called to separate himself from his kindred, Sarah went with him. She would adopt the separated life, too, and the same caravan that traveled across the desert with Abraham as its master had Sarah as its mistress. She continued with him, believing in God with perseverance. Although they had no city to dwell in, she continued the roaming life with her husband, looking for *a city which hath foundations, whose Builder and Maker is God* (Hebrews 11:10). She believed God's promise with all her heart, for although she laughed once because when the promise neared its realization, it overwhelmed her (Genesis 18:12), it was only a slip of the moment, for it is written in the eleventh chapter of Hebrews, *Through faith also Sarah herself received strength to conceive seed, and was delivered of a child when she was past age, because she judged Him faithful who had promised* (Hebrews 11:11).

She did well to her parents, well to her husband, well to her household, well to her guests, and well before her God. Oh, that all professing Christian people had a faith that showed itself in doing well!

Never let it be forgotten, though, that although we preach faith as the great means of salvation, yet we never say that you are saved unless there is a change worked in you and good works are produced in you, for *faith, if it hath not works, is dead, being alone* (James 2:17). Faith saves, but it is the kind of faith that causes people to do well. If there is a faith (and there is such a faith) that leaves a man just what he was and permits him to indulge in sin, it is the faith of devils – and perhaps not even as good as that, for the devils believe and tremble (James 2:19), whereas these hypocrites profess to believe, yet dare to defy God and seem to have no fear of Him whatsoever. Sarah had this testimony from the Lord, that she did well, and if you believe and do well, you are her daughters. Do not be a discredit to your queenly mother. Take care that you honor your spiritual parentage and maintain the high prestige of the elect family.

CHAPTER 14

AFTER TWENTY-FIVE

And he went out about the third hour, and saw others standing idle in the marketplace, and said unto them; Go ye also into the vineyard, and whatsoever is right I will give you. And they went their way. (Matthew 20:3-4)

FOR YOUNG MEN AND WOMEN

No parable teaches all sides of truth. It is wrong to attempt to make a parable run on all fours. It is intended to convey one lesson, and if it teaches that, we must not attempt to draw everything else out of it. This parable sets forth the great God as a householder going forth to find men to work for Him – but let no one imagine that God needs any of us. He was perfect – perfectly happy and perfectly glorious – long before any angel's wing moved in space, or before time even existed. God always was and still is self-contained and all-sufficient. If He chooses to make any creatures, or to preserve or use any of the creatures He has formed, that is not because He needs them or is in the least degree dependent upon them. If God comes forth in wondrous grace to call any of us to work in His vineyard, it is not because He needs us, but because we need Him. He does not set us to work because He needs workers, but because we need work. He does not call us because He requires us, but because we require to be called.

Out of the various men who are mentioned, no one went to the vineyard, either early in the morning or later in the day, and requested to be employed. The householder went out into the marketplace and employed his men. At the third hour, the sixth hour, and the ninth hour, not one man had come of his own free will, but in every case the first overture was from the householder: he went out *to hire laborers into his vineyard* (Matthew 20:1). At the eleventh hour, although the day was coming to a close and the sun was almost down, even then men were not wise enough to want to end the day in the right service, but they still remained, as they had been all day, idling in the marketplace until the generous employer came out, reasoned with them, and convinced them to enter the vineyard.

No man ever comes to God until God first comes to him, so it is my earnest desire that the impulses of divine grace may even now be felt in many hearts. God the Holy Spirit is able to work upon the judgment, the understanding, the affections, the fears, the hopes, and the will of men. As He works upon them, He makes men willing in the day of God's power (Psalm 110:3) so that they turn to Him and enter into His service. That is, I think, the first meaning of God's going out.

Personally, to most people there is a time of God's going forth when they are especially moved to holy things. It happens to some in childhood. While they are still young, God speaks with them as He did with Samuel. He might even appear to them on their little bed at night and say, "Samuel, Samuel," and then helps them to answer, "Here am I, for You called me" (1 Samuel 3:5). To others, God comes a little later in life, when it is the second hour of the day, while they are still in the prime of their youth. It was the great privilege of some of us for the Lord to call us while we were still young men, and it is a great blessing when God comes to us at that important period of our history.

To others, God appears when they are advanced in life. Blessed be God, He comes also to some when the day is nearly over, when the furrows of care are on their brows and the snows of age are on their heads. He comes with power, by the effectual calling of the Holy Spirit. He speaks to them, and they yield to His speaking and give themselves up to be His servants for the rest of their lives.

I have heard or read a good number of sermons to the young, or I have heard of them – sermons to those who are called by God early in the morning – and I know there have been a great many sermons to those who have reached the eleventh hour. Therefore, I thought that

I would specifically address those who have come to the third hour. What kind of people are those who are at the third hour? What is the third hour? Let us calculate a little. To the Jews, there were always twelve hours in the day, whether it was summer or winter, so the hour was different every day. It was a very difficult way of computing time, for as the day lengthened or shortened, they still divided the daylight into twelve hours.

Well, think of human life as a period of twelve hours, and then form a calculation of what each hour must be. Take the whole of life roughly at seventy, seventy-two, seventy-three, seventy-five, or whatever you want. Then you have to leave out the very earliest hours – that period of life in which God does not call children to intelligent faith because they do not yet have enough understanding to be capable of intelligent faith. Take off a little for that. I would calculate the first three hours of life to be over at about the age of twenty through twenty-four, or something close to that, and I would say that the third hour of life would range from twenty-five to thirty-five. That is the period in which the man has come to perfection, and in which the woman has reached the fullness of her strength. There will be little growing after this. If this is not the pinnacle of life, yet certainly a considerably developed period of life has now been reached. Very earnestly do I pray for the Master to come out to you who have come to the third hour of your day, and to say to you, *Go ye also into the vineyard, and whatsoever is right I will give you* (Matthew 20:4).

Now, my friends, you who are between twenty and forty years of age, I want you to become the servant of my Lord and Master. You have already wasted some of the best hours of the day. There are no hours of the day like the early morning – when the dew is upon everything and the smoke of care and trouble has not yet dimmed the landscape. Give me the earliest hours of a summer morning for enjoyment – when the birds are singing at their sweetest, and all nature seems to be adorned with her wedding jewels, her most delightful ornaments. There is no time for work like the first hours of the day, and there is no time for serving the Lord like the very earliest days of youth.

I remember the joy I had in the little service I was able to render to God when I first knew Him. I was employed in a school during the week, but there was Saturday afternoon – and that Saturday afternoon, although I could have justly used it for rest, and although I was only a boy myself, was committed to a certain district of town and to visiting the very poor within my reach. I devoted the Lord's Day to teaching a class, and later on, addressing the Sunday school. Oh, but how earnestly I did it all! I often think that I spoke better then than I did in later years, for I spoke so tremblingly, but my heart went with it all.

When I began to talk a little in the villages on Sundays, and afterward every night in the week, I know that I used to speak then what came fresh from my heart. There was little time for gathering much from books. My primary library was the Word of God and my own experience, but I spoke from my very soul. I have no doubt that I spoke with much blundering, weakness, and youthful folly, but oh, I spoke with such an intense desire to bring people to Christ! I remember that I felt I could cheerfully lay down my life if I could only save a poor old man, or bring a boy of my own age to the Savior's feet.

There is nothing later in life quite like those early morning works. Yet, my friend, you have let that period pass away. You are twenty-five, you are thirty, you are even thirty-five, and you are still unsaved! Do not waste any more precious time. Go at once to the Crucified One, my dear Lord and Master. There He stands, with a crown of thorns about His brow. Give Him, at least, the rest of your days. Beg Him to pardon you for having lived so long without loving and serving Him.

Besides, I must plead with you at this age that you come to Christ because habits of idleness are already forming in you. "No," you say, "it is not so." I am referring to spiritual idleness. You have not yet done anything for Christ. You have not even looked to see what you could do. You have not meditated upon what place in the vineyard you could occupy – whether you could trim the vines, water them, gather the grapes, or tread the wine vat. No, you have done nothing as yet. I am afraid that soon you will get settled down into this do-nothing style, and you will go back to the dust from where you came, having achieved nothing for Him who gave Himself that He might save us from our sins. Do not stay in that condition a moment longer. The wax is not very soft now. It is beginning to harden. Before it is completely set, let the stamp of sovereign grace be pressed upon it so that your life may yet bear the impress of Christ.

Moreover, Satan is very ready with his temptations. You know how he is:

Satan finds some mischief still,
For idle hands to do.[15]

I hope you have not gone into any blatant, open sin. Like the young man in the narrative we read, possibly you have been kept quite pure and clean outwardly. That is good, but do you not see that as good of a person as you are in your own estimation, you are extremely likely to be assailed by Satan? If he can get you to indulge the lusts of the flesh, or some other vain and sinful pleasure, he will take great delight in ruining you. Oh, how I wish that I could get you enlisted into my Lord's army! Here, take the pay. I mean, believe on the Lord Jesus Christ. Accept Him as your Savior and become His faithful servant. I wish I could put a rake into your hands, or a pruning knife, or something with which you should be persuaded to go into the vineyard of my Master to serve Him. You who have reached the age of twenty-five, or thirty, or thirty-five, I want you to come to Christ because your sun may go down at noon. Such things do happen.

It seems to me that if God will spare you, there is a decent opportunity of work yet before you. As I look at men and women in the prime of life, and know that many of them are not yet converted to God, I feel that Satan must not have you, and the world must not have you, and sin must not have you – but Christ must have you. He is such a glorious Savior and Lord that I would gladly have all the world at His feet. He deserves so much that He would well deserve if all kings fell down before Him and all princes called Him blessed. It would only be right for you to fall down before Him and call Him blessed. What a life you may yet lead! What usefulness, what happiness, what blessedness may yet be your portion! If you could look through a telescope that could reveal what you might be if your heart were consecrated to God, what a heaven below and what a heaven above awaits you, I feel sure that you would now yield to the calling of the Great Householder and enter His vineyard.

---

15 This is from a hymn from *Divine Songs for Children* (also titled *Divine and Moral Songs for Children*) by Isaac Watts (1674-1748). This hymn is "against idleness and mischief," and begins with "How doth the little busy bee."

In a literal sense, many are completely idle. There are still many who should be Christians who are really idle. When I have been by the seaside, I have sometimes seen a great many well-to-do folk who had nothing wrong with them; they were perfectly well, yet they were idling their time away day after day. I have almost thought, "If they were thrown into the Mediterranean, who would lose anything by them?" Are there not plenty of people just like that, even among those who come to our places of worship? They consume so much bread and meat, and if they are not careful, they will get consumed one of these days, for they do no good to anybody. What a pity it is that a man who stands nearly six feet tall would be doing nothing, and that a woman who is made for love and kindness would not be scattering that love and kindness on all sides and serving the Lord!

To those of you who are of the ages from thirty to forty, who are still idle, I want to say in the name of the Lord Jesus Christ, with all earnestness, to come to Him by faith, confess your idleness and all your other sins, seek His grace and mercy, and then enter His vineyard and serve Him while you may.

There are also others who are laboriously idle, wearied with work that accomplishes nothing of real worth. The man who is spending all his life in his business, living simply to get money, has only frivolous goals, for temporary objects preoccupy him. He who lives for God, for Christ, and for the good of men lives for a purpose worthy of an immortal being; but he who lives only for his own increase lives for such a temporary and shallow purpose that he may be said to be idle, even though he wears himself to death with his labor.

Oh, if this is all you do, the Master thinks you are idle! You are doing nothing for Him, nothing worth doing, nothing that can be written in the roll and record of history as a great feat done by a soul redeemed by the blood of Christ. Oh, you laborious idlers, I pray that you may be made to go and work in the Master's vineyard.

There are some who are idling because of their constant indecision. They are not entirely bad, but they are not good. They do not serve the devil except by neglecting to serve God. Although they are idle, they are full of good intentions, but they have been so for a long while. If they were now what they resolved to be ten years ago, there would be a great change in them. But they are not, and apparently in ten years' time, they will be as they are now – that is to say, if God spares them. They will go no farther, for they are the kind of people who resolve, and resolve, yet remain the same. I almost wish that they would say that they want to be lost rather than say that they hope to be saved, yet not mean it. For if they said that they wanted to be lost, they would draw back with horror after having said it. But now they play with God, and with eternity, heaven, and hell, and say, "I will, I will, I will." It is always, "I will," yet they never will to make "I will" a thing of the present moment.

If a house were on fire, and you were in the upper story, it would be a pity to say, "I will escape later when the flames have reached another story, but I must wait a little while." No; you would be eager to escape at once. I am sure that you would be. Wisdom dictates that a person should not always contemplate and hesitate and say, "I will," without ever coming up to the mark. Wisdom dictates that, by the grace of God, he should say, "I have reached the end of my indecision. I will begin to live for God if He will give me spiritual life. I will cast off the works of darkness if God will give me spiritual light. I will lay myself at Jesus's feet and cry, 'Save me, O Lord, for I long to escape from my sin and to be an idler no longer.'"

From what you hear from some people, one would think that the service of God was a very difficult, dreary, dismal, hard, toilsome business; but it is not so. The work that the Lord has for us to do is very proper and appropriate for us. He wants us to recognize that we are sinners, and therefore He wants us to come and be washed. After we are washed, He wants us to realize that it is our joy, our duty, our privilege, and our delight to show forth the praises of Him who has thus saved us. The service of God is the most proper employment for a man to be engaged in. It never degrades him and never wearies him, for we gain fresh strength in the service of God, and the more we serve Him, the more we can serve Him.

The Lord invites you to a service in which He will give you all the tools and all the strength you need. When He sends you to His vineyard, He does not expect you to go home and bring back a basket of tools. God does not expect sinners to bring their own Savior. He never sends His soldiers on a warfare at their own expense. He who surrenders himself to be a servant of God will find himself exceptionally prepared and particularly helped to do all that God asks him to do.

More than that, if you will come into God's vineyard, you will work with God, and will so be honored. It seems to me that the most wonderful thing about our service is that we are workers together with God (2 Corinthians 6:1) – to bend the stems of that vine and find an almighty hand softly working with our own; to take the sharp pruning knife and cut off the too-luxuriant bough, and feel that there is a knife sharper than ours cutting as we cut; to take a spade and dig around the vine, and all the while to feel and know that there is a secret Worker digging deeper than we are digging, and so making what we do productive. If you are building for God, and you lift the trowel or the hammer and feel that there is another hand lifting another trowel and another hammer, building with you and building by you, you are divinely honored. If God works with you, you are of the nobility of heaven, and it is to that position He invites you when He says, *Go ye also into the vineyard* (Matthew 20:4).

Let me tell you that if you engage in this work, it will be increasingly pleasant to you. The little difficulties at the beginning will soon be gone. The service of God may at first seem like swimming against the stream, but later you will discover that there is a pleasure even in the opposing element, for the live fish always prefer to swim up the stream. You will find a delight in your difficulties, a sacred joy in that which seems at first so difficult. As you live and labor for your Lord, it will become joy upon joy to serve Him and glorify His holy name.

We must remember that the householder went out again at the sixth hour. We might say these are those who are thirty-five to forty-five. He called those whom he found then, and when he called them, they went into the vineyard. You who are between thirty-five and fifty, in the very strength of your days, Christ will not refuse to use you if you will come at His call.

Then the householder went out again at the ninth hour – to those who are fifty, fifty-five, sixty, or even sixty-five. It was getting late, but they could still do a good amount of work if they threw all their energy into it. No one needs to despair of doing a lifework even now. If you cannot do long work, you can do strong work. There are some people who begin work very late, but they go at it with such vigor and earnestness that they accomplish a good deal. I do not see why you should not. At any rate, come in now. Old men have done great things in the past. If they do not have the exuberance of youth, they have more wisdom. If they do not have all the strength, they have more common sense. There is a place for you to fill, even though so many years have flown over your head. If you come to Christ even now, He will use you in His vineyard.

But best of all, the householder even went out at the eleventh hour. He might have said, "It is of no use to go out now, for if I bring them in, there is only one hour left for them in which to work." Still, as I have told you, he did not employ them because he needed men, but because they needed the money. So to show that, since he did not need them at the first hour, and did not need them at the third, or the sixth, or the ninth hour, much less would he need them at the eleventh hour – yet he would still go out.

There they are! I see them. They are a group of old men and old women. You would not employ them, I am sure. You would say, "They will take half their time for talking, and the other half for wiping the sweat from their brows and doing nothing. There is not any strength left in the poor old souls. They would be better off in a poorhouse eating a bowl of oatmeal and sitting by the fireside."

But this good householder's employment of the men was not for his own sake, but for their sakes. He felt that he might as well engage these men as he had done the rest, so he said to them, "It is the eleventh hour, but go and work in my vineyard, and whatsoever is right, I will give you." I feel it to be a great joy to have been called to work for my Lord in the early hours of life's day. I hope in time to be able to say, "O God, You have taught me from my youth, and up to this time I have declared Your wondrous works. Now also when I am old and gray-headed, O God, do not forsake me. Let me still show Your strength unto this generation, and Your power to everyone who is to come."

It is the best and the happiest thing of all if we have served our Lord from our youth, but if you have missed that privilege (to your own grief and sorrow), if you are old, yet even now the Lord invites you. He calls you. He urges you to come. He will welcome you. If you only come to Him, He will give you your wages, too, even as He gives the wages to those who have begun their working day so early.

If I remember correctly, there was a man who was converted at the age of 103. He was sitting under a hedge, I think in Virginia, and he remembered a sermon that he had heard Rev. John Flavel preach at Plymouth. He recalled a powerful part of it, turned to God, and found peace and pardon. He was spared to live three years more, and when he died, this inscription was put on his grave: "Here lies a babe in grace, aged three years, who died, according to nature, aged 106."

CHAPTER 15

JOASH AND HIS FRIEND JEHOIADA

There is a book called *The Museum of Natural History,* and the most remarkable "animal" listed in that "museum" is man. It would be much easier to understand any other creature than to understand a human being. He is worthy of great study. The more he is studied, the more he will surprise you. There are certain characters who are great curiosities. There are also other characters who are great monstrosities! You can never tell, from what a man is, what he will be.

The case before us is a very extraordinary one because here is a man with every possible advantage, who through a number of years exhibited the brightest form of character. Yet in the end, he was not thought worthy to be laid in the sepulchers of his fathers with other kings of Judah. Nor was he worthy of any royal burial, for the latter part of his life stained and defiled his whole career, and he who began his reign like the dawning of the day ended it like the middle of the night.

I wonder whether anyone we know will turn out to be very sinful and wicked before life is over. I am referring to those who have begun well, who are now the hope and joy of those who know them, but who will end badly, in dishonor to themselves and grief to their households. Probably you can find these people by this one test. Those who say, "It is impossible that it would be so with us" are probably the people, while those who are afraid lest it should be so, and who ask for grace that it may not be so, are probably those who will be preserved and whose path will shine brighter and brighter unto the perfect day (Proverbs 4:18).

There is much need to go below the surface in the examination of moral and spiritual character! In appearance, Joash was all that we could wish (2 Chronicles 24). However, if he had really been what he seemed to be, he would have continued so. If there had been that work of grace within his soul that there appeared to be in his life, he would not have turned aside as he did, for where a work of grace is real and true, it is known by its abiding influence throughout the entire life. Where godly principles have been imparted, and a divine life has been infused, these things are not taken from a person. *They went out from us, but they were not of us*, said the apostle John, *for if they had been of us, they would no doubt have continued with us: but they went out, that they might be made manifest that they were not all of us* (1 John 2:19). So it was with Joash. He turned aside from God because he had never truly known the Lord at all, and his last end was worse than the first because his beginning was not really what it had seemed to be.

Although Joash came from a bad family, he had a good aunt. She was married to the high priest, and the aunt and the uncle took care of young Joash. When he was only an infant, they hid him away so that Athaliah would not kill him with the rest of the royal seed. Thus, Joash had this remarkable privilege that *he was with them hid in the house of God six years* (2 Chronicles 22:12). It is a splendid beginning for any life to be hid in the house of God six years.

I do not think we ever value enough those first six years of a child's life. Impressions made then have a remarkable influence over the rest of one's life. Joash was where God's praise was sung from day to day and where holy prayer was perpetually offered. He was seldom beyond the fragrance of the perfumed incense or away from the sight of the white-robed priests. He heard nothing that could defile him, but everything that could instruct and purify him. He was hidden in the house of the Lord so as not even to go out of it, concealed with godly people for the first six years of his life.

The first thing that you might remember is your mother taking you to a place of worship. You can never forget the time when your father also led you there. He did not seem to be happy unless his boy was scampering by his side when he went to hear the gospel. Among our earliest recollections are the memories of holy hymns and the sayings of gracious people, in whom, as children, we took an interest when they came to our father's house. It is a splendid thing that the first days of one's life would bear the impress of the divine finger. It is good when the vessel begins to revolve upon the wheel, and the clay is soft and malleable, that the first fingers that touch and shape it would be the fingers of God's servants. May God grant that they may be as the very finger of God upon our souls!

Joash began his career by being hid in the house of the Lord six years. After he was seven years of age, he began his life's business in a very admirable way. He was to be the king, but there had to be great care taken to sweep away the usurper from the throne and to put the little king upon it, and Jehoiada managed the whole affair with great skill. He also drew up a covenant for the king to sign. It was a covenant with God that he would be obedient to Jehovah as the supreme King, and also a covenant with the people that he would rule according to equity and right and would not tyrannize over them. It was all done so well that no objection was ever taken to it. Joash reigned with great prosperity and happiness over a people who were blessed by his rule. The whole time, Jehoiada was his faithful prime minister and guide. It is a splendid thing to be started in life properly. To begin well is half the battle.

Some young men, and some young women, too, are launched in life wrongly. It seems almost a matter of course that they should be too strongly tempted, and in all probability yield to the temptation. But many of you did not begin in such a way. You began with a father's blessing and a mother's prayers. You remember your first time going out into life. Some of us remember the ride when, early in the morning, we had to leave our father's house for the first time. Perhaps it was a cold and bitter frosty morning when we started in those old days to go across the country. We remember it well, and how God cared for us and blessed us. We desire to praise Him that He has preserved us even unto this day.

I am showing you the bright side of Joash's career first. After six years in the house of God, he had a great start in life with everything to his advantage. It is very heartbreaking that with such a bright beginning, he would come to such a sad end!

Notice also that beginning so well, *Joash did that which was right in the sight of the LORD all the days of Jehoiada the priest* (2 Chronicles 24:2). While that good man lived, the king was under his influence. He consulted him in every matter of importance. He even seems to have been guided by him to some extent in the matter of his marriage. He was malleable under his uncle's hand, and not only did he do that which was right in the sight of good people, but he did that which was right in the sight of the Lord. His life seems to have been at least outwardly obedient to the law of Jehovah, and he yielded himself up, apparently, at any rate, to be a loyal servant of the great King. He did not just do that for a short time only, but all the days in which Jehoiada lived.

Have we not known men and women whose lives have been under the gentle influence of some kind elderly person – uncle or aunt, father or mother – and they have done what was right year after year, as long as their godly relatives lived? They have been diligent in going up to God's house, apparently devout in Bible reading and prayer, willing to assist in holy work in the school and in all kinds of service for the Lord. They outwardly led most useful, admirable lives all the time that these higher influences were over them.

More than this, Joash was zealous for the externals of religion: *It came to pass after this, that Joash was minded to repair the house of the LORD* (2 Chronicles 24:4). He actually admonished Jehoiada, his uncle, because of the slowness of the Levites: *The king called for Jehoiada the chief, and said unto him, Why hast thou not required of the Levites to bring in out of Judah and out of Jerusalem the collection?* (2 Chronicles 24:6).

There are some people whose hearts are not right toward God, who nevertheless are very zealous about the externals of divine worship. It is much easier to build a temple for God than it is to be a temple for God. It is much more common for people to show zeal in repairing temples than in reforming their own manners. So this young man, Joash, went even beyond his uncle in intense zeal for the cause of God, just as there are many who are trained up in the ways of the Lord and are tireless in rendering some external service to the cause of the Lord Jesus Christ. They will give to the building of a church. They will work hard to promote the paying for it, and so forth; but sadly, you may give, and you may work, and you may devote yourself to all the externals of religion, yet have no *part nor lot in the matter* (Acts 8:21)!

John Bunyan says that when he was an ungodly man, he still had such a reverence for the outward things of religion that he would gladly have kissed the ground that the clergyman walked upon. He said that every nail in the door of the church seemed holy to him.[16] That is all very good, but unless there is a great deal more than that in us, we will fall far short of the requirements of God.

All this time, Joash influenced other people for good. As king, he kept back the nation from worshipping idols. As king, he threw the cloak of his patronage over those who worshipped Jehovah. Things seemed to go well for years – *all the days of Jehoiada the priest* (2 Chronicles 24:2). As long as Jehoiada lived, Joash seemed to be all that he should be.

---

16   For John Bunyan's autobiographical conversion story, see *Grace Abounding to the Chief of Sinners*, available from Aneko Press.

CHAPTER 16

THE LAST DAYS OF JOASH

EARLY PROMISE NOT REALIZED

Joash had given his heart to Jehoiada, but perhaps he never gave it to Jehovah. It is very easy to be outwardly religious by giving your heart to your mother, or your father, or your aunt, or your uncle, or some good person who helps you to do what is right. You are doing all this out of love to them, which is at best only a very secondary motive. God says, *My son, give Me thine heart* (Proverbs 23:26). If you follow your religion to please any creature, it is not the religion that pleases the Creator. Your devotion is not due to anyone here below, but to Him who *sitteth in the heavens*, whose *kingdom ruleth over all* (Psalm 2:4; 103:19).

People can give in to godly influences without any personal, vital godliness whatsoever. You may meet with God's people, yet not be one of God's people. You may give attention to God's servant, yet not be yourself God's servant. A young man may adhere to his mother's advice, yet never really be repentant because of his sin. He may listen to his father's word and pay respect to the externals of his father's religion, yet never have believed in the Lord Jesus Christ.

You must repent yourself, and you must believe in Christ yourself, or else all the rest will aggravate your sin by increasing your responsibility, but it will not go even a hair's breadth toward your salvation. I want everyone to examine himself to see whether his religion gives life to his own soul. Have you been born again? I am not now asking about your mother or father or friends, but about you. Have you been born again? Are you now condemned under sin, or are you justified by faith in Jesus Christ? There can be no substitutes or representatives here, but every person must give account for himself to God. Each man and each woman must come to the Savior personally and accept Him and be saved by Him, or else eternal ruin is certain.

I also believe that a character like that of Joash, a pliant character, an externally pious character, may even prevent people from being saved at all. You may take it for granted that you are saved, but you must not take anything for granted between God and your soul. I direct you to make certain work here. Take your wealth for granted if you want to, and take the title deeds of your estate for granted if you please – but between God and your soul, let everything be settled, straight, clear, and sure, and have no mistakes about this matter.

It is so easy to have been under religious influence from our youth up, and then to go on, year after year, never having raised the question whether we are true Christians or not, saying to ourselves, "Of course it is all right." You will be much nearer the truth if you say, "Of course it is all wrong." You will be much more likely to come to an honest conclusion if you instead suspect yourself too much than believe in yourself too much. In speaking like this, I am sure that I am giving you sound teaching.

After all, to be under godly influences year after year, without any great trial or temptation, may leave the personal character entirely undeveloped. Some people put children under restraint continually, never allowing them to have any sort of temptation. It is sometimes so with children in large institutions. They do not have any money, and they cannot steal any, because there is no one else who has any. They are kept completely out of the world, they live only among their own company, and there is very much of prayer and everything that is good. Often then, when they go out into the world, those who have trained them are completely disappointed with them; yet they need not very much wonder.

If a person on dry land thinks he can swim, it is not certain that he will swim when he gets into the sea. We must have some kind of test, or else we cannot be sure of the character. We cannot know whether a child is honest or not if he never has any chance to take that which is not his own. You cannot be sure about principle being in any young man if he has been kept under a glass case, and if his principles have never been tested. That was the condition of Joash. The real character of the man had never come out at all because Jehoiada, as it were, covered him. He was guided and influenced by the high priest, but his own character only needed an opportunity of developing itself.

I have heard of an officer in India who had raised a young leopard. It was completely tamed. Apparently it was as tame as a cat, and the officer had no fear of his leopard. It went up and down the stairs and entered into every room of his house. He never suspected for a single moment that it would be guilty of shedding blood, but while he was asleep in his chair one afternoon, the leopard licked his hand in all tenderness as a cat might have done. After licking for a while, it licked too hard, and a little blood began to flow. It no sooner tasted blood than the old leopard spirit was up, and his master was his master no more.

The same kind of thing happens to many people who, by being shut in and tamed, as it were, but not changed; subdued, but not renewed; kept in check, but not converted – there has come a time later when the taste of blood has called out the old nature, and away the man has gone. You would never have thought that he could act as he did, but he did so because he did not have a new nature. It was human nature held in check for a while, but it was not the Spirit of God creating a new life and infusing a new character into the soul.

Do you see where I am going? I am speaking to those who have not *passed from death unto life* (1 John 3:14), to you who have never been *renewed in the spirit of your mind* (Ephesians 4:23). I ask you not to imagine that natural religion is spiritual religion. Do not mistake the lessons learned at your mother's knee for the teachings of the Holy Spirit. Do not confuse *a* change with *the* change. Do not think that anything that can come to you by your first birth can help your situation without a second birth. *Ye must be born again* (John 3:7), or else, even though you spent the first six years of your life in the house of God, and although you began under the most sacred influences, you only need an opportunity, a temptation, or a specific stress laid upon you, and you will go wherever the old nature carries you. You will find out for yourself, and to the horror of others, that all your early training had produced nothing because it stopped short of the kingdom of God and His righteousness.

We like young people to be obedient. We are very glad to work with those moldable characters who are easily shaped, but at the same time, we should never be too sure about them. A person with grit in his character, if really affected by the grace of God, may turn out to be a far better man than your too adaptable, pliable character. How many people we know who are very good, but there is nothing in them at all! We have known some others who were dreadfully hard to manage and to get at, but when at last a change has been worked by divine grace, that very stubbornness and persistence of theirs, when sanctified, has given strength to their character, and instead of being a drawback, it has been a benefit.

This young Joash was exceedingly pliant in the hand of Jehoiada, but now Jehoiada was dead. Other counselors came and flattered him: *Now after the death of Jehoiada came the princes of Judah, and made obeisance to the king* (2 Chronicles 24:17). Can you not picture those gentlemen coming to Joash and bowing and scraping a hundred times before they get up to him? They *made obeisance to the king.* Jehoiada had not often made much obeisance to him. He had treated him with due respect as his king, but he had also spoken to him honestly and faithfully. Joash had somebody to look up to while Jehoiada lived, and now he found himself a great man with everybody looking up to him. The princes of Judah, the fashionable part of the realm, the respectable people who had never been worshippers of Jehovah, but who had always preferred the more mystical, ritualistic, and sensuous service of Baal, the philosophical god, came and bowed and *made obeisance to the king.*

I think I can hear what they said: "Royal sir, we congratulate you upon being released from being directed by others. Now you can think for yourself. It is a fine thing for a young man to be delivered from the power of his old uncle. He was undoubtedly a very excellent person. We were present at his funeral, and we paid him all due respect, but still, he was a regular old fossil, one who had never made any progress at all. He clung to the worship of Jehovah and served the God of his fathers. Royal sir, we congratulate you in regard to the liberty that you have attained. Besides that, we fear that you have been considerably controlled by the priests. Jehoiada was a priest, and of course you respected and venerated his character, but you could not indulge yourself as long as he lived. We have always had high thoughts of you, royal sir. We always believed that you would break out one of these days, and now that the good man is laid asleep, we are sure that you will not let his dead hand rest upon you, but you will wake up, be mindful of the age, and keep up with the spirit of the times."

You know how they do it. It is always being done – this pouring of drops of poison into the ear, these soft, subtle flatteries. Even when a man has reached Joash's age, he is not beyond the power of flattery. I wonder how old a man would be when he would be too old to love flattery. Of course, he always likes to be told, "Ah, dear sir, I know that you could not bear flattery," being at that moment more highly flattered than at any other time in his life. That is what these princes of Judah did, and poor Joash, good Joash, Joash who repaired the temple, Joash who was even more intensely earnest than Jehoiada himself, was led astray by the soft words of the deceivers, and we find him burying his religion with his uncle. He buried all his piety in Jehoiada's grave. Some people I have known, and over whom I have wept, have acted in the same way.

After that, Joash went off to sin. The images that he had broken down were set up again. The groves that he had cut down were planted again. He who seemed to be such a zealous servant of Jehovah had now become a worshipper of the abominable Ashtaroth, and bowed before the accursed Baalim. Oh, sad, sad, sad wickedness this is!

There was a lack of principle in Joash, and I want to warn all people about this. Do not be satisfied with the practice of piety without the principles of piety. It is not enough to have a correct creed; you must have a renewed heart. It is not sufficient to have an ornate ritual; you must have a holy life, and to be holy, you must be renewed by the Holy Spirit. If this change is not brought about in you by the Holy Spirit, you who yield so easily to good will yield just as quickly to evil.

What happened next? Joash refused reproof. God sent prophets to the people, and they came and warned them, testifying against the idolaters – *but they would not give ear* (2 Chronicles 24:19). This Joash, who had spent his first six years in the temple, would not now give ear to the Lord's prophets. He had always been ready to listen to Jehoiada, but now he would not give ear. He was a tremendous zealot for repairing the temple, with the most costly architecture, and gold and silver without limit; but now he will not give heed to God's servants at all. They may speak with all their heart and soul, but he is as the deaf adder that will not hear the voice of the charmer, no matter how wisely he charms.

He was once your good young man, your pious young man! Oh, how London has often sifted too many like Joash! I remember many whose story was like this. They had been to the house of God always. They were brought up where there was a family altar in the house. Everybody considered them to be Christians. Then they went to London or another big city. At first, they went where their father exhorted them to go – to some humble place where the gospel was preached; but after a time, they thought it was not wrong to go on Sunday to see one of the more showy religious places. Having done that, they went to some showy place that was not religious. They worked so hard all week that they thought they must go out a little into the fresh air on Sunday. Then they found companions who led them, little by little, from the path of integrity and chastity until "the good young man" was as wicked and immoral as any on the streets of London, and he who seemed to be a saint became not only a sinner, but the maker of sinners.

What did Joash do next? He slew his friend's son (2 Chronicles 24:22). Old Jehoiada's son, Zechariah, one of those who had helped to put the crown upon young Joash's head, was at last moved to speak out in the midst of the temple service to the people, as he had a right to do. He began to upbraid them for turning aside from Jehovah to the worship of the foul idol gods. See now that the tiger's blood is up! Joash tells them to kill him. How dare Zechariah testify against his king? It is true that he is the son of his best friend; he is his own cousin; he is one who helped him to ascend the throne – but what does all that matter to this once good young man? The milk of human kindness is soured now. The oil that was so soft burns fiercely once it takes fire. "Let Zechariah die. Kill him in the temple. Splatter the sacred altar with his blood. Stone him. He has dared to speak against me." See how hard and coarse and rough your soft clay has become!

I have seen this change come over people. I believe that the worst persecutors in the world are generally made of those who once were tender and softhearted. Nero would at first hardly sign the death warrant of a criminal, yet he went on to delight in mass murder. When the was desired to betray his Lord (John 17:12), the raw aitor was found in an apostle. You cannot make an an except from one who seems to be good. You must has been six years in the temple, the man who has done that which is right in the sight of the Lord all the days of Jehoiada, to make such a devil as Joash turned out to be when he killed the son of his benefactor in the court of the house of the Lord.

I could look steadily in the face of some people, and in the spirit of prophecy I could burst out into tears to think of what they will yet be, what they will yet do, and what they will yet say! Perhaps you ask, *Is thy servant a dog that he should do this . . . thing?* (2 Kings 8:13). Oh, sir, you are worse than a dog. There lurks within you a heart *deceitful above all things, and desperately wicked: who can know it?* (Jeremiah 17:9). Oh, that you did know it, and would turn to God and say, "O Lord, renew me! Lord, make a new creature of me! Lord, save me so that I may never do such things that now, today, I think it impossible that I would ever do!"

Joash, who was perishing, miserable, and having no faith in God, robbed the temple and gave all the gold and treasures unto Hazael the Syrian. Personally, he was full of disease, and in time, his own servants, disgusted with him for his conduct toward Jehoiada's son, slew him on his bed. What a death for the young man who was six years hidden away in the house of the Lord!

Oh, if I could tell some of you what will become of you, you would be so angry with me! If I could prophesy to some good young fellow – I mean, outwardly good, as Joash was at first, but without a new heart and without the grace of God in his soul – if I could prophesy to him what he will be, he would spit in my face in indignation that I would dare to foretell such a thing.

There is not a man or woman who is safe from the most abominable sin until they surrender themselves to Christ. There is not one who is sure that the deepest damnation of hell will not be your portion unless you come and commit your soul into the hands of Jesus, who is a faithful Keeper of those who put their trust in Him.

Can there be a Character Insurance Society? There can be no such society formed by men that can insure our character, yet God has formed one. *The righteous also shall hold on his way; and he that hath clean hands shall be stronger and stronger* (Job 17:9). The Lord will ke. him and preserve him from evil, for *the path of the just is as the shining light, that shineth more and more unto the perfect day* (Proverbs 4:18).

I do advise you, by the living God, my hopeful young friend, to surrender yourself to Jesus Christ and to seek His guardian care lest the fair blossom of today never brings forth fruit, but ends in disappointment!

CHAPTER 17

A BOLD AND EARNEST PROFESSION

David said, *O LORD, truly I am Thy servant* (Psalm 116:16). *Truly.* The word of caution is that if you become the servant of God, become the servant of God *truly. God is not mocked* (Galatians 6:7). It is the curse of our churches that we have so many merely nominal Christians in them. It is the plague of this age that so many people put on Christ's uniform, yet never do a single thing for Him. Oh, if you serve God, mean it! If a man serves the devil, let him serve the devil; but if he serves God, let him serve God. Some people serve their business very actively, but not their God.

Years ago, there was a brother who used to pray at the prayer meeting occasionally in a low tone, as if he had no lungs left. You could seldom hear what he said, and if you listened and strained your ear, there was still nothing to hear. I thought that the brother had a bad voice, and so I stopped calling on him to pray. But stepping one day into his shop, I heard him say in a commanding voice, "John, fetch that half-hundred!"

I thought, "That is the kind of voice he has in his business, but when he comes into the service of God, that little squeak is all he can give." Is there not much of this hypocrisy all over the world? God is to have the leftovers of a person's life, and he flings these down as if they were all that God was worth; but he gives to the world the strength of his life and the best of his being. God does not want servants in name only. *O LORD, truly I am Thy servant*, said David. He who does not intend to *truly* be God's servant, let him not pretend to be one at all.

I want every young man who is a Christian to make it known by an open declaration of his discipleship. There should not be anyone who follows the Lord Jesus Christ in an inferior, private, indistinct, questionable way. It has become the custom of many to try to be Christians and never say anything about it. This is beneath contempt. I urge you true servants of Christ to be open about it and never be ashamed of it, because if ever a bold profession was required, it is required now. You may not be burned at the stake for saying that you are a Christian, but I believe that the old enmity to Christ is not removed, and a true believer will still be called upon to take up the cross.

In many houses in London, a young man will have to run the gauntlet if he is known to be a Christian. He will be attacked and criticized and have to prove himself. Run the gauntlet, then! You have an honorable opportunity. It is a grand thing to be permitted to endure reproach for Christ's sake. You should look at it as a great privilege that you are counted worthy not only to believe in the Lord Jesus Christ, but also to suffer for His sake.

These days the world needs decided men. It seems to be imagined everywhere that you may believe what you like, or believe nothing; and that you may do as you like, or do nothing, and the result will be just the same both to the unbeliever and the man of faith. But it is not so. It is time for the outright servant of the Lord to put down his foot and say, "I have believed, and that is why I have spoken. I am a Christian, and while I leave you to your individual liberty, I intend to have mine, and I intend to exercise that liberty by being openly and unquestionably on the side of Christ, and on the side of that which is pure, straightforward, right, true, and good."

Is not this well deserved by Christ? If He was never ashamed of us, we should never be ashamed of Him! If the Lord of life and glory lowered Himself to die for us, could we ever lower ourselves at all even if we rolled into the mire or dropped into the grave for Him? Surely our blessed Lord deserves to be followed by heroes. Every man in the presence of the cross-bearing Jesus should feel that to take up his cross and follow Christ is the simplest and most natural thing that he can do. He should resolve in God's strength that he will do it, and that he will continue to obey the Lord, even if all the world would ridicule.

Let me tell you that it is the easiest thing to do, after all. As compared with compromise, it is simplicity itself. I have known many young Christians who have come up to London and have determined that they would serve God if they could, but would keep it very quiet. They have attempted to be private Christians, but they have failed. If you are a genuine Christian, it will be found out as certainly as you are alive.

If you go down to Mitcham when the lavender is ripe, you may shut all your windows, but you will find that the scent of the lavender will somehow get into your house. Christianity has a perfume about it that will spread abroad so that all in the house inquire, "What is all this?" The wicked gossips will whisper that you are "a Christian young man," and if you have not been open about it at first, it will be very hard for you afterward.

Begin as you intend to continue, young man. Do not hide your flag and try to sail under false colors, for both the good and the bad will be against you in that case. You will be hunted from place to place if the dogs find that you will run. You will make rare sport for the hunters if you take to your heels. Come straight out and let them do their best or their worst. Live a most consistent life, and the other young fellows will know where you stand. They will soon see what you are, and if you are sincere, they will leave you alone before long. If they do not, patience is still yours. If they continue to persecute you, so much the worse for them, for you, by your quiet and holy life, will make them feel that it is hard for them to oppose and resist the truth of your life. In any case, be bravely open about following Jesus.

Some young fellows are like rats behind the walls; you do not mind coming out at night to eat the crumbs on the floor, but you quickly go back in hiding again. By this I mean that you will join in religious exercises if it is not known to the people you work with, but you would not for the world become suspected of real religion. Is that how true Christians should act? No; put on your uniform.

"But I do not care about joining a church," someone says. That may be true, but do you not know that it is found to be a convenient and proper thing in warfare that a soldier should wear a uniform? At first Oliver Cromwell's Ironsides were dressed any which way, but in the battles with the Cavaliers, an Ironside was sometimes struck down by mistake by the sword of one of his own brethren, and so the general said, "You wear red coats, all of you. We must know our own men from the enemy." Cromwell meant what he said, and the men had to come in their red coats, for it is found essential in warfare that men should be known by some kind of uniform.

You who are Christ's – do not go around as if you were ashamed of His Majesty's service. Put on your red coats. Come out clearly as acknowledged Christians. Unite with a body of true Christian people, and be distinctly known to be Christ's. How are the ordinances of the Lord's house to be sustained if everyone is to go to heaven alone by the back way? Come out boldly. If anyone wants to laugh at a Christian, step out and say, "Laugh at me. If anybody wants to abuse a fellow and call him a hypocrite, or anything else, come on! I am ready for you." Once you have done that and have taken a clear stand, you will find it the easiest thing in life to bear the reproach of Christ.

Young men, if you meet with any reproach for Christ, a reward awaits you. Shall I tell you a parable? There was once a king's son who went upon a journey incognito, and he journeyed into a far country. However, he was poorly treated there, and because of his language and his appearance, the people of the land set him in the pillory, which was used in the past as a place of scorn. They set him there, and the mob gathered around him and threw all kinds of filth and waste upon him. This unknown prince must necessarily be pelted in this manner and be made as the *offscouring of all things* (1 Corinthians 4:13). But there was among them one man who loved the prince and who recognized him, and he was determined to be associated with him. He mounted the pillory, stood by the prince's side, wiped his face with his handkerchief, and whenever he could, he put himself in the way of the mire and dirt so that it would hit him instead of the prince.

Years went by, and it came to pass that the prince was back in his kingdom in all his glory, and the attendants were standing around the throne. This man who had been a poor man in his own country was summoned to the court, and when he arrived at the palace, the prince saw him and said to the peers of the realm, "Stand aside and make way for this man. He was with me when I was poorly treated and scorned, and now he will be with me in my glory, highest among you here."

Do you not know the story of how our Lord Jesus came down to earth and suffered many things, and how He was *despised and rejected of men* (Isaiah 53:3)? Young man, are you the man who would wipe His blessed face and share His shame, and take half turns with the man of Nazareth in all the abuse and scorn? Are you that man? Then there will come a day when the great Father on His throne will see you and say, "Make a path, you angels! Stand back, seraphim and cherubim! Make way for this man. He was with My Son in His humiliation, and now he will be with Him in His glory."

Will you receive that mark of honor? Not unless you are prepared to put on the badge of Christ and say, "I am His servant and His follower from this day until life's end." May God help you to do it! O Lord, lead hundreds of young men to shoulder the cross!

Were you ever in chains? Did you ever feel the chains of guilt? Are you believing in Christ? If so, then those chains are loosed, for your sin is forgiven you for Christ's sake, and you are delivered from all condemnation. You are completely delivered from the bonds of guilt and despair. You are also saved from the power of sin. The habits that were your masters are now destroyed. The lusts that lorded it over you are now slain, and you are free. Do you not want to be bound to Christ from now on because He has loosed your chains?

I know some men in this world who talk a great deal about being free, but they are always in chains. There is a man I know for whom the devil makes a nauseous mixture (at least to me it is very nauseous), and he says, "Drink a quart of it," and he drinks. "Drink another," says the devil, and he does so. "Drink another," says the devil, and his brain begins to reel, and he is all on fire. "Drink it," says the devil, and he lets it run down his throat, for he is in chains. I know another man who, against his better self, will go into sin, which he knows to be sin and knows to be harmful to him. Yet he goes in a foolish manner and harms himself more and more. He is led by the nose by the devil, and he says that he cannot resist. He is a slave in the worst sense.

Blessed is the man who can say, "You have loosed my bonds. No evil habit enslaves me now. No passion controls me. No lust enchains me"! Young friend, if you can stand up and say, "I am free from myself. I am no longer the slave of sin," then you are a blessed man, and you may well be God's servant forever!

What a mercy it is to be delivered from the bonds of the fear of man! Some young men dare not call their souls their own for fear of their employers. A great many more are dreadfully in fear of the young man who is near them. They dare not do what is right! Poor babies that they are, they must ask permission to keep a conscience! When they are about to do anything, they are always saying, "What will So-and-so think of it?" Does it matter to any true man what all the world thinks about him? Has he not risen out of that? Is he still a slave?

"Go," says the brave man. "Think what you will and say what you will. If I serve God, I am not your servant. I will not fall by your criticism, and I will not rise by your praise." Will I be afraid of such a thing myself, and ask permission of another man what I should think, what I should believe, and what I should do? I will die first! When God brings a man to know himself and to be His servant, He sets him free from this cowardly crime of being afraid of a man who will die.

So, too, He sets him free from all the practices and customs of the world. Young man, when you go into business, they will tell you that you must do so-and-so because it is "the custom of the trade." You respond, "That is lying!" You will be told that it is not exactly lying because your customer is used to your tricks, and he quite understands that a hundred means eighty and that the best quality means a second-class article. I am told that half the business in London is robbery in some form or another if the customs of the trade are not understood.

If it is true that it is all understood, it might just as well be done honestly, and it would pay just as well. Yet somehow, people feel as if they must do what others have done, or else they will not be able to compete. Slaves! Serfs! Be honest! He is not free who does not dare to be honest. Will I not speak my mind? Will I not act out my integrity? If I cannot, then I cannot say with David, *Thou hast loosed my bonds* (Psalm 116:16).

What a blessing it is when God frees us from the fear of death! *Thou hast loosed my bonds.* What will it matter to you, young man, if you become the servant of God by faith in Jesus Christ, whether you live or die? If you die early, you are so much sooner in heaven. If you live long, you have that much longer to serve God on earth. Give your heart to Christ. Trust your salvation in those dear hands that were pierced for sinners. Become the servant of God, and you will be provided for, for His children will not lack (Psalm 34:10). You will be led, guided, taught, educated, and prepared for heaven. One of these bright days, a convoy of celestial spirits will think it is an honor to be permitted to bear your joyful spirit up to the throne of God.

Who, then, will be the servant of the Most High? I always wish when I have a sermon that I could preach it over again, because I have not done well enough; but all I care to preach for is that I may touch your hearts. I would not care a snap of the fingers to be an orator or to speak sentences elegantly. I want to declare the truth in such a way that some young man will say, "I will serve God."

I remember young men who began life when I began, who are now – I will not say what. I remember hearing their names mentioned as good examples. They were such fine young men and had just gone up to London. Yes, and if they are not in jail tonight, they are in the poorhouse. It all came about in this way: the young man sent word home to his mother what the text was on Sunday, yet he had not been to hear a sermon at all. He had been to some amusement to spend a happy day. Wherever he went, he had neglected the house of God. Little by little, there was a little wrong in his small accounts. It seemed like just a little matter, but once that man had lost his character, he could not pick himself up again. There was another man. There was nothing wrong in his accounts, but his habits were loose. In time, he became ill. Who could wonder? When a man plays with sharp tools, he is very likely to cut himself. It was not long before he was so sick that he could not attend to business, and before long, he died. It was said of him (and I fear it was true) that he killed himself by vice. That is what happens with thousands of young people in the big cities.

Oh, if you become the servant of God, this will not happen to you! You may not be rich, you may not be famous, and you may not be great, but you do not need to want these things. They are very often mere decorated, worthless trinkets. To be a man to the fullness of your manhood; to be free and to dare to look every other man in the world in the face and speak the truth and do what is right; to be a man who can look God in the face because Christ has covered him with His glorious righteousness – this is the passion with which I would inspire the spirit of every young man. I pray that the flame may burn in his life by the power of the Divine Spirit. Come then, and bow your heads and say, "We will be servants of the living God from this time forth and forever."

CHAPTER 18

LYDIA OF THYATIRA

There are many points of interest in Lydia's conversion. Notice that it was brought about by providential circumstances. She was a seller of purple in Thyatira. That city was famous for its dyeing trade, which had flourished there ever since the days of Homer. The mode of producing an unusually delicate and valuable purple seems to have been known to the women of Thyatira. It may be that Lydia had come to Philippi upon a journey, or that while her articles were made at Thyatira, she resided during a part of the year at Philippi to dispose of her goods. The communication between the two places was very easy, and she may have frequently made the journey.

In any case, Providence brought her there when the hour of her conversion was come. You might remember that Thyatira was situated in that part of the country into which Paul was forbidden by the Spirit to go and preach (Acts 16:6). Therefore, if Lydia had been at home, she could not have heard the truth, and since *faith cometh by hearing, and hearing by the Word of God* (Romans 10:17), she would have remained unconverted. But Providence brought her to Philippi at the right time. This is the first link of the chain.

But how is Paul to be brought there? First of all, he must be kept out of Bithynia, and he must be silenced in his journey through Mysia (Acts 16:7). He must be brought to Troas, close by the shore of the sea (Acts 16:8). He must look across the blue sea and think about Europe's needs. Then he had to fall asleep, and in the visions of the night, he must be prompted to cross to Macedonia (Acts 16:9-10). He then had to ask for a ship, a ship headed for Samothracia, and for no other place, before landing at Neapolis (Acts 16:11). By the same instinct, he had to make his way to Philippi (Acts 16:12). He cannot go in any other direction. He must be brought there at the very time when Lydia is present. He must find out about the times of prayer by the river's side, for God ordained that Lydia will be saved. Notice how many different threads were all interwoven here to make up the fabric of her providential conversion! In this case, God rules and overrules all things to bring that woman and that apostle to the same spot. Everything in God's providence is working together for the salvation of the elect.

Not only was there preventing providence in Lydia's case, but there was also grace in a certain manner preparing the soul. The woman did not know the Savior. She did not understand the things that made for her peace, yet she knew many truths that were excellent stepping stones to a knowledge of Jesus. If not a Jewess by birth, she was a "proselyte of the gate,"[17] and therefore was well acquainted with the oracles of God. She was one who worshipped God. She was one of the most devout of God's worshippers among the Jews. Although she was far away from the synagogue (some forget the Sabbath when they travel in foreign lands), yet when the day came around, she was found with that little handful at the riverside prayer. I do not doubt that she had read Isaiah the prophet and could carry in her heart and remember such words as these: *He is despised and rejected of men; a man of sorrows, and acquainted with grief. . . . He is brought as a lamb to the slaughter, and as a sheep before her shearers is dumb, so He openeth not His mouth* (Isaiah 53:3, 7).

As in the case of the Ethiopian eunuch (Acts 8), although the Scriptures she had read were not understood for lack of some man to guide her, they had prepared her mind. The ground had been plowed and was ready for the good seed. It was not a hard rock, as in the jailer's case (Acts 16). Lydia worshipped God, she worshipped Him in sincerity, and she worshipped Him looking for the coming of the Messiah, Israel's consolation (Luke 2:25) – and so her mind was prepared for the reception of the gospel.

---

17   A "proselyte of the gate" was sort of a half-convert to Judaism. The convert was not required to be circumcised or to follow the Mosaic ceremonial law, whereas a "proselyte of righteousness" followed all of the Mosaic laws.

Undoubtedly, in many of us there was a preparation for Christ before Christ came to us in life-giving grace. I know that in some of our cases, the pious example of a godly father and the loving instruction of a tender mother had softened us somewhat so that although we were still unsaved and still out of Christ, we were yet like the man who laid at the pool of Bethesda (John 5). We were close by the edge of the healing stream, and there was not that sudden, astounding change in our case that we have seen in others.

Still, we should attribute all this preparatory work to sovereign grace, for grace – free favor – does much in which no grace of practical salvation is discernible. What I mean is that before grace renews the heart, there is grace that prepares us for grace. Grace may be setting the mind in activity, clearing us from preconceptions, and ridding us of a thousand unbelieving and skeptical thoughts, thereby raising a platform from which divine grace conducts us into the region of the new life. Such was the case of Lydia, and such is the case of many others. Providence and grace work together before the operative time is come.

On the Sabbath, Lydia went to the gathering of her people. Although God works great wonders and calls people when they are not hearing the Word, we usually must expect that, *being in the way*, God will meet with them (Genesis 24:27). It is somewhat extraordinary that the first convert in Europe was converted at a very small prayer meeting. There were only a few women there. We have no reason to think that there were any more males than just Paul and his friend Luke, who had stopped by unexpectedly and had been moved to speak at the prayer meeting – and that talk was the means in God's hand of opening her heart.

Let us never neglect the means of grace. Wherever we are, let us not forget *the assembling of ourselves together, as the manner of some is* (Hebrews 10:25). May you ever have, even if as yet you are unconverted, a love for the courts of the Lord's house and for the place where His people meet together. Love the prayer meeting. Do not say about it that it is only a prayer meeting. God loves to put honor upon prayer, upon the assembly of His people directly for His worship. You may hope that even if the sermon has not been useful, and if the common Lord's Day service may not have been blessed, yet perhaps on the Monday evening, maybe in that little cottage when there are only a few women present, you may meet with God, who did not appear to you in the larger assembly. Be diligent in going to church. Be constantly in God's house, as often as the doors are open and your duties will permit, for Lydia's conversion took place in the gathering of God's people.

It was clearly a work of grace, for we are specifically told, *whose heart the Lord opened* (Acts 16:14). She did not open her own heart. Her prayers did not do it. Paul did not do it. The Lord Himself must open the heart to receive the things that make for our peace (Luke 19:42; Romans 14:19). It belongs to God alone to savingly work upon human hearts. We can get at human brains, but God alone can awaken human affections. We may reach them, we grant you, in the natural and common way, but to reach them so that the enemy of God will become His friend, and so that the stony heart will be turned into flesh (Ezekiel 36:26), is the work of grace – and nothing short of divine power can accomplish it.

Lydia was baptized, but her good works did not end at the water. She then had the apostles come to her house. She would bear the shame of being thought to be a follower of the crucified Jew and a friend of the despised Jewish apostle, the renegade, the turncoat. She would have him in her house, and although he said no out of his hesitation to receive anything, yet she constrained him, for love was in her heart, and she had a generous spirit. While she had even a crust of bread, it would be broken with the man who brought her to Christ. Not only would she give him the cup of cold water in the prophet's name (Matthew 10:41-42), but her house would shelter him.

I do not think much of a conversion where it does not touch a person's substance. Those people who pretend to be Christ's people, yet live only for themselves and do nothing for Him or for His church, give only sorry evidence of having been born again. A love to the people of God has always been a distinguishing mark of the true convert. Look, then, at Lydia, and remember that she is one example of many. Let her case rest before you, and let the prayer go up, "Lord, bring in other Lydias according to Your mighty grace."

The Lord opened Lydia's heart to attend to the things that were spoken (Acts 16:14). No doubt the Lord removed prejudice. This prejudice is an evil that we have to fight against in very many people. In Lydia's case, it would be Jewish prejudice. Maybe the report had reached her, as it had most of the Jews, concerning Jesus of Nazareth. She knew that her race had hounded Him to the death, and that her nation had even said, *His blood be on us, and on our children* (Matthew 27:25).

God removed all this prejudice from Lydia's mind. She sat down to listen to Paul with a determination to give him a fair hearing and to weigh the matter and see whether these things were so or not – somewhat like the Bereans of old, who also had their hearts in a measure opened, for they searched the Scriptures to see whether things were so (Acts 17:11).

The devil often covers men from head to foot in a coat of armor so that when they go where the arrows of God are flying, there is very little hope of their being wounded because there is hardly a joint of the harness that the devil has not protected by an iron rivet of prejudice.

When Lydia's heart was opened, her desires were awakened. She now felt a wish to understand this matter, and if there was anything in what the apostle was saying about eternal salvation, about complete pardon by the blood of Him who was *the Lamb slain from the foundation of the world* (Revelation 13:8), she said to herself, "I would like to know about it. I hope it may be true. I want to get an interest in these things."

So she listens, anxiously desiring to be influenced by the Word. She has a hunger and a thirst, and those people have this blessing: *they shall be filled* (Matthew 5:6). When, by God's grace, people begin hungering and thirsting, then we are very thankful to say that this is the opening of the heart. As the oyster opens its shell when the tide comes up, so when the tide of grace is coming, God often makes people open their hearts so that they may now get the spiritual supply.

Well, there was a desire awakened, but this was not all. There came another kind of opening. Her understanding was now enlightened. Her understanding was opened. She had a clear view of the gospel. She could see in its height, depth, and length that which her soul needed.

Then came something else. Lydia's affections were now moved. She felt growing within her a love to Him who, though He was equal with God, yet took upon Himself the form of a servant (Philippians 2:6-7). As she heard Paul describe His sufferings, and as she pictured to herself the scene around the cross, she thought she could hear the death shriek and see the flowing blood. She seemed to think, "Yes, I love that Man. I love Him. My heart goes after Him. Oh, that He were mine!" Then she thought, "Yes, I love that preaching. Those doctrines of mercy are sweet to my ears." She began already to rejoice. *Blessed are the people that know the joyful sound* (Psalm 89:15), for if they do not yet walk in the light of God's countenance, yet they will, for so the promise runs.

All this, I think, is included in the words that her heart was opened (Acts 16:14). Her affections were now burning toward divine things. Then came faith. She believed the entirety of the record. She accepted it as absolutely true, as Paul had stated, that there had been a Messiah; that He, according to Scripture, was the Son of God and was also the Son of man; that He had suffered, *the just for the unjust* (1 Peter 3:18); and that she, believing in Him, had her sins forgiven. Faith came now through hearing (Romans 10:17). She took God at His word. She simply and humbly put her soul at the feet of that cross where the blood was dripping, believing that, as it fell from heaven, it pleaded for her; and as it dropped on her, it gave her peace with God through Jesus Christ (Romans 5:1).

Once faith had been given, all the graces followed. Now she hated her sins. She repented. Now she loved righteousness. She sought after holiness. Now she had a bright hope of the many mansions in the Father's house. Now she began to run with holy and happy feeling in the ways of obedience to Christ's commands. She became not merely a believer in the basic truths of Christianity, but she went on toward perfection (Hebrews 6:1-2), adding to her faith courage, and to her courage experience, and to experience brotherly kindness, and to brotherly kindness love (2 Peter 1:5-7). Onward she went in the way of her God. All this the Master did by opening her heart to seriously consider the things that were spoken of by Paul.

CHAPTER 19

THE QUEEN OF SHEBA, SOLOMON'S PUPIL

Queens have many cares, and they have countless duties and engagements, but the Queen of Sheba neither considered it beneath her dignity to search into the wisdom of Solomon, nor a waste of valuable time to journey to his dominions. How many offer the vain excuse that they cannot give due attention to the religion of Jesus Christ for lack of time! They say that they have a large family or a very difficult business to manage. This woman rebukes such people, for she left her kingdom and threw off the cares of state to take a long journey so that she might listen to the royal sage.

Her royal court was undoubtedly already stored with wisdom. The princes of the Eastern realms were always careful to gather to themselves a band of wise men, who found in their patronage both provisions and honor. In the court of such a great lover of learning as the Queen of Sheba was, there would certainly be a little society of magi and wise men. However, not being content with what she already knew, she was determined to search after this divine wisdom about which she had heard the fame.

In doing so, she rebukes those of you who think you know enough and who suppose that your own homespun intelligence will suffice without sitting at the feet of Jesus. If you dream that human wisdom can be a sufficient light without receiving the brighter beams of revelation; if you say, "These things are for the unintelligent and for the poor; we will not listen to them," then this queen, whose court was full of wisdom, yet who left it all to find the wisdom that God had given to Solomon, rebukes you. The wisdom of Jesus Christ as much surpasses all human knowledge as the sun outshines a candle. There can be no comparison, although there is much contrast. He who will not come to the fountain that brims with wisdom, but trusts to his own leaking cisterns, will wake up too late to find himself a fool.

Consider, too, that the queen came from a very great distance to hear the wisdom of Solomon. The journey from Arabia Felix, or from Abyssinia, whichever the country may have been, was a long and dangerous one. It was a much more serious matter than it would be in these times. Performed by the slow process on the backs of camels, the journey must have taken a very long time. Coming *from the uttermost parts of the earth*, as Matthew says (Matthew 12:42), there were doubtless mountains to be climbed, if not seas to be navigated and deserts to be crossed; but none of these difficulties could keep her back. She heard of wisdom, and wisdom she will have. So she boldly set out on the journey with her large entourage, no matter how far she may have to travel.

Very many people have the gospel brought to their doors, yet will not leave their chimney corners to listen to it. The Queen of Sheba, toiling across the desert and of the weaker gender though she was, *shall rise up in the judgment* against those who neglect the great salvation and who treat the Savior as though it were nothing to them that Jesus would die (Matthew 12:42).

Do not forget, also, that this woman was a foreigner to Solomon, and that she had a religion already – probably one of the older forms of idolatry, perhaps the Sabean worship of the sun. Many people argue in these times, "Are you trying to have me change my religion?" Yes, that is what I want if your religion is false. If your religion has not changed you, I want you to change your religion, for a religion that does not renew a man's character and make him holy, that does not change his beliefs and make him rest upon Christ, that does not make a completely new man of him from top to bottom, is a religion of no value, and the sooner he gives it up, the better.

Because my mother or my grandmother happened to be blind, why am I to be blind, too, if there is sight to be had? Remember, to your own Master you stand or fall on your own account (Romans 14:4). Each soul enters through the gate of life alone, and it departs alone through the iron gate of death. Every person should search in solitary earnestness, apart from all the rest of the world, to know what the truth is; and knowing it, it is his duty to come out alone on the Lord's side. Yes, we would like you to give attention to the things of God, even though you might have been brought up in other customs and have honestly followed another form of religion. *Try the spirits whether they are of God* (1 John 4:1). If your soul has been deceived, there is still time to be set right. May God help you that you may find out the truth!

It is worthy of observation that this woman, the Queen of Sheba, coming from afar, made a journey that cost her very much expense. She came with a great entourage, with camels bearing spices and very much gold and precious stones. She looked upon the treasures of her kingdom as only valuable because they would cause her to be admitted into the presence of the keeper of the storehouse of wisdom.

Our Lord Jesus Christ asks nothing of people except their hearts. He does not sell the truth to any of them, but gives it freely *without money and without price* (Isaiah 55:1). If people will not have it, if they refuse to lend their ears and to give their thoughts to divine things, will they not be utterly inexcusable when this heathen queen will rise up and declare that she gave her rubies and her pearls, her spices and her camels, to King Solomon so that she might learn his human wisdom?

The gospel presents freely to every needy soul just that which he requires. It cries, *He that hath no money; come ye, buy, and eat; yea, come, buy wine and milk without money and without price* (Isaiah 55:1). If you have refused the invitation of Christ's gospel, you may well tremble at the thought that the Queen of Sheba will rise up in judgment against you.

Note that this queen had received no invitation. King Solomon never asked her to come. She came unsought for and unexpected. You, however, have been asked to come: *The Spirit and the Bride say, Come* (Revelation 22:17). The Bible is God's written invitation, and you may search it if you will. Therefore, if you who received invitations and were urged with line upon line and precept upon precept (Isaiah 28:10, 13) will not come when God's providence brings the gospel to your very gates, if you will not seek King Jesus, then you indeed will be condemned by this Queen of Sheba. The object that she journeyed after was vastly inferior to that which is proposed to our inquiry.

We urge the careless soul to consider the Son of God. The Queen of Sheba went that distance to see a son of man. She journeyed all that way to see one who was wise himself, but who had power to impart only a very small portion of his wisdom. We, however, invite the sinner to come to One who is made of God unto us *wisdom, and righteousness, and sanctification, and redemption* (1 Corinthians 1:30). We tell him that Christ is ready to give all that He has, that His abundance is only an abundance for others, and that His fullness is that out of which all of us have received (John 1:16).

The Queen of Sheba went to hear a man who had wisdom, but we plead with you to come to One who is wisdom – wisdom itself consolidated. Do you talk of the royalty of Solomon? We invite you to a greater King than he, One who is Lord of heaven and earth and hell. Do you speak of Solomon's riches? We tell you of One who has unspeakable riches of grace and glory. It is true that the Queen of Sheba might benefit by the journey, but that was only a probability. Whosoever comes to Christ, however, becomes rich to all the intents of delight. No soul ever transacted with our Solomon without being at once enriched. If he came empty-handed, poor, weak, naked, and sinful to accept from our Jesus His great salvation, he was never sent away empty.

Let us now observe, to this queen's worthy commendation, how she conducted the inquiry. Observe that she did it in person. She did not appoint an ambassador to go and search into the matter, but personally, and on her own account, she set out to see Solomon himself. Was it not the Duke of Wellington who, on one occasion, rebuked one of his officers for criticizing the Bible by asking him if he had ever read it, and when the other honestly confessed that he had not, he showed him how ignoble it was to find fault with that which he did not understand? Most people who object to the religion of Christ have never investigated it. I am sure that no one has ever had an intelligent idea of the person of the Savior and of the graciousness of His work who could ever think or speak against Him afterward. Isaac Watts is correct when he says:

> His worth, if all the nations knew,
> Sure the whole world would love Him too.[18]

---

18   This is from a hymn by Isaac Watts (1674-1748) that begins with "The wondering world inquires to know."

The queen went first of all to Solomon. She went, and she went to Solomon. The way to learn the faith of our Lord Jesus Christ is to go to Him. She told him all that was in her heart! This is the way to know the Lord. Tell Him all that is in your heart – your doubts, your fears, your hardness of heart and impenitence – confess it all. That person is near to knowing Christ who begins to know himself. He who will confess as much as he knows of his own corruption and depravity, of his sinfulness and needs and inabilities, will soon have a gracious answer of peace.

Do not wait simply because your heart is wicked – it is more wicked than you think it is – but go with it just as it is, and tell Jesus everything. Are you like the woman with the issue of blood? I implore you to tell Him *all the truth*, and He will say, *Thy faith hath made thee whole* (Mark 5:33-34). Why do you try to hide anything from Omniscience? He knows the corners of your heart. The deep places and the dark places thereof are in His hands. If you would tell Him everything, He already knows it, so why, then, do you hesitate? Tear off the veil from your heart, and then you will find mercy.

Moreover, the Queen of Sheba proposed to Solomon her hard questions. I do not know what they were, and I do not particularly care. The Jewish rabbis have invented a few very stupid ones that they say were her hard questions. I know, though, that if you come to our Solomon, to Christ, these will be your hard questions: "My Lord, how can mercy and justice kiss each other? How can God forgive sin and yet punish it?" Jesus will point you to His wounded hands and feet. He will tell you of His great atonement, how by a substitution, God is fearsome in His justice and boundless in His love.

Then you will ask Him the question, "How can a sinful creature be accepted in the sight of a holy God?" He will tell you of His righteousness, and you will see how a sinful person, covered with the imputed righteousness of the Redeemer, is as acceptable before the Lord as though he had never offended.

You will say to Him, "Can you tell me, Jesus, how it is that a weak soul with no power will still be able to fight with the devil and overcome the world, the flesh, and the devil?" Jesus will answer, "My grace is sufficient for you, for My strength will be perfect in your weakness" (2 Corinthians 12:9). All the difficult questions will be answered.

This good woman, in pursuing her inquiry, listened carefully to what Solomon told her. It is said that he *told her all her questions* (1 Kings 10:3; 2 Chronicles 9:2). There is a blessed communion between Christ and a trembling soul. If you will tell Him all your failings, He will tell you all His merit. If you will tell Him your weakness, He will tell you all His strength. If you will tell Him your distance from God, He will tell you His nearness to God. If you will show Him how hard your heart is, He will tell you how His heart was broken so that you might live. Do not be afraid. Simply make a clear revelation to Him and trust in Him, and He will make a sweet revelation to you.

The Queen of Sheba then did what was the best proof of her truthfulness: she gave to Solomon of her treasures. *She gave the king a hundred and twenty talents of gold, and of spices very great store, and precious stones: there came no more such abundance of spices as these which the Queen of Sheba gave to King Solomon* (1 Kings 10:10). Those who know the beauty of Christ give Him all they have. There are no such spices as those that come from newly converted souls.

Nothing gives Christ greater delight than the love of His people. We think that our love is a very poor and common thing, but He does not think so. He has set such a value on us that He gave His heart's blood to redeem us, and now He looks upon us as being worth the price He paid. He will never think that He made a bad bargain of it, and He looks upon every grain of our love as being even choicer spices than archangels before the throne can render to Him in their songs.

What are we doing for Christ? Are we bringing Him our talents of gold? Perhaps you do not have 120 talents, but if you only have one, bring that. You may not have very many spices, but bring what you have. Bring your silent, earnest prayers, your holy, consistent life, the words you sometimes speak for Christ, the training up of your children, the feeding of His poor, the clothing of the naked, the visitation of the sick, the comforting of His mourners, the winning of His wanderers, the restoring of His backsliders, and the saving of His blood-bought souls. All these will be like camels laden with spices – an acceptable gift to the Most High.

After the Queen of Sheba had given Solomon her gifts, Solomon made her a present of his royal bounty. She lost nothing. She gave all she had, and then Solomon gave her just as much again, for I will be obliged to say that King Solomon was such a noble-hearted prince and was so rich that he would not be outdone in generosity.

I tell you that Jesus Christ will never be in your debt. It is a great gain to give to Christ. We give Him pennies, and He gives us dollars. We give Him years of labor, and He gives us an eternity of rest. We give Him days of patient endurance, and He gives us ages of joyous honor. We give Him a little suffering, and He gives us great rewards. *I reckon that the sufferings of this present life are not worthy to be compared with the glory which shall be revealed in us* (Romans 8:18).

Besides what He gives us in the covenant of grace, notice that He does for us what Solomon did for her: He gives us all that is in our heart, all that we can desire. What a King our Savior is, who will not let His people have one ungratified wish if that wish is a good one! Knock, and the gate will open (Matthew 7:7). *Open thy mouth wide, and I will fill it*, says the Lord (Psalm 81:10). *According to your faith be it done unto you* (Matthew 9:29). *What things soever ye desire, when ye pray, believe that ye receive them, and ye shall have them* (Mark 11:24).

What precious promises – and all these are given to those who come with a humble inquiry, willing to get Christ first and then to get the rest afterward!

CHAPTER 20

HE PROPHESIETH OF THE TIMES THAT ARE FAR OFF

Son of man, behold, they of the house of Israel say, The vision that he seeth is for many days to come, and he prophesieth of the times that are far off. (Ezekiel 12:27)

One would have thought that if the glorious Lord condescended to send His servants to speak to people about the way of salvation, all mankind would delight to hear the message. We should naturally conclude that the people would immediately run together in eager crowds to catch every word and would be obedient at once to the heavenly command. But sadly, this has not been the case.

Man's opposition to God is too deep and too stubborn for that. The prophets of old were compelled to cry, *Who hath believed our report?* (Isaiah 53:1). The servants of God in later times found themselves face to face with a stiff-necked generation who resisted the Holy Spirit as their fathers did. People display great ingenuity in making excuses for rejecting the message of God's love. They display marvelous skill, not in seeking salvation, but in coming up with reasons for refusing it. They are skillful in avoiding grace and in securing their own ruin. They hold up first this shield and then the other to ward off the gracious arrows of the gospel of Jesus Christ, which are only meant to slay the deadly sins that lurk in their hearts.

The evil argument that is mentioned in the text has been used from Ezekiel's day right down to the present moment, and it has served Satan's cause in ten thousand cases. By its means, people have delayed themselves into hell. The sons of men, when they hear of the great atonement made upon the cross by the Lord Jesus, and are urged to lay hold upon eternal life in Him, still say concerning the gospel, *The vision that he seeth is for many days to come, and he prophesieth of the times that are far off.* That is to say, they pretend that the matters whereof we speak are not of immediate importance, but may safely be postponed. They imagine that the Christian religion is for the weakness of the dying and the infirmity of the elderly, but not for healthy men and women.

They meet our urgent invitation, "All things are now ready. Come now to the supper" (Luke 14:17) with the reply, "Religion is meant to prepare us for eternity, but we are far away from it as yet. We are still in the prime of our life. There is plenty of time for those dreary preparations for death. Your religion smells of the grave and the worm. Let us be merry while we may. There will be room for more serious considerations after we have enjoyed life a little, or have become established in business, or can retire to live upon our savings. Religion is for the dry and yellow leaf of the year's fall, when life is fading, but not for the opening hours of spring, when the birds are mating and the primroses are smiling upon the returning sun. You prophesy of things that are *for many days to come*, and *of the times that are far off.*"

Very few young people may have said as much as this, but that is the secret thought of many, and with this they resist the admonition of the Holy Spirit, who says, *Today, if ye will hear His voice, harden not your hearts* (Hebrews 3:15). They put off the day of conversion as if it were a day of tempest and terror, and not, as it really is, a day most calm and most bright, the marriage of the soul with heaven.

Let every unconverted person remember that God knows what his excuse is for turning a deaf ear to the voice of a dying Savior's love. You may not have spoken it to yourself so as to put it into words; you might not even dare to do so lest your conscience would be too much startled – but God knows it all. He sees the emptiness, the folly, and the wickedness of your excuses. He is not deceived by your vain words, but makes short work with your apologies for delay.

Remember the parables of our Lord, and notice that when the man of one talent professed to think of his master as a hard man, he took him at his word and condemned him out of his own mouth (Matthew 25:24-26). In the case of the invited guests who pleaded their farms and their merchandise as excuses, no weight was attached to what they said, but the sentence went forth, *None of those men that were bidden shall taste of my supper* (Luke 14:24). God knows the frivolity of your plea for delay. He knows that you yourself are doubtful about it and that you dare not hold to it so as to give it anything like a solemn consideration. You try very hard to deceive yourself into an easy state of conscience concerning it, but in your inmost soul, you are ashamed of your own falsehoods.

Suppose that you are spared for seventy years. Young man, suppose that God spares you in your sins until the snows of many winters whiten your head. Young woman, suppose that your now youthful countenance will still escape the grave until wrinkles are upon your brow. Yet still, how short your life will be! You might think of seventy years as a long period of time, but those who are seventy, in looking back, will tell you that their age is a handbreadth.

I feel that every year flies more swiftly than the last, and months and weeks are compressed into twinklings of the eye. The older one grows, the shorter one's life appears. I do not wonder that Jacob said, *Few and evil have the days of the years of my life been* (Genesis 47:9), for he spoke as an extremely old man. Man is short-lived compared with his surroundings. He comes into the world and goes out of it as a meteor flashes through the distant skies that have remained the same for ages. Listen to the brook that murmurs as it flows, and the meditative ear will hear it warble:

> Men may come and men may go,
> But I go on forever.[19]

Look at that venerable oak that has battled with the winds for five hundred years, and what an infant one seems when reclining beneath its shade! Stand by some giant rock that has confronted the tempests of the ages, and you feel like the insect of an hour. There are people of

---

19   This is from "The Brook," a poem by Alfred Lord Tennyson (1809-1892).

seventy years of age who look back to the days of their boyhood as if they were but yesterday. Ask them, and they will tell you that their life seems to have been little more than a wink of the eye. It has gone like a dream or a lightning's flash.

> What is life? 'Tis but a vapor,
> Soon it vanishes away.[20]

Therefore, do not say, "These things are for a far-off time" for even if we could guarantee to you the whole length of human existence, it is only a brief time.

But there comes upon the heels of this a reflection never to be forgotten – that not one among us can promise, with anything like certainty, that he will ever live to be seventy. We may survive, and by reason of strength, we may creep up to eighty years old (Psalm 90:10), yet not one of us can be sure that we will do so. Most of us will certainly be gone long before that age. Even more, we cannot promise that we will see half that length of time.

Young men and women cannot be certain that they will reach middle age. You cannot be certain that you will see this year out and hear the bells ring in a new year. Yes, as close upon you as tomorrow is, boast not yourselves of it, for it may never come; or if it does come, you do not know what it may hold for you (Proverbs 27:1) – perhaps a coffin or a burial garment. Yes, and this very night, when you close your eyes and rest your head upon your pillow, do not think for certain that you will ever again see that familiar room, or go forth from it to the pursuits of life. It is clear, then, that the things that make for your peace are not matters for a far-off time. The frailty of life makes them necessities of this very hour. You are not far from your grave. You are nearer to it than when this chapter began. Some of you are much nearer than you think.

To some people, this reflection comes with remarkable emphasis, for your occupation has enough danger about it every day to furnish death with a hundred roads to bring you to his prison house in the sepulcher. Can you look through a newspaper without meeting with the words "fatal accident" or "sudden death"? Traveling has many dangers, and

---

20   These are the first lines of a hymn written by Thomas Kelly (1769-1855).

even to cross the street is perilous. Many people die at home. Others die when engaged in their lawful callings. How true this is of those who go down to the sea in ships or descend into the earth in mines!

Truly no occupation is secure from death. A needle can kill as well as a sword. A scald, a burn, or a fall may end our lives quite as readily as a disease or a battle. Does your business lead you to climb a ladder? It is not a very dangerous matter, but have you never heard of anyone who missed his footing and fell, never to rise again? You work amid the materials of a rising building. Have you never heard of stones that have fallen and have crushed the workers?

> Dangers stand thick through all the ground
>> To push us to the tomb;
> And fierce diseases wait around
>> To hurry mortals home.[21]

Despite all that can be done by sanitary laws, fevers are not unknown, and deadly strokes that cause men to fall to the ground in an instant, as a butcher slays an ox, are not uncommon. Death has already removed many of your former companions. You have ridden into the battle of life, like the soldiers in the charge at Balaklava, and as young as you are in this warfare, you have seen saddles emptied right and left around you. You survive, but death has grazed you. The arrow of destruction has gone whizzing by your ear to find another mark. Have you never wondered that it spared you? There are people of delicate constitutions. It grieves me to see so many fair daughters of our land with the mark of consumption upon their cheeks. I know very well that pale flame upon the countenance and that strange luster of the eye – signs of exhausting fires feeding upon life and consuming it too soon.

From the condition of your bodily frames, many of you young men and women can only struggle on until middle life, and barely that, for you cannot survive beyond thirty or forty years of age. I fear that some of you have, even in walking, sometimes felt a suspicious weariness that foretells exhaustion and decline. When we talk to you about preparing

---

21   This is a stanza from a hymn by Isaac Watts (1674-1748) that begins with "Thee, we adore, eternal name."

to die, how can you say that we are talking about things that are far off? Do not be so foolish. I implore you to let these warnings lead you to decision.

Far be it from me to cause you needless alarm, but is it needless? I am sure I love you too well to distress you without cause, but is there not cause enough? Come now; I urge you most affectionately to answer me and tell me. Does not your own reason tell you that concern for you is not misplaced? Should you not at once take to heart your Redeemer's call and obey your Savior's appeal? The time is short. Catch the moments as they fly, and hurry to be blest.

Remember, also, that even if you knew that you would escape from accident and fever and sudden death, yet there is one great event that we too often forget that may put an end to your day of mercy suddenly. Have you never heard that Jesus Christ of Nazareth, who was crucified on Calvary, died on the cross and was laid in the tomb? Do you not know that He rose again on the third day, and that after He had spent a little while with His disciples, He took them to the top of the Mount of Olives, and there before their eyes ascended into heaven with a cloud hiding Him from their view? Have you forgotten the words of the angels, who said, *This same Jesus, which is taken up from you into heaven, shall so come in like manner as ye have seen Him go into heaven* (Acts 1:11)? Jesus will certainly come a second time to judge the world.

Of that day and of that hour knoweth no man, no, not the angels of heaven (Matthew 24:36). He will come *as a thief in the night* to an ungodly world (1 Thessalonians 5:2). They will be eating and drinking, and marrying and giving in marriage, just as they were when Noah entered into the ark, and they did not know until the flood came and swept them all away (Matthew 24:37-39). In a moment – we cannot tell when, perhaps it may be before the next words escape my lips – a sound far louder than any mortal voice will be heard above the clamors of worldly traffic and above the roaring of the sea (1 Corinthians 15:52). That sound as of a trumpet will proclaim the day of the Son of Man. *Behold, the Bridegroom cometh: go ye out to meet Him* will sound throughout the church (Matthew 25:6). This clear call will ring out to all the world. *Behold, He cometh with clouds; and every eye shall see Him, and they also which pierced Him* (Revelation 1:7).

Jesus may come tonight. If He were to do so, would you then tell me that I am talking of far-off things? Did not Jesus say, *Behold, I come quickly* (Revelation 22:12)? His tarrying may be long to us, but to God it will be brief. We are to stand hourly watching and daily waiting for the coming of the Lord from heaven.

Oh, please do not say that the Lord delays His coming, for that was the language of the wicked servant who was cut in pieces (Luke 12:46), and it is the mark of the mockers of the last days that they say, *Where is the promise of His coming?* (2 Peter 3:4). Do not be mockers lest your chains are made strong, but listen to the undoubted voice of prophecy and of the Word of God: *Behold, I come quickly.* As Jesus Himself said, *Be ye also ready, for in such an hour as ye think not the Son of man cometh* (Matthew 24:44).

Now, then, it is clear enough that even if the gospel message concerned only our life in another world, it is still unwise for people to say, *The vision that he seeth is for many days to come, and he prophesieth of the times that are far off* (Ezekiel 12:27).

CHAPTER 21

SOMETHING TO DO WITH THE FUTURE

The gospel of Jesus Christ deals with all of life. If you receive Jesus Christ, you will have that faith that will operate upon your whole existence throughout time and eternity. If you are saved while you are still young, you will find the Christian religion to be a great preventative of sin. What a blessing it is not to have been daubed with the slime of Sodom, never to have had our bones broken by actual degeneracy. Many who have been saved from a life of crime will nevertheless be spiritual invalids for life! To be rescued out of the vortex of vice is cause for great gratitude, but to have been kept out of it is better. It is doubly well if the grace of God comes upon us while we are still unstained by the pollution of the world (James 1:27) and have not gone into *excess of riot* (1 Peter 4:4). Before corrupt habits have undermined our character and self-indulgence has degraded the mind, it is above all things well to have the heart renewed. Prevention is better than cure, and grace gives both. Thank God that you are still young, and pray earnestly that you may now receive grace to cleanse your way *by taking heed thereto* according to His Word (Psalm 119:9).

Grace will act as a preservative as well as a preventative. The good thing that God will put in you will keep you. I thank God that I do not have to preach a temporary salvation. That which charmed me about the gospel when I was a boy was its power to preserve from sinning. I saw some of my school companions who were a little older than myself, and had been highly commended for their character, become sad offenders when they left home. I used to hear sad stories of their evil actions after they had gone to London to be apprenticed or to take positions in large establishments. I reasoned thus with myself: "When I leave my father's house, I will be tempted, too, and I have the same heart that they have. Indeed, I have not been even as good as they have been. It is likely, therefore, that I will plunge into sin as they have done." I felt horrified with that. I could not bear the thought that I would cause my mother to shed tears over a degenerate son, or that I would break my father's heart with immorality and overindulgence. I could not endure that thought, and when I heard that whosoever believed in the Lord Jesus Christ would be saved, I understood that he would be saved from sinning, and I laid hold upon Jesus to preserve me from sin – and He has done it. I committed my character to Christ, and He has preserved me to this day – and I believe He will not let me go.

I recommend to you, young men, a character insurance in the form of believing in Jesus Christ. Dear young woman, may that modest cheek of yours never need to blush for any deeds that would bring you shame. May your delicate purity of feeling never be lost through impure, defiling sin. Remember, though, that it may be so unless the Lord keeps you. I commend to you the blessed preserving power of faith in Jesus Christ, which will secure for you the Holy Spirit to dwell in you and abide in you and sanctify you all your days.

I know I speak to some who shudder at the thought of depravity and immorality. As trained as you have been by Christian parents, and under the holiest influences, you would rather die than act as some who disgrace their father's name; I know you would. However, you must not trust your own hearts. You may still become as bad as others, or worse than they are, unless your natures are renewed – and only Jesus Christ can do that by the power of the Holy Spirit. Whosoever believes in Him has passed from death unto life (John 5:24). He will not live in sin, but he will be preserved in holiness even to the end.

You have not fully entered into the battle of life yet. You have your way to make, your professions and trades to choose. You, young women, are still under the parental wing. You have domestic relationships yet to form. Consider how well prepared you will be for life's work and service if you give your hearts to Jesus. Young man, you will be the right man to enter a large business, and with the grace of God in your heart, you will be a blessing there. Although surrounded by her snares in this wicked city, the strange woman will hunt in vain for your precious life. Other vices will be unable to pollute you.

Young woman, you will have wisdom to choose for your life's companion no mere vain man and fool, but one who loves the Lord as you will do, with whom you may hope to spend happy and holy days. You will have placed within yourself resources of joy and pleasure that will never fail. There will be a well of living water within you that will supply you with joy and comfort and consolation, even amid trial and distress. You will be prepared for whatever is to come.

A young Christian is qualified to be made an emperor or a servant, if God should call him to either post. If you want the best material for a model prince or a model peasant, you will find it in the child of God. Only notice that the man who is a child of God is less likely to sink into utter destitution because he will be saved from the vices of extravagance and idleness, which are the frequent causes of poverty. On the other hand, he is probably less likely to become a prince, for seldom has God lifted His own children to places so perilous. You will be ready, young man, for any future if your heart is right with God. When I think about you and about what the Lord may make of you, I feel an intense respect, as well as love, for you. I hope none of us will be lacking in respect to old age. It is honorable, and it is to be esteemed and reverenced, but I also feel frequently inclined to show respect to youth.

When a well-known teacher entered his schoolroom, he always took off his hat to his boys because, as he said, he did not know which of them might yet turn out to be a poet, a bishop, a lord chancellor, or a prime minister. When I look at young men and women, I feel much the same, for I do not know what they will become. I may be addressing a David Livingstone or a Robert Moffat. I may be speaking to a John Howard or a William Wilberforce. I may be addressing an Ann Judson or an Elizabeth Fry. I may be speaking to some whom God will kindle into great lights to bless the sons of men for many days, and afterward to shine *as the stars forever and ever* (Daniel 12:3).

However, you cannot shine if you are not lighted. You cannot bless God and bless the sons of men unless God first blesses you. Unregenerate, you are useless. Born again, you will be born for usefulness. While you are unconverted, though, your usefulness is being lost. I will not insinuate that I expect everyone to become famous. It is not even desirable; but I do know that everyone whose heart will be given to Jesus will be so useful and so necessary to the church and to the world that this world without them would lack one who would benefit mankind, and heaven's company would be incomplete unless they joined its ranks.

That is enough about this life, but now let me remind you, dear young friends, that if your hearts are given to Christ, you do not need to fear about the end of life. You may look forward to it with hope. It will come. Thank God, it will come! Have you never wished that you could ride to heaven in a chariot of fire like Elijah (2 Kings 2:11)? I did once, until I considered that if a chariot of fire would come for me, I would be more afraid to get into it than to lie down and die upon my bed. Of the two options, one might prefer to die, for to die in the Lord is to be made like to our glorious Head.

I see no joy in the hope of escaping death. Jesus died, and so let me die. On His dear face, the seal of death was set; so let it also be on mine so that I may talk of resurrection as those cannot who will be changed at His coming. You do not need to be afraid to depart and be with Christ, *which is far better* (Philippians 1:23). Young people, whether you die in youth or in old age, if you are resting in Jesus, you will sit upon the banks of Jordan singing, "Never mind the river."

The parting song will be sweet, but oh, the glory! Oh, the glory! I will not try to describe it. Who can? The judgment will come, but you will not tremble at it. You will stand on the right hand, for who can condemn those for whom Christ has died? The burning of the globe will come. *The elements shall melt with fervent heat* (2 Peter 3:10, 12), but you will not fear, for you will be *caught up together* with the Lord, and so you will be forever with the Lord (1 Thessalonians 4:17). Hell will swallow up the unjust, and they will go down alive into the pit; but you will not tremble for that, for you are redeemed by the precious blood.

The millennial glory, whatever that may be; the reign with Christ; the triumph over death and hell; the giving up of the kingdom to God, even the Father, when God shall be all in all; and eternity with all its infinite glory – these will all be yours. If you had to go through hell to reach this glory, it would be worth the cost! But you do not have to do any such thing. You only have to believe in Jesus, and even faith is the Lord's own gracious gift. *Look unto Me, and be ye saved, all the ends of the earth* (Isaiah 45:22). This is the gospel.

CHAPTER 22

A MESSAGE FOR THE PRESENT TIME

We plead with you, young men and women, and tenderly remind you that you are at this hour acting unjustly and unkindly toward your God. He made you, yet you do not serve Him. He has kept you alive, yet you are not obedient to Him. He has sent the word of His gospel to you, yet you have not received it. He has sent His only begotten Son, yet you have despised Him. This injustice is a thing of the present, and the appeal we make to you about it is that in all reason, such conduct should come to an end. Oh, may God's Holy Spirit help you to end it!

If I feel that I have done anyone an injustice, I am eager to set it right. I would not wait until tomorrow. I want to make things right at once. Even when I have forgotten to deliver assistance to some needy widow, I scold myself and feel uneasy until I have attended to the matter. Do you not feel the same? Would you willingly wrong or neglect another? I feel sure you would not. How is it, then, that you can be content to be unjust to God, cruel to the dear Lover of the souls of men, and hostile to the loving pleadings of the Holy Spirit?

How fascinating that first chapter of Isaiah is! If people had hearts that were at all tender, it would break them. *Hear, O heavens, and give ear, O earth: for the LORD hath spoken. I have nourished and brought up children, and they have rebelled against Me. The ox knoweth his owner, and the donkey his master's crib: but Israel doth not know; My people doth not consider* (Isaiah 1:2-3). It is the lament of God Himself over man's unkindness to his Maker!

Young man of honor, young man of integrity, does nothing speak to your conscience in this? *Will a man rob God?* (Malachi 3:8). You would not rob your employer. You would not like to be thought unfaithful or dishonest toward others, yet is your God to be treated so dishonorably despite all His goodness? As Jesus said, *For which of those works do ye stone Me?* (John 10:32). Jehovah also says, "I have made you. I have kept breath in your nostrils. I have fed you your entire life. For which of all these good things do you live without Me, neglect Me, perhaps curse My name, and sin so boldly against My sacred law?"

Can you think it is right to remain in such an openly unjust way of life as this? Can it be right to continue to wrong your God and grieve His matchless love? Provoke Him no more. Let conscience lead you to feel that you have dealt wrongly with the Lord, and go to Him for forgiveness and change of heart. O Spirit of God, make this appeal to be felt by all our beloved young men and women!

Again, our message has to do with the present, for we would affectionately remind you that you are now at enmity with your best Friend – the Friend to whose love you owe everything. You have grieved Him, and without cause, you are His enemy. Can you bear this thought? I know a little child who had done something wrong, and her kind father talked to her. At last, as a punishment, he said to her in a very sad voice, "I cannot kiss you tonight, for you have grieved me very much." That broke her little heart. Though not a hand had been laid upon her, she saw sorrow in her dear father's face, and she could not endure it. She pleaded and wept, and pleaded again to be forgiven. It was thought wise to withhold the kiss, and she was sent to bed, for she had done very wrong; but there was no sleep for those weeping eyes, and when the mother went up to that little one's room, she heard frequent sobs and sighs. Then a sorrowful little voice said, "I was very, very naughty, but please forgive me, and ask dear father to give me a kiss." She loved her father, and she could not bear that he would be grieved.

Child of mercy, erring child of the great Father of spirits, can you bear to live forever at enmity with the loving Father? You ask, "Would He forgive me?" What makes you ask the question? Is it that you do not know how good He is? Has He not portrayed Himself as meeting His prodigal son and falling upon his neck and kissing him (Luke 15:20)?

Before the child had reached the father, the father had reached the child. The father was eager to forgive, and therefore, when the son was yet a great way off, his father saw him, and ran, and had compassion. Do not say any longer that we are talking of things of a far-off time. It is not so. I am speaking of that which I pray may be true of you now so that you may not remain enemies to God even another hour, but may now become His dear repenting children and run into your tender Father's arms.

I have to remind you, however, of much more than this – namely, that you are in danger. Because of your treatment of God, and remaining an enemy to Him, He will surely visit you in justice and punish you for your transgressions. He is a just God, and every sin committed is noted in His book – and there it stands recorded against His judgment day. The danger you are in is that you may this moment go down into the pit. You may bow your head in death and appear before your Maker in an instant to receive the just reward of your sins.

We tell you that there is immediate pardon for all the sins of those who will believe in the Lord Jesus Christ, and that if you will believe in Jesus, your sins, which are many, will all be forgiven you. Do you not know the story (you have heard it many times) that the Lord Jesus took upon Himself the sins of all who trust Him, and that He suffered the penalty due to their sins in their place? He was our substitute, and as such, He died, *the just for the unjust*, to bring us to God (1 Peter 3:18). He laid down His life for us so that *whosoever believeth in Him should not perish, but have everlasting life* (John 3:16).

Will you refuse the salvation so dearly purchased but so freely presented? Will you not accept it here and now? Can you bear the burden of your sins? Are you content to abide for a single hour in danger of eternal punishment? Can you bear to be slipping down into the open jaws of hell as you now are?

Remember that God's patience will not last forever. You have provoked Him long enough. All things are weary of you. The very earth on which you stand groans beneath the indignity of bearing a sinner upon its surface. As long as you remain an enemy to God, the stones of the field are against you, and all creation threatens you. It is a wonder that you do not sink at once to destruction. Because of this, we want you to be pardoned now and made free from divine wrath now. The danger is immediate, and we pray that the Lord will grant the rescue to be immediate also!

I hear you say, "But may pardon be obtained at once? Is Jesus Christ a present Savior? We thought that we might perhaps find Him when we came to die, or might obtain a hope of mercy after living a long life of seeking." It is not so. Free grace proclaims immediate salvation from sin and misery. Whosoever looks to Jesus at this very moment will have his sins forgiven. At the moment he believes in the Lord Jesus, the sinner will cease to be in danger of the fires of hell. The moment a person turns his eye of faith to Jesus Christ, he is saved from the wrath to come. It is present salvation that we preach to you, along with the present comfort of that present salvation.

Many other reasons tend to make this serious matter exceedingly urgent, and among them is that there is a disease in your heart – the disease of sin – and it needs immediate cure. When people discover a developing disease in their bodies, I do not hear them say that they will wait a while until the disease is more fully developed, and then they will go see a physician. Most of us have enough sense to try to stop a disease at once.

Young man, you have a leprosy upon you. Young woman, you have a terrible disease within your heart. Do you not desire to be healed now? Jesus can give you immediate healing if you believe in Him. Will you hesitate to be made whole? Do you love your deadly affliction? Is hideous sin so dear to you? Oh, that you would cry out to be saved immediately, for then Jesus will hear you. His Spirit will descend upon you and cleanse you. He will give you a new heart and a right spirit, and will make you whole from this time forth and forevermore. How can you want to have such a great blessing postponed? Surely a sick person can never be cured too soon.

The gospel will also bring you present blessings. In addition to present pardon and present justification, it will give you present regeneration, present adoption, present sanctification, present access to God, present peace through believing, and present help in time of trouble. It will even make you doubly happy in this life. It will be wisdom for your way, strength for your conflict, and comfort for your sorrow.

If I had to die like a dog, I would still want to be a Christian. If there were no hereafter (even though that idea is not to be tolerated), I would still want to live for and with Jesus, my beloved Lord. Balaam chose the righteous man's death (Numbers 23:10). I choose it, too, but just as much do I choose in this life to have the love of God in the heart, to have peace with God, to be able to look up to heaven with confidence, and to talk to my heavenly Father in childlike trustfulness. This is a present joy and comfort worth more than worlds.

Young men and women, in preaching to you the gospel, we are preaching that which is good for this life as well as for the life to come. If you believe in Jesus, you will be saved now – this moment – and you will now enjoy the unchanging blessing of God. You will go your way from that moment on not to live as others do, but as the chosen of God, beloved with special love and enriched with special blessings, to rejoice every day until you are taken up to dwell where Jesus is.

Present salvation is the theme of the Lord's message to you. Therefore, it is not true, but is notoriously false, that the vision is for many days to come, and that the prophecy is for times that are far off. Is there not reason in my pleadings? If so, yield to them. Can you answer these arguments? If not, I plead with you to stop delaying. Again I pray that the Lord will lead you to immediate decision!

CHAPTER 23

A STORY OF AN ECCENTRIC WOMAN

*Verily I say unto you, Wheresoever this gospel shall be
preached in the whole world, there shall also this, that
this woman hath done, be told for a memorial of her.*
(Matthew 26:13)

The Evangelists, the writers of the Gospels, are the historians of the
time of Christ, of course, but what strange historians they are! They
leave out just that which worldly historians would write, and they record
just that which the worldly historians would have passed over. What
historian would have thought of recording the story of the widow and
her two mites? Would a David Hume or a Tobias Smollett have spared
half a page for such an incident? Do you think that even a Thomas
Macaulay could have found it in his pen to write down a story of an
eccentric woman who broke an alabaster box of precious ointment upon
the head of Jesus? But so it is.

Jesus does not value things by their glare and glitter, but by their
intrinsic value. Christ was sitting, or reclining, at the table of Simon
the leper. A sudden thought struck this woman. She went to her home,
got her money, and spent it on an alabaster box of ointment; or perhaps
she had it already prepared and waiting at home. Anyway, she brought
it and hurried into the house. Without asking anyone's permission or
explaining her intention, she broke the alabaster vase (which was itself

of great value), and a stream of the most precious ointment, with a very refreshing fragrance, flowed forth. She poured this on His head. So plentiful was the outpouring that it streamed right down to His feet, and the whole house was filled with the aroma of the ointment.

The disciples murmured, but the Savior commended. What was there in the action of this woman that was worthy of commendation, and of such high commendation, too, that her memory must be preserved and passed down with the gospel itself throughout all ages?

In the first place, I think this act was done from the impulse of a loving heart, and this is what made it so remarkable. The heart is better than the head, after all, and the renewed heart is infinitely superior to the head. Somehow or other, although grace will undoubtedly renew the understanding, yet it takes longer to sanctify the understanding than it does the affections. At least the heart is first affected. It is that which is first touched, and being swifter in its progress than the head, it is generally more uncontaminated by the atmosphere around, and so more clearly perceives that which is right.

In our day, we fall into the habit of calculating whether something is our duty or not, but do we never have an impulse of the heart that is more powerful and more expressive than the mere calculation of moral obligations? Our heart says to us, "Get up and go visit such and such a one who is sick." We stop and say, "Is it my duty? If I do not go, will not somebody else go? Is my visit absolutely necessary?" Perhaps your heart has once said, "Devote all that you have substantially to the cause of Christ." If we obeyed the heart, we would do it at once; but instead of that, we stop and shake our heads, and we begin to calculate the question whether it is precisely our duty.

This woman did no such thing. It was not her duty (I speak broadly); it was not her positive duty to take the alabaster box and break it on the head of Christ. She did not do it from a sense of obedience, but she did it from a higher motive. There was an impulse in her heart that gushed forth like a pure stream overflowing every objection and question: "Duty or no duty, go and do it." She took the most precious things she could find, and out of simple love, guided by her renewed heart, she went at once and broke the alabaster box and poured the ointment on His head. If she had stopped a minute to consider, she would not have done it at all. If she had pondered and considered and reasoned, she never would have accomplished it – but this was the heart acting, the invincible heart, the force of a spontaneous impulse, if not of very inspiration, while the head with its various parts had not been allowed time to hold a council. It was the heart's dictate that fully and entirely carried it out.

In these times, we lace ourselves so tight that we do not give our hearts room to act. Instead, we just calculate whether we should do it – whether it is specifically our duty. Oh, I wish to God that our hearts would grow bigger! Let our heads be as they are, or let them be improved, but let the heart have full opportunity, and how much more would be done for Christ than has ever yet been done! I want you to see that this woman, acting from her heart, did not act as a matter of formality or ceremony.

Will you give to Christ no more than His due, just as you give to Caesar when you pay your taxes? What if the tax is only a shekel; is the shekel all He is to have? Is such a Master as this to be served by calculations? Is He to have His required pay every day, just as the common laborer? God forbid that we should indulge such a spirit! Sadly, the majority of Christians do not even rise as high as that, and if they do get there, they fold their arms and are quite content. They say, "I do as much as anybody else. In fact, I probably do a little more. I am sure that I do my duty. Nobody can find any fault with what I do. If people were to expect me to do more, they would be really unreasonable." If this is how you feel, then you have not yet learned this woman's love in all its heights and depths. You do not know how to do an unreasonable thing – a thing that is not expected of you – out of the divine impulse of a heart fully consecrated to Jesus.

The first era of the Christian church was an era of wonders because then Christian men obeyed the prompting of their hearts. What wonders they used to do! A voice within the heart said to an apostle, "Go to a heathen country and preach." He never counted the cost – whether his life would be safe or whether he would be successful. He went and did whatever his heart told him. To another it said, "Go and distribute all that you have," and the Christian went and did it, and gave all that he had into the common supply. He never asked whether it was his duty. His heart told him to do it, and he obeyed at once.

Now we have become stale. We have ourselves in the same rut as everyone else. We all do what other people do. We are content with just performing the routine and accomplishing the formalism of religious duties. This is very much unlike this woman, who went out of all order because her heart told her to do so, and she obeyed from her heart. This, I think, is the first part of the woman's act that won a deserved commendation.

The second commendation is that what this woman did was done purely to Christ and for Christ. Why did she not take this spikenard ointment and sell it and give the money to the poor? "No," she might have thought, "I love the poor. I would help them at any time. I would clothe the naked and feed the hungry to the utmost of my ability, but I want to do something for Him."

Well, why did she not get up and take the place that Martha did, and begin to wait at the table (John 12:2)? "Ah!" she thought, "Martha is at the table dividing her services. Simon the leper, and Lazarus, and all the rest of the guests have a share in her attention. I want to do something directly for Him – something that He will have all to Himself, something that He cannot give away, but which He must have and which must belong to Him."

I do not think that any other disciple, in all Christ's experience, ever had that thought. I do not find in all the Evangelists another instance like this. Jesus had disciples whom He sent out two by two to preach, and they did so very boldly, for they desired to benefit their fellow men in the service of their Lord. He had disciples, too, I do not doubt, who were very, very happy when they distributed the bread and the fish to the hungry multitudes because they felt they were doing an act of humanity in supplying the needs of the hungry. However, I do not think He had one disciple who thought about doing something exactly and directly for Him – something of which no one else could partake, something that would be Christ's and Christ's alone.

The very beauty of this woman's act lay in the fact that she did it all for the Lord Jesus Christ. She felt that she owed Him everything. It was He who had forgiven her sins. It was He who had opened her eyes and had given her the ability to see the light of the heavenly day. It was He who was her hope, her joy, and her all. Her love went out in its common actions to her fellow men. It went out toward the poor, the sick, and the needy, but, oh, it went in all its intensity to Him.

That Man, that blessed Man, the God-Man, she must give something to Him. She could not be content to put it in that bag there, but she must go and put it right on His head. She could not be content that Peter or James or John would have a part of it, but it all must go on His head. Even if others might say it was wasteful, yet she felt it was not, but that whatever she could give to Him was well given because it went to Him to whom she owed her all. The scene is a very simple one, but it is extremely captivating. You will do your acts in religion far better if you can always develop the desire to do them all for Christ.

This woman did an extraordinary thing for Christ. Not content with doing what other people had done, nor caring to find a precedent, she set out to reveal her intense devotion, even though she might have known that some would call her crazy, and all would think her foolish and wasteful; yet she did it – an extraordinary thing – for the love she had for her Lord. It seems to me that Jesus praised this woman and handed down this memorial because her act was so beautifully expressive. There was more virtue in it than you could see. The manner, as well as the matter, of her willing sacrifice might well excite the rebuke of people whose practical religion is miserly and frugal. It is not enough that she pours out the ointment with such reckless abundance, but she is so rash and extravagant that she actually broke the box. Do not be surprised at this, but admire the absorbed enthusiasm of her godly soul.

Love is a passion. If you only knew and felt its intensity, you would never marvel at an act so expressive. Her love could no more wait to conform to the customs of service than it could count the cost of her offering. A mighty impulse of devotion carried her soul far above all ordinary routine. Her conduct simply symbolized the inspiration of a grateful devotion and reverence. A sanctified heart, more beautiful than the transparent vase of alabaster, was broken that hour.

Only from a broken heart can the sweet spices of grace give forth their rich perfume. We sometimes sing, "Love and grief, our heart dividing,"[22] but let me say that love, grief, and gratitude – the spikenard,

---

22   This is from a hymn by James Allan (1734-1804) that begins with "Sweet the moments, rich in blessing."

myrrh, and frankincense of the gospel – blend together here. The heart must expand and break or the perfume would never fill the house. Every muscle of the woman's face, every involuntary motion of her body, as delirious as it might appear to the unsympathizing observers, was in harmony with her heart's emotion. Her every feature gives evidence of her sincerity. What they could coldly criticize, Jesus delivers to them for a study.

Here is one on whom a Savior's love has produced its appropriate effects. Here is a heart that has brought forth the most precious fruits. Not only admiration for her, but kindness to us moved our Lord when He resolved to illustrate the gospel from then on, wherever it is published and proclaimed, with this portrait of saintly love that broke the delicate vase and burst the tender heart in one moment. That woman was saying to Christ, "Dear Lord, I give myself away." She went home and brought out the most precious thing she had. If she had possessed anything worth ten thousand times as much, she would have brought that. In fact, she really did bring Him everything.

She hath wrought a good work upon Me (Matthew 26:10). Note these two last words: *upon Me!* Some people might say, "It is not a good work to go and spill all that ointment and bring about so much waste."

"No," says Jesus, "it is not a good work in relation to you, but it is a good work upon Me." After all, the best sort of good work is a good work that is done for and upon Christ – an act of devotion that faith in His name and love to His person would dictate. A good work upon the poor is commendable; a good work upon the church is excellent; but a good work upon Christ is certainly one of the very highest and noblest kinds of good works. I am obligated to say that neither Judas nor the disciples could comprehend this. There is a mystic virtue in the acts of some Christian people that common Christians do not and cannot comprehend. That mystic virtue consists in this – that they do it *as to the Lord, and not unto men* (Colossians 3:23), and in their service, they serve the Lord Jesus Christ.

Additionally, our Lord protects the woman with another explanation. He says, "Do not trouble her. Do not reflect upon what might have been done for the poor, *for ye have the poor always with you; but Me ye have not always.* You can always do good to them whenever you please" (Matthew 26:10-11). He seems here to respond to her accusers: "If there are any people around who are poor, give to them yourselves. Empty that bag of Mine out, Judas. Don't hide that away in your pocket. *Whensoever ye will, ye may do them good* [Mark 14:7]. Don't begin talking about the poor and about what might have been done. Go and do what might have been done yourselves. This poor woman has done a good thing for Me. I will not be here long. Don't trouble her." So if you complain about people because they do not do what people normally do because they venture a little out of the regular line, there is plenty for you to do. Your errand might not be exactly the same as what someone else has done, but there is plenty for you to do. Go and do it, and do not blame those who do extraordinary things.

There are multitudes of ordinary people to attend to ordinary things. It is those who give all they have who are different. Do not trouble those people. There are not many of them. They will not trouble you. You will have to travel from here to John o' Groat's house before you come against many dozen.[23] They are rare creatures not often discovered. Do not trouble them; they may be enthusiastic and they may be excessive, but if you would build an institute to put them all in, it would require only a very small sort of a house. Leave them alone. There are not many who do much for their Master. There are not many who are irrational enough to think that there is nothing worth living for but to glorify Christ and magnify His holy name.

This woman thought she was just anointing Christ. "No," says Christ, "she is anointing Me for my burial" (Matthew 26:12; Mark 14:8). There was more in her action than she knew of, and there is more in the spiritual promptings of our heart than we will ever discover to the day of judgment. When the Lord first said to George Whitefield, "Go and preach out on Kennington Common," did Whitefield know what the result was to be? No; he undoubtedly thought that he would just stand once on the top of a table and speak to about five thousand people.

However, there was a greater intent in the heart of Providence. The Lord meant that to set the whole country in a blaze and to bring forth a glorious renewal of Pentecostal times, the like of which had not been

---

23 John o' Groats is a village in the far north of Scotland. The village is named after a fifteenth century Dutchman by the name of Jan de Groot.

seen before. Only seek to have your heart filled with love, and then obey its first spiritual dictate. Do not stop. However extraordinary the command may be, go and do it. Have your wings outstretched like the angels before the throne, and the very moment that the echo vibrates in your heart, fly, fly, and you will be flying you know not where. You will be carrying out an errand higher and nobler than your imagination has ever dreamed.

CHAPTER 24

GRACE - A MATTER OF GROWTH

In the Christian church, there is a class of Christians who have grown so much that they can no longer be called babes in grace, yet they are not so mature that they can be exactly called fathers. Those men who form this middle class of the spiritually minded are called young men. Age, according to the flesh, often differs much from the condition of the spirit. Many old men are still no more than infants in Christ. Some children in years are even now young men in grace, while not a few young men are fathers in the church while still young in years.

God has endowed certain of His servants with great grace, and He has made them mature in their youth. Some examples of such people are Joseph, Samuel, David, Josiah, and Timothy. It is not age according to the family register that we speak about, but age according to the Lamb's Book of Life.

Grace is a matter of growth, and therefore we have among us babes, young men, and fathers, whose position is not determined according to this fleeting, dying life, but according to that eternal life that has been brought about in them by the Spirit of God. It is a great mercy when young men in the natural sense are also young men in the spiritual sense. The fathers do not need to be ashamed of their spiritual seed.

In speaking to young men in Christ, I am speaking to a large body of Christians who make up a very efficient part of the army of Christ. I would ask them not to be either so modest or so proud as to decline to be classed in this way. You are no longer weaklings. Therefore, do not consider yourselves to be babes lest you plead exemption from hard service. You are hardly yet mature enough to be included with the fathers. Do not forget the duties of your real place because you are aspiring to another. It is honor enough to be in Christ, and certainly it is no small thing to be in spiritual things a man in the prime of life.

These young men are not infants. They have been in Christ too long for that. They are no longer novices and strangers to the Lord's house. Most have been born unto God for years now. The things for which they hoped at first they have to a large extent realized. They know now what once they could not understand. They are not confined to a diet of milk, for they can now eat meat and digest it well. They have discernment, having had their senses exercised by reason of use, so that they are not so likely to be misled as they were in their infancy. While they have been longer in the way, they have also now grown stronger in the way. It is not a weak and timid faith that they now possess. They believe firmly and strongly, and are able to do battle for the *faith which was once delivered unto the saints* (Jude 1:3), for they are *strong in the Lord and in the power of His might* (Ephesians 6:10). They are wiser now than they used to be.

When they were children, they knew enough to save them, for they knew the Father, and that was a blessed knowledge; but now they know far more of the Word of God, which abides in them through their earnest, prayerful, believing acceptance of it. They now have a clearer idea of the breadth and length and depth and height of the work of redemption, for they have been taught by God. They even venture to enjoy the deep things of God, and the covenant is by no means an unknown thing among them. They have been under the blessed teaching of the Spirit of God, and from Him they have received an unction so that they know *all things* (John 14:26). In knowledge, they are no longer children, but they are men in Christ Jesus. Thus they are distinguished from the first class, which contains the babes in Christ.

They are not yet fathers because they are not yet so established, confirmed, and settled as the fathers are, who know what they believe, and who know it with a certainty of full assurance that nothing can shake. They have not yet had the experience of fathers, and consequently they do not have all their wisdom and foresight. They are richer in zeal than in judgment. They have not yet acquired the skill to nurture others in the faith that is so precious in the church and is the result of growth, experience, maturity, and affection. They are going on to that, and in a short time they will have reached it, but as yet they have other work to do that is more suitable to their strength.

Do not suppose that when we say they are not to be called fathers, that they are not, therefore, very valuable to the community, for in some senses they are quite equal to the fathers, and in one or two respects they may even be superior to them. The fathers are for contemplation. They study deep and see far, and so they *have known Him that is from the beginning* (1 John 2:14), but a part of their energy for action may have gone through stress of years.

These young men are born to fight. They are the militia of the church. They have to contend for her faith and extend the Redeemer's kingdom. They should do so, for they are strong. This is their lot, and may the Lord help them to fulfil their calling. These must be our active spirits for years to come. They are our strength and our hope. The fathers must soon leave the stage. Their maturity in grace shows that they are ready for glory, and it is not God's way to keep His shocks of corn in the field once they are fully ripe. Mature men will be gathered up with the mature, and they will enter into their proper sphere. The fathers, therefore, must soon be gone, and after they are gone, we must look to these young men for a succession. We hope to have them with us for many years – valiant for the truth, steadfast in the faith, ripening in spirit, and growingly made ready to take their seats among the glorified saints above.

Judge whether you are deservedly to be ranked among the young men. Have no regard to the matter of gender, for there is neither male nor female in Christ Jesus (Galatians 3:28). Judge whether you are ready to be ranked among those whose full-grown and vigorous life entitles them to stand among the soldiers of the church, the vigorous manhood of the seed of Israel.

These Christians of the middle group are emphatically strong. This does not imply that any measure of spiritual strength was in them by nature, for the apostle Paul clearly says otherwise concerning our natural state: *When we were yet without strength, in due time Christ died for the ungodly* (Romans 5:6). By nature, we are without strength to do anything that is good and right. We are as strong as a wild bull to dash headlong into everything that is evil, and we are as strong as a lion to fight against all that is good and godlike, but for all spiritual things and holy things, we are entirely weak and incapable. We are as dead men until God the Holy Spirit deals with us.

Neither does the apostle here at all allude to the strength of the body of young men, for in a spiritual sense, this is their weakness rather than their strength. The man who is strong in the flesh is too often for that very reason strongly tempted to sins of the flesh. Therefore, the apostle urges his young friend to *flee also youthful lusts* (2 Timothy 2:22).

The time of life in which a young man is found is full of danger, and so is the spiritual condition of which it is the type. The young man might almost wish that it were with him as with the older man in whom the forces of the flesh have declined, for although age brings with it many infirmities, it also has its gain in the decline of the passions. So you see that the young man cannot depend upon strength of the flesh as contributing toward real strength. Instead, he must ask for more strength from on high lest the physical strength that is within him would drag down his spirit. He is glad to be in robust health so that he may bear much toil in the Lord's cause, but he is not proud of it, for he remembers that the Lord *delighteth not in the strength of the horse; he taketh not pleasure in the legs of a man* (Psalm 147:10).

These young men in grace are strong, first of all, in faith according to that exhortation, *Be strong and of a good courage; be not afraid* (Joshua 1:9). They have known the Lord now for some time, and they have enjoyed that perfect peace that is a result of forgiven sin. They have observed the work of the Spirit within themselves, and they know it is no delusion, but a divine change. Now they not only believe in Christ, but they know that they believe in Him. They know whom they have believed, and they are persuaded that He is able to keep that which they have committed to Him (2 Timothy 1:12). That faith that was once a healing touch has now become a satisfying embrace. That enjoyment that was once a sip has now become a full glass, quenching all thirst. Yes, and that which was once a full glass has become an immersion into the river of God, which is full of water. They have plunged into the river of life and find waters to swim in.

Oh, what a mercy it is to be strong in this way! Let him who is strong take heed that he glory only in the Lord (Jeremiah 9:23-24; 1 Corinthians 1:31), who is his righteousness and strength, but in Him and in His strength he may indeed make his boast and defy the armies of the strangers. Paul said, *I can do all things through Christ which strengtheneth me* (Philippians 4:13). Take care that you never lose this strength. Pray to God that you may never sin so as to lose it, that you may never backslide so as to lose it, and that you may never grieve the Spirit so as to lose it. I suppose that to be endowed with power from on high and to be strong in faith, giving glory to God, is the truest glory and majesty of our manhood, and it would be sad to lose it, or even to impair it. Oh, that all Christians were so much advanced as to enter the enlisted battalion of the Lord's young men!

This strength makes a man strong to endure. He is a sufferer, but notice how patient he is! He is a loser in business, and he has a hard task to earn his daily bread, but he never complains, for he has learned to be content in every condition and situation (Philippians 4:11). He is persecuted, but he is not distressed by it (2 Corinthians 4:9). People revile him, but he is not moved from the even tenor of his way. He does not pay much attention to either flattery or slander. As long as he can please God, he is not concerned if he displeases men. He dwells on high and lives above the smoke of human opinion. He bears and forbears. He bows his neck to the yoke and his shoulders to the burden, and has fellowship with Christ in His sufferings (Philippians 3:10).

Blessed is that man who is so strong that he never complains of his trials, never complains and agonizes because he is made to share in the humiliations and griefs of His covenant head. He expected to bear the cross when he became a follower of the Crucified, and he is not now made weary and faint when it presses upon him. It is a fine sight to see young Isaac bearing the wood for the sacrifice; young Joseph bearing the chains in prison with holy joy; young Samson carrying away the gates of Gaza, bars and all; and young David praising God with his harp even though Saul is reaching for his javelin. Such are the exploits of the young men who *count it all joy* when they fall into manifold trials for

Christ's sake (James 1:2). O young man, be strong. Be as strong as an iron column that bears the full stress of the building and is not moved.

This strength shows itself next in laboring for Christ. The young man in Christ is a great worker. He has so much strength that he cannot sit still. He would be ashamed to leave the burden and heat of the day that others bear. He is up and working according to his calling and ability. He has asked his Lord as a favor to give him something to do. His prayer has been, "Show me what You want me to do," and having received an answer, he is found in the vineyard trenching the soil, removing the weeds, pruning the vines, and attending to such labors as the seasons demand.

His Master has said to him, *Feed My sheep*, and *Feed My lambs* (John 21:15-17), and therefore you will see him through the entire day and far into the night watching over the flock that is committed to him. He greatly rejoices in all this toil, for he is strong. He can run and not be weary; he can walk and not faint (Isaiah 40:31). *By my God have I leaped over a wall*, he says (Psalm 18:29). Nothing is hard to him, or if it is, he remembers that the diamond cuts the diamond, so he sets a harder thing against a hard thing, and he overcomes by a firm and stern resolve. That which should be done, he declares will be done in the power of God, and it is indeed accomplished!

Blessed is the church that has her *quiver full* of these men; she will speak with her *enemies in the gate* (Psalm 127:5). These are the men who work our reformations. These are the men who conduct our missions. These are the men who launch out into the deep for Christ. They make the front line of the host of God, and largely compose the main body of her forces.

These young men are also strong to resist attack. They are assaulted, but they carry with them the shield of faith which with they quench the fiery darts of the enemy (Ephesians 6:16). Wherever they go, if they meet with others who are tempted, they rush to the front to take up their cause. They are ready in the day of battle to meet attacks upon the faith with the sword of the Spirit. They will not give up any point of faith, but will defend the truth despite all danger. Clad in the armor of truth, they meet no deadly wound, for they are so preserved by grace that the Wicked One does not touch them. They resist temptation, and are unharmed in the midst of danger. Do you want an example?

Look at Joseph! Where ten thousand would have fallen, he stands in snow-white purity. Joseph, as contrasted with David, is an example of how a young man may bring greater glory to God than an older man when assailed by a similar temptation. Joseph is still young, and the temptation forces itself upon him while he is in the path of duty. He is alone with his temptress, and no one needs to know of the sin if it is committed. On the other hand, if he refuses, then shame, and possibly death, may await him through the false statements of the offended woman – yet he bravely resists the assault and overcomes the Wicked One. He is a bright contrast to the older man, a father in Israel, who went out of his way to perform an evil deed and committed a crime in order to fulfil his wicked desire. From this case, we learn that neither years, nor knowledge, nor experience can preserve any one of us from sin. Both old and young must be kept by the power of God or they will be overthrown by the Tempter.

Furthermore, these young men are not only strong in defense, but they are strong in attack. They carry the war into the enemy's territory. If there is anything to be done, they are like Jonathan and his armor-bearer, eager for the fight. They are very zealous for the Lord of hosts, and are quick to undertake toil and travail for Jesus's sake. They smite down error and set up truth. They believe great things, attempt great things, and expect great things, and the Lord is with them. *The archers have sorely grieved* them and shot at them and hated them, but their bows abide in strength, for the arms of their hands are made strong *by the mighty God of Jacob* (Genesis 49:23-24). One of them shall *chase a thousand, and two put ten thousand to flight* (Deuteronomy 32:30).

CHAPTER 25

OPEN THE YOUNG MAN'S EYES

Elisha prayed, and said, LORD, I pray thee, open his eyes, that he may see. And the LORD opened the eyes of the young man; and he saw: and, behold, the mountain was full of horses and chariots of fire round about Elisha. (2 Kings 6:17)

For certain of our friends, we pray that their eyes may be opened to see the Enemy of their souls under the many disguises that he assumes. We fear that many are *ignorant of his devices* (2 Corinthians 2:11). Young men, especially, are too inclined to mistake the great Enemy for a friend. They believe his false and flattering words, and are seduced to ruin. He holds forth to them the sparkling cup, but in its beaded bubbles, death is lurking. He talks of pleasure, but in the lusts of the flesh, the pleasure is a shadow and misery is the substance. He wears the mask of caution, and he admonishes young men to take care of themselves first and leave religion until after they have made their fortunes. However, the gain that comes from casting God aside will prove to be an everlasting loss. The devil as a serpent does more harm than he does as a roaring lion. If we had to meet the devil, and knew him to be what he really is, we could far more easily conquer him; but we have to deal with him disguised as an angel of light, and we have need of a hundred eyes, each one opened by God so that we may see.

Even worse than this is the fact that, at times, he does not meet us at all, but he undermines our path. He digs pits for our feet, he shoots his arrows from afar, or he sends forth a pestilence that travels in darkness. We then have need of a better sight than nature gives. For the young man who is just leaving home to go into the world, I would pray, "O Lord, open the eyes of the young man so that he may see!"

I would pray that he would be able to detect the falsehood that may hide itself beneath the truth, the malice that may wrap itself about with pride, the foolishness that may robe itself in learning, and the sin that may clothe itself in the garments of pleasure! I would not want him to be taken like a bird in a snare. I would not have the youth led by the hand of temptation like a bullock to the butcher's shop. Let us breathe such a prayer as that of Elisha for each person who is beginning life. May God grant that his eyes may be opened to see sin as sin, to see that evil can never be good, that a lie can never be true, and that rebellion against our God can never be the way to happiness!

We want people's eyes to be opened to see God as everywhere, observing all things. What an opening of the eyes this would be to many! It is a sad but true saying that God may be seen everywhere, but that most people see Him nowhere. He is blind indeed who cannot see Him to whom the sun owes its light. Until our eyes are opened, we rise in the morning and we fall asleep at night, but we have not seen God all day, even though He has been around us and within us every moment. We live from the first day of January to the last day of December, and while the Lord never ceases to see us, we do not even begin to see Him until He opens our eyes by a miracle of grace. We dwell in a wonderful world that the great Creator has made. He has filled it with His own handiwork and inspired it with His own presence, yet we do not see Him. Indeed, some people are so blind as to argue that there is no Creator and that they cannot perceive any evidence that a supremely wise and mighty Creator exists.

Oh, that the Lord Jesus would open the eyes of the willfully blind! Oh, that you also, you who are blinded by forgetfulness rather than by error, may be made to cry with Hagar, *Thou God seest me* (Genesis 16:13), and with Job, *Now mine eye seeth Thee* (Job 42:5)! If God will graciously convince people of His own divine presence, what a blessing it will be to them, especially to the young who are setting out in life! A clear perception that the Lord observes all that we do will be a very useful protection in the hour of temptation. When we remember the divine eye, we will cry, like Joseph, *How can I do this great wickedness, and sin against God?* (Genesis 39:9). To see yourself is good, but to see God is better. Let us pray, "O Lord, open the young man's eyes so that he may see You!"

When a man begins to see his great Enemy and also his best Friend, we may next pray, "Lord, open his eyes to see the way of salvation through the appointed Savior." We cannot see the Lord Jesus except by His own light. We look to Him with a look that comes from Him. I have tried to explain salvation to people many times in simple words and figures, but there is a great deal more needed than an explanation. It is right to be very plain, but more is needed than a clear statement.

No matter how bright the candle, a blind man does not see any better. I continually pray, "Lord, open my mouth!" but I perceive that I must also pray, "Lord, open men's eyes!" Until God opens a person's eyes, he will not see what faith means, nor what atonement means, nor what regeneration means. That which is as plain as a spear to a seeing man is invisible to the blind. "Believe and live": what can be plainer? Yet no one understands it until God gives grace to perceive His meaning.

It is the duty of preachers to put the gospel as plainly as possible, but we cannot give anyone spiritual understanding. We declare, in the plainest and boldest terms, *Believe on the Lord Jesus Christ, and thou shalt be saved* (Acts 16:31), but people ask without understanding, "What do you mean?" We cry out, "Look unto Jesus and live," but when our explanations are over, we learn that they have mistaken our meaning and are still looking to themselves and turning their backs on the Lord Jesus. To believe, or trust, is no mystery, but it is the simplest of all simplicities. For that very reason, people cannot be persuaded to think that we mean what we say, or that God means what He says. We need to pray, "Lord, open their eyes so that they may see; for seeing, they do not see; and hearing, they do not understand" (Matthew 13:14).

Blessed be the Lord – how sweetly they see it the moment their eyes are opened by His own omnipotent touch! Then they wonder how they did not see it before, and they call themselves ten thousand fools for not perceiving what is so plain. Faith in the Lord Jesus is the most complete ABC of divine revelation. It belongs to the fundamentals and basics of heavenly knowledge, and we are fools indeed not to take it as we find it in the Word, but begin bewildering ourselves over such a plain matter. Once the miracle-working power of God opens our eyes, we see well enough, but until then we fumble around in the noonday for that which is right before us. Sin cannot so darken the mind that God cannot pour light into it. If we cannot make people see, we can at least lead them to the Master Ophthalmologist, who can rectify their sight.

We should pray that our friends may have their eyes opened to see all manner of spiritual truth. These optics of ours can only see natural objects; that is all they are intended for. We should be very grateful that our eyes can see as much as they do see, but spiritual objects are not discernible by the eyes of the body, which are for material objects only. The things that pertain to the spiritual kingdom must be perceived by eyes of a spiritual kind – eyes opened by the Lord. God must give spiritual senses to us before we can discern spiritual things. Let this never be forgotten.

The flesh cannot grasp, perceive, or discern the things of the Spirit. We must become spiritual and receive spiritual capabilities before we can perceive spiritual things. In a word, we *must be born again* (John 3:7). *The natural man receiveth not the things of the Spirit of God: for they are foolishness unto him: neither can he know them, because they are spiritually discerned* (1 Corinthians 2:14). This is why the prayer is needed: "Lord, open the eyes of the young man so that he may see!"

Already the horses and chariots of fire were round about Elisha, but his servant could not see any of them because they were spiritual chariots and spiritual horses – angelic beings belonging to the purely spiritual domain. As yet, the youth had not entered the spiritual region and had no eyes with which to see into it. Once God had given him spiritual eyes, then there began to break upon his vision that strange sight – celestial, aerial, no, spiritual, yet most real. It was sight that revived his soul with the conviction that the prophet was safe since the ministers of God, as flames of fire, flashed to and fro, and like an army with horses and chariots, showed themselves strong for the defense of the servant of Jehovah. How surprised he was! How great was his amazement! How content was his mind! He and his master were mysteriously defended beyond all fear of danger.

If you were strangers to the things of God, and the Lord would open your eyes at once, you would be astonished indeed, for as yet you have no idea, you cannot have any idea, what the spiritual life is, nor what spiritual realities must be. Neither can you have any true idea of them until you are given life by the Lord. You may talk about spiritual subjects, and discuss them, and think yourselves theologians – but you resemble deaf people criticizing music, and blind people describing pictures. You are not qualified to even express an opinion upon the matter until you are made new in Christ Jesus and are brought within range of the spiritual and the heavenly. *Except a man be born again, he cannot see the kingdom of God* (John 3:3). Let the prayer go up, then, from all enlightened hearts, for those who are not yet walking in the light: "Lord, open the eyes of the young men so that they may see!"

Elisha's prayer for this young man was not, and our prayer for others is not, that they may do something that they can do, that they may use some ability that they already have. Rather, our prayer is that a new sight may be granted to them and that a new nature may be created within them by a power altogether above and beyond themselves. We call in the hand of God. We ask the Lord to work a miracle. We want you to receive what no education can ever give you and what no graduation at any university can ever bestow upon you. We want you to obtain what no number of years of experience or of study can achieve. We want you to possess what no imitation of other people will gain for you. We want you to experience a change that only the Lord Himself can work in you. We want you to pass from nature's darkness into God's marvelous light (1 Peter 2:9), from a dreadful blindness into a clear vision of things otherwise invisible.

CHAPTER 26

PRAYER FOR YOUNG MEN – THE REASONS FOR IT

Elisha prayed, and said, LORD, *I pray thee, open his eyes, that he may see. And the* LORD *opened the eyes of the young man; and he saw: and, behold, the mountain was full of horses and chariots of fire round about Elisha.*
(2 Kings 6:17)

The first reason for our prayer is because we ourselves have been made to see. If this miracle of grace had not taken place within us, we would have had no thought of prayer for you, but now our whole heart goes with the plea. Once we were as you are. Our eyes were once blinded so that we saw neither our enemies in all their dread, nor the glory of the Lord round about us.

Like blind Samsons, we went through the weary drudgery of earth surrounded by our enemies. At last, a glimmering of the light fell upon us like a lightning flash, showing us our sin. After the light shined upon us, we endured a great fight of afflictions. *Without were fightings, within were fears* (2 Corinthians 7:5). Our enemies were round about us, and we did not know what to do. But some man of God prayed for us, and one day our eyes were turned toward the hills from where comes all aid to terror-stricken men (Psalm 121:1). The Lord was there, although we did not know Him. Still, we looked to Him and were enlightened, and our faces were not ashamed (Psalm 34:5), for round about Him the mountain was full of chariots and horses of fire. *For God, who commanded the light to shine out of darkness, hath shined in our hearts, to give the light of the knowledge of the glory of God in the face of Jesus Christ* (2 Corinthians 4:6).

We also call upon the Lord because only by His power can people be made to see. We found this to be true in our own experience. We struggled in vain to behold the salvation of God. We sought in vain the help of godly people. No sight came to our souls, nor were the eyes of our understanding enlightened (Ephesians 1:18), until the Lord Himself washed our eyes in the waters that go softly (Isaiah 8:6). Then we came seeing.

We also see this when we try to lead others to the light. We speak to them of the glories we ourselves behold, and we set before them the truth of God, but we cannot make them see. To bestow spiritual vision is as great a wonder as to make a world, and it requires the same decree of omnipotence. Only He who created the eye can give this second sight. *Since the world began was it not heard that any man opened the eyes of one that was born blind* (John 9:32). What absurdity, then, to attempt the greater task of bestowing the sight of the heart! How vain is the boast of those who attempt to invade God's prerogative and imagine that human ordinances or rituals can open blind eyes!

After we have done our best to make the people see the glory of the gospel, let us ever fall back on the God of the gospel and plead with Him to do His own blessed work. Do not try to hold up your wax candles to reveal the chariots of fire, nor parade your vain philosophy as if that could clear away the darkness of the soul. Leave room for God to work, and in a moment, at the touch of His finger in response to the prayers of His people, the wondrous work will be accomplished.

We pray most urgently when we see the people inquiring. The cry, "What shall we do?" sends us to our knees, for we know that what is necessary is not something to be done, but something to be seen. We feel convinced that the Lord who awoke the desire in the hearts of the seekers will also certainly open their eyes to behold His glory. The very fact that we feel drawn to pray for them is already a token to us that before long the scales will fall from their eyes, and through their vision of the splendor and sufficiency of the provision that God has made for those who trust in Him, the name of the Lord will be greatly glorified. Therefore, with much expectancy, we again utter our prayer: "Lord, open their eyes so that they may see!"

Another reason for this prayer is that you are not aware of your own blindness. You are trusting in yourselves that you can see well enough all that you need to see. That young man of whom I am now thinking has no idea whatsoever that his eyes are completely blind to eternal things. He thinks of himself as a sharp and clever fellow, and I do not deny that he is so in his own line of things. I am glad that he has such bright abilities for this life. May God bless him, and may he prosper in his business and in the enterprise upon which he is just entering! May the Lord be with him concerning the matter on which his heart is set!

Still, though, I am rather afraid of your cleverness. I am somewhat frightened at that sharpness of yours because I have seen sharp men cut themselves, and I have seen some who are self-reliant become miserable failures. Something is to be said for confidence in its proper place, but self-congratulation is a proof of inward weakness, and it foretells a breakdown. If you are depending on an arm of flesh, at the very best you are resting on a broken reed. You require strength beyond your own to fight the moral and spiritual battle of life. In this case, your self-reliance is a piece of groundless self-conceit.

Remember Hazael, who, when he was forewarned of what he would do, exclaimed in astonishment, *Is thy servant a dog, that he should do this great thing?* (2 Kings 8:13). Hazael could not think of himself as capable of such crimes, yet he no sooner had the opportunity than he fell into the evil up to his very neck. He was dog enough to be cruel, for he was dog enough to flatter himself.

Young man, you do not believe that you will ever be dishonest, yet that little gambling venture of yours will lead to it. You cannot think that you will ever be godless, yet you are even now departing from the good old ways of your home and are mocking sacred things when in certain company. Those who trust in themselves are storing up the fuel for a great fire of sin. The pride that lifts itself up will throw itself down. Because the fine young fellow does not know how blind he is, we therefore lament his blindness, and we are even more earnest in bringing him to Jesus so that he may receive his sight. "Lord, open his eyes so that he may see!"

Next, we pray this prayer because we have reason to fear that you are surrounded by people who will mislead you. We know the young man well. He has come to London from that sober, orderly country home, and he has no idea of the snares that will be laid for him by both male and female. Oh, you who have no experience and little discretion, hear the voice of warning! Satan has shrewd servants around him who hunt for the precious life with double diligence.

Our Lord Jesus has servants around Him who too often slumber, but the devil's servants are not slothful in their dreadful business. They will ambush you in the streets outside, and will gather around you in the houses of pleasure within. They are everywhere, and they leave no stone unturned as they try to entrap the unwary. What if this blind young man is placed in the midst of all these predators? They will devour him if they can. What if he is left to be their victim? It is like turning out a sheep among a pack of wolves. "Lord, open the eyes of the young man so that he may see!"

We pray this prayer for some of you because you are going away from those who have until now watched over you, and this is a dangerous change for you. Your mother – we can never tell what a blessing a godly mother is to a young man. Your mother parts from you with great concern. Will you ever forget her tender words? Our fathers are all very well. God bless them! A father's godly influence and earnest prayers are of untold value to his children, but the mothers are worth two of them – mostly as to the moral training and religious inclination of their sons and daughters. Well, you are going right away from your mother's holy influence and from your father's restraining admonitions. You will now have nobody to encourage you in the right way. You will miss your sister's holy kiss and your grandmother's loving persuasions. You are going out of the greenhouse into a night's frost. We may well pray concerning you that you may carry with you well-opened eyes to see your way and to look before you leap. The young man is now to walk alone: "Lord, open his eyes so that he may see!" If he does not look before he leaps, he will soon be in the ditch – and who will pull him out?

We pray this prayer with even more pleasure because you will do

so much good if your eyes are opened. What can a blind man do in the midst of such a world as this? He cannot help other travelers, for he has to seek help for himself. You want to give rather than to take, do you not? Some people have great abilities, and I want them to use them appropriately. I am convinced that I am speaking to young people whom God has ordained to be of great service to their age.

That youth over there does not yet know what is in him. He is playing around. He is making a fool of himself. He is throwing his pearls before swine. He is wasting his strength. If the Lord would open his eyes, he would see what he is doing. What a man he would make if he were only right with God! Think of how Saul of Tarsus harassed the church of Christ, but when the scales fell from his eyes, the Lord had no better servant under heaven than that once-furious persecutor. With both hands, he diligently built up the church that he once labored to cast down. *The thing that has been, it is that which shall be* (Ecclesiastes 1:9).

Pray, therefore, for our young men who have sinned that they may be restored. Pray for those who are still ignorant that they may be enlightened. The cause of God has need of these men, and in these the church will find her champions! Little do we know the wealth of comfort for the faithful that may lie in one young life. Certainly we should pile on our prayers and make our intercession flame like some great beacon light for the rising youth of our time.

There is yet another reason that comes from the other side of the case. We should pray for the blinded one since he may sin terribly if not soon made to see. How capable of doing harm is a man who is blinded by ignorance, passion, greed, or any other form of sin! Who knows the capacities for evil that lie within a single soul? That once bright spirit, Satan, when he first thought of raising revolt against the God of heaven – it was, perhaps, a single momentary flash of rebellious thought. Before long, though, he had become proudly antagonistic to his Maker, and the Dragon had drawn down with his tail *a third part of the stars of heaven* to quench them in the eternal night of endless wickedness (Revelation 12:4). Then he came to this earth, corrupted paradise, and seduced our first parents from their happy innocence so that they became the progenitors of an unhappy race that was steeped up to their lips in sin. How filled with innumerable evils was that one first thought of sin!

It is the same way with us. A boy, his mother's pride, to whom she looks forward as the honor of the family, may for a while appear to be everything that love can hope; but he falls into the hands of one of those tempters to unbelief who are so abundant in this great city. He is taught to pour ridicule upon his mother's piety, and soon he casts off the perceived shackles of his father's God. He forgets the sanctity of God's holy day, and he forsakes the house of prayer. Then he learns the way to the houses of strange women and to the palace of strong drink. He plunges into one sin after another until he is himself leading others down to the abyss. That boy who used to kneel at his mother's knee, say his childish prayer, and then stand up and sing of Jesus and His love, was fondly regarded as one who would honor Jesus in his life; but see him now. He staggers home after midnight spewing profanity! He is wicked both in soul and in body, and those who love him best are saddest at the sight of him.

If we do not want to see children or friends running to this *excess of riot* (1 Peter 4:4) and sinking in this *superfluity of naughtiness* (James 1:21), let us in agony of spirit plead with God at once on their behalf. Oh, for an immediate entrance of the light into their souls! *Lord, open their eyes so that they may see! Lord, cause them to back away from the beginnings of sin, which are as the breaking out of the waterfloods! O Savior, quench in them the spark of evil before it grows into a fire and rages to an inferno!*

We want people's eyes to be opened so that they may know, first, that spiritual forces really exist. The things that we see are not the only real things, nor even the most real things. The things that are seen are temporal; they are, in truth, only shadows of the unseen. The substantial realities are not seen by these poor eyes. The substance is only perceived by our true selves. All that is visible is the mere shadow. The very image of the things is out of sight.

Faith teaches us to believe in the existence of the most glorious of all spirits, the great God, in whom *we live, and move, and have our being* (Acts 17:28). Faith reveals to the heart the existence of that divine and ever-cherished Person, the Lord Jesus Christ, who is at this hour with His church, and will abide with her to the end of the world. Faith also makes us know the existence, power, and presence of the Holy Spirit, who dwells with believers and is in them, working out the eternal purpose of God in their sanctification.

No knowledge is more marvelous than to know the Trinity in Unity: Father, Son, and Holy Spirit, yet one Jehovah. When we come to realize that the Lord God is the source of all things, that God *hath made us, and not we ourselves* (Psalm 100:3), and that all things come into being by His sovereign will and power, then we come to recognize His presence, consult His will, and lean upon His might. God becomes real in our thought and understanding. Since He whom we cannot see nevertheless supports all things that are, we feel that the invisible is the basis of all things.

Oh, that we could get people's minds out of these timeworn ruts of things seen, these narrow bounds of space, time, seeing, and touching! Oh, that they could rise into the region where the dim senses, which are bounded by so small a circle, would give place to awareness that knows the infinite, the eternal, the true, the divine! Oh, that the human mind, which was made in the image of God, could find itself at home with God, whose child he may become by a second birth, of the living and incorruptible seed, *by the Word of God, which liveth and abideth forever* (1 Peter 1:23)!

CHAPTER 27

THE SWIFTNESS OF LIFE

Let me speak to you about the frailty of human life, the fleeting nature of time, how swiftly it passes away, how soon we will all fade as the leaf, and how quickly the place that knows us now will know us no more forever. The apostle James asks, *What is your life?* (James 4:14), and thanks to inspiration, we are at no great difficulty to give the reply, for Scripture, being the best interpreter of Scripture, supplies us with many very excellent answers. I will attempt to give you some of them.

It is a common fact that although life to the young man, when viewed from his perspective, appears to be long, to the old man it is ever short. To all people, life is really only a brief period. Human life is not long. Compare it with the existence of some animals and trees, and how short human life is! Compare it with the ages of the universe, it is just a moment. Especially if we measure it by eternity, how short life seems! It sinks like one small drop into the ocean, and it becomes as insignificant as one tiny grain of sand upon the seashore. Life is swift. If you want to picture life, you must turn to the Bible, and we will walk through the Bible gallery of old paintings.

You will find its swiftness spoken of in the book of Job, where we are furnished with three illustrations. In the ninth chapter, in the twenty-fifth verse, we find, *Now my days are swifter than a post.* Most of us are familiar with the swiftness of post transportation. Sometimes, in an emergency, I have taken post horses where there has been no railway, and I have been amused and pleased with the quickness of my journey. But since there can be no allusion to modern posts in this ancient Book, we must turn to the manners and customs of the East. In doing so, we find that the ancient monarchs astonished their subjects by the amazing rapidity with which they received intelligence. By well-ordered arrangements, swift horses, and constant relays, they were able to attain a speed which, although slow in these days, was a marvel of marvels in those slower ages. To someone in the East, one of the greatest ideas of swiftness was that of a post.

Well does Job say our life is like a post. We ride one year until it is worn out, but there comes another just as swift, and we are carried by it, and it is gone. Then another year serves us for a steed. We pass posthouse after posthouse as birthdays successively arrive. We do not loiter, but vault at a leap from one year to another, and still we hurry onward, onward, onward still. Our life is like a post – not like the slow wagon that drags along the road with tiresome wheels, but, like a post, it attains the greatest speed.

Job further says that his days *are passed away as the swift ships* (Job 9:26). He increases the intensity of the metaphor. If anything could excel the swiftness of a post in the mind of someone in the East, it was the swift ship. Some translate this passage as "ships of desire;" that is, the ships are hurrying home, anxious for the haven, and therefore spreading all its sail. You may well conceive how swiftly the sailor flies from a threatening storm or seeks the port where he will find his home. You have sometimes seen how the ship cuts through the waves, leaving a white furrow behind her and causing the sea to boil around her.

Such is life, says Job, like the swift ships when the sails are filled by the wind and the vessel dashes on, dividing a passage through the crowding water. Swift are the ships, but swifter far is life. The wind of time carries me along. I cannot stop its motion. I may direct it with the rudder of God's Holy Spirit. It is true that I may take in some small sails of sin that might hurry my days on faster than they would otherwise go, but nevertheless, like a swift ship, my life must speed on its way until it reaches its haven.

Where is that haven to be? Will it be found in the land of bitterness and barrenness, that dreary region of the lost – or will it be that sweet haven of eternal peace where not a troubling wave can ruffle the restful glory of my spirit? Wherever the haven is to be, that truth is the same: we are like *the swift ships*.

Job also says that our days are *as the eagle that hasteth to the prey* (Job 9:26). The eagle is a bird noted for its swiftness. I remember reading an account of an eagle attacking a fish hawk that had obtained some treasure from the deep and was carrying it toward the sky. The hawk dropped the fish, which fell toward the water. However, before the fish had reached the ocean, an eagle had flown more swiftly than the fish could fall, and catching the fish in its beak, the eagle flew away with it. The swiftness of the eagle is almost incalculable. You see it, and it is gone. You see a dark speck in the distant sky. It is an eagle soaring. Let the hunter imagine that he will overtake it on some mountain's craggy peak, but it will be gone long before he reaches it.

Such is our life. It is like an eagle hurrying to its prey. It is not merely like an eagle flying in its regular way, but it is like an eagle rushing to its prey. Life appears to be rushing to its prey. The prey is the body. Life is always flying from unappeasable death, but death is too swift to be outrun. As an eagle overtakes his prey, so will death.

If we require a further illustration of the swiftness of life, we must turn again to Job, upon which I will not dwell. It will be found in the seventh chapter. Job says that it is *swifter than a weaver's shuttle* (Job 7:6), which the weaver throws so quickly that the eye can hardly discern it. Job gives us a still more excellent metaphor in the seventh verse of the same chapter, where he says, *O remember that my life is wind* (Job 7:7). This excels in speed all the other illustrations we have examined. Who can outrun the winds? Proverbially, the winds are rapid. Even in their gentlest motion, they appear to be swift. But when they rush in the tornado, or when they dash madly on in the hurricane – when the tempest blows and destroys everything – how swift then is the wind!

Perhaps some of us may have a gentle gale of wind, and we may not seem to move so swiftly. With others, though, who are only born and then snatched away to heaven, the swiftness of it may be compared to the hurricane, which soon snaps the ties of life and leaves the infant dead. Surely our life is like the wind.

Oh, if you could only understand these ideas! You know we are all really in motion. This world is turning around on its axis once every twenty-four hours, and besides that, it is moving around the sun all 365 days of the year. We are all moving. We are all speeding along through space. As we are traveling through space, so we are moving through time at an incalculable rate. Oh, what an idea it is if we could comprehend it! We are all being carried along, as if by a giant angel with broad, outstretched wings, which he flaps to the wind, and flying before the lightning, he makes us ride on the winds. The whole multitude of us are hurrying along. Where we are going remains to be decided by the test of our faith and the grace of God, but it is certain that we are traveling.

Do not think that you are anchored and steady creatures. Do not think that you are standing still. You are not. Each moment, your pulse beats the funeral marches to the tomb. You are chained to the chariot of rolling time. There is no bridling the steeds or leaping from the chariot. You must be constantly in motion.

We have abundant illustrations concerning the uncertainty of life. *For what is your life? It is even a vapor, that appeareth for a little time, and then vanisheth away* (James 4:14). If I were to ask for a child's explanation of this, I know what he would say. He would say, "Yes, it is even a vapor, like a bubble that is blown upward." Children sometimes blow bubbles and amuse themselves by doing so. Life is even as that bubble. You see it rising into the air. The child delights himself by seeing it fly about, but it is gone in a moment. *It is even a vapor, that appeareth for a little time, and then vanisheth away.*

But if you ask the poet to explain this, he would tell you that in the morning, sometimes at early dawn, the rivers send up a steamy offering to the sun. There is a vapor, a mist, an exhalation rising from the rivers and brooks, but very soon after the sun is risen, all that mist is gone. Therefore, we read of the morning cloud and the early dew that passes away. A more common observer, speaking of a vapor, would think of those thin clouds you sometimes see floating in the air that are so light that they are soon carried away. Indeed, a poet uses them as the picture of feebleness:

Their hosts are scatter'd, like thin clouds
Before a Biscay gale.[24]

---

24   This is from "The Battle of Ivry," a poem by Thomas Babington Macauley (1800-1859). The line from the actual poem is, "Their ranks are breaking like thin clouds before a Biscay gale."

The winds move them, and they are gone. *What is your life? It is even a vapor, that appeareth for a little time, and then vanisheth away.* So uncertain is life!

If you read the sixth chapter of the book of Ecclesiastes, you will there find life compared to something else that is even more fragile than a vapor. The wise man there says that it is even *as a shadow* (Ecclesiastes 6:12). What can there be that is less substantial than a shadow? What substance is there in a shadow? Who can lay hold of it? You may see it, but the moment the person goes away, it is gone. Yes, and who can grasp his life? Many people depend upon having a long existence, and they think they are going to live forever – but who can calculate upon a shadow?

Go, you man who says to your soul, "Eat, drink, and be merry; I have much goods laid up for many years" (Luke 12:19) – go and fill your room with shadows. Go and pile shadows up and say, "These are mine, and they will never depart." However, you say, "I cannot catch a shadow." No, and you cannot depend on a year, for it is as a shadow, which soon melts away and is gone.

The prophet Isaiah also furnishes us with a comparison, where he says that life is like a thread that is cut off: *Mine age is departed, and is removed from me as a shepherd's tent: I have cut off like a weaver my life* (Isaiah 38:12). The weaver cuts off his thread very easily, and so is life soon ended. I could continue my illustrations at will concerning the uncertainty of life. We could find, perhaps, a couple dozen more examples in Scripture if we would look. Take, for instance, the grass, the flowers of the field, etc.

Although life is swift, and although it is to pass away so quickly, we are still generally very anxious to know what it is to be while we have it. For we say, if we are to lose it, while we still live, let us live; and while we are to be here, no matter how short a time, let us know what we are to expect in it.

CHAPTER 28

THE CHANGES OF LIFE

If you want illustrations of the changes of life, turn to this wonderful book of poetry, the Sacred Scriptures, and there you will find metaphors piled on metaphors. First, you will find life compared to a pilgrimage by good old Jacob in Genesis 47:9. That gray-headed patriarch, when he was asked by Pharaoh how old he was, replied, *The days of the years of my pilgrimage are an hundred and thirty years: few and evil have the days of the years of my life been, and have not attained unto the days of the years of the life of my fathers in the days of their pilgrimage.* He calls life a pilgrimage.

A pilgrim starts out in the morning, and he has to journey many days before he gets to the shrine that he seeks. What diverse scenes the traveler will behold on his way! Sometimes he will be on the mountains. Later he will descend into the valleys. At one time he will be where the brooks shine like silver, the birds warble, the air is balmy, the trees are green, and luscious fruits hang down to gratify his taste. At another time he will find himself in the arid desert where no life is found and no sound is heard except the screech of the wild eagle in the air, where he finds no rest for the sole of his foot. The burning sky is above him and the hot sand is beneath him. He finds no shade from trees and no house where he can find rest. Later he finds himself in a sweet oasis, resting himself by the springs of water and plucking fruit from palm trees. One moment he walks between the rocks in some narrow gorge, where all is darkness. At another time he ascends the hill of Miza, then he descends into the valley of Baca. Later he climbs the hill of Bashan, a *high hill as the hill of Bashan* (Psalm 68:15), and then going into a den of leopards, he suffers trial and affliction. Such is life – ever changing. Who can tell what may come next?

Today it is fair, but the next day there may be thunderstorms. Today I may lack nothing, but tomorrow I may be like Jacob, with nothing but a stone for my pillow and the heavens for my curtains (Genesis 28:18). What a happy thought it is, though, that while we do not know where the road winds, we know where it ends! It is the straightest way to heaven to go round about. Israel's forty years of wanderings were, after all, the nearest path to Canaan. We may have to go through trial and affliction. The pilgrimage may be a tiresome one, but it is safe. We cannot trace the river upon which we are sailing, but we know it ends in floods of delight at last. We cannot track the roads, but we know that they all meet in the great metropolis of heaven, in the center of God's universe. May God help us to pursue the true pilgrimage of a pious life!

In Psalm 90, we have another picture of life in its changes: *We spend our years as a tale that is told* (Psalm 90:9). David understood about tales that were told. I daresay he had been annoyed by them sometimes. There are professed storytellers in the East who amuse their hearers by inventing tales such as those in that foolish book, the *Arabian Nights*. When I was foolish enough to read that book, I remember sometimes you were with fairies, sometimes with genies, sometimes in palaces, and sometimes you went down into caverns. All sorts of strange things are conglomerated into what they call a tale. Now, says David, *We spend our years as a tale that is told.*

There is nothing as wonderful as the history of the odds and ends of human life. Sometimes it is a merry rhyme, and sometimes a dreary subject. Sometimes you ascend to the sublime, and then soon you descend to the ridiculous. No one can write the entirety of his own biography. I suppose that if the history of a man's thoughts and words could be written, the world itself could hardly contain the words that should be written, so wonderful is the tale that is told. Our lives are all unique, and much of might be said must seem strange to us. Our life is *as a tale that is told.*

We get another idea from Isaiah 38:12: *Mine age is departed, and is removed from me as a shepherd's tent.* The shepherds in the East build temporary huts near the sheep. The huts are soon removed when the flock moves on. When the hot season comes, the shepherds pitch their tents, and each season has its suitable position. My life is like a shepherd's tent. I have pitched my tent in a variety of places already, but where I will pitch it in the future, I do not know. I cannot tell. Present probabilities seem to say:

> Here shall I make my settled rest,
> And neither go nor come;
> No more a stranger or a guest,
> But like a child at home.[25]

However, I cannot tell, and you do not know the future. You have been opening a new shop lately. You are thinking of settling down in trade and managing a thriving concern. Do not paint the future too brightly. Don't be too sure. Someone else has been engaged in an old establishment for a long time. Your father always carried on business there, and you have no thought of moving. Here you have no abiding city. Your life is like a shepherd's tent. You may be here, there, and almost everywhere before you die. It was once said by Solon, "No man ought to be called a happy man until he dies." That is because he does not know what his life is to be. However, Christians may always call themselves happy people here because wherever their tent is carried, they cannot pitch it where the cloud does not move and where they are not surrounded by a circle of fire. *For I, saith the* LORD, *will be unto her a wall of fire round about, and will be the glory in the midst of her* (Zechariah 2:5). They cannot dwell where God is not householder, protector, and fortress of salvation.

> All my ways shall ever be
> Ordered by His wise decree.[26]

I know that my tent cannot be removed until God says, *Go forward* (Exodus 14:15), and it cannot stand unless He makes it firm. If any

---

25 These lines are based upon a hymn by Isaac Watts (1674-1748) that begins with "My Shepherd will supply my need," based upon Psalm 23.

26 These lines are from a hymn by John Ryland (1753-1825) that begins with "Sovereign ruler of the skies."

who are God's people are going to change their condition, if they are going to move out of one situation into another to take a new business or move to another county, you do not need to fear. God was with you in the last place, and He will be with you in this new situation. *Be not dismayed; for I am thy God* (Isaiah 41:10).

There is a frequently told story of Caesar during a storm. The sailors were all afraid, but he exclaimed, "Fear not! You carry Caesar and all his fortunes." It is the same with the poor Christian. There is a storm coming on: "Fear not! You are carrying Jesus, and you sink or swim with Him." Well may we say, "Lord, if You are with me, it does not matter where my tent is." *If I make my bed in hell, behold, Thou art there* [Psalm 139:8]. All must be well, even if my life is removed like *a shepherd's tent.*

Our life is also compared in the Psalms to a dream. If a tale is strange, certainly a dream is more so. If a tale is changing and shifting, what is a dream? As for dreams, those meanderings of the nighttime thoughts, those revelries of the imagination – who can tell what they consist of? We dream of everything in the world, and a few things more! If we were asked to tell our dreams, it would be impossible. You dream that you are at a feast, and behold, the food changes into a Pegasus, and you are riding through the air; or you are suddenly transformed into a morsel for a monster meal.

That is how life is. The changes occur as suddenly as they happen in a dream. People have been rich one day, and have been beggars the next. We have witnessed the exile of monarchs and the flight of a king. In another direction, we have seen a man who is neither reputable in company nor honorable in station exalted to a throne in a single step, and you who would have shunned him in the streets before were foolish enough to crowd your thoroughfares to stare at him.

Such is life. Leaves of the Sybil were not more easily moved by the winds,[27] nor are dreams more variable. *Boast not thyself of tomorrow, for thou knowest not what a day may bring forth* (Proverbs 27:1). How foolish are those men who desire to pry into the future. The telescope is ready, and they are looking through – but they are so anxious to see

---

27   In Greek mythology, one story about the Sybil was that she had the gift of prophecy. She would write her prophecies on oak leaves and put them in order. However, if the wind blew the leaves out of order, she did not put them back in order.

THE CHANGES OF LIFE

that they breathe on the glass with their hot breath, and they fog it over so that they can discern nothing but clouds and darkness. Oh, you who are always dreaming up evil monsters from the deep unknown, and foolishly troubling your mind with your imagination, cast aside those figments of your imagination and begin to rest on never-failing promises. Promises are better than premonitions and predictions. *Trust in the LORD, and do good; so shalt thou dwell in the land, and verily thou shalt be fed, . . . and dwell therein forever* (Psalm 37:3, 29).

What is to be the end of this life? We read in Samuel that we are *as water spilt upon the ground, which cannot be gathered up again* (2 Samuel 14:14). Man is like a large icicle that the sun of time is continually thawing, and that will soon be *water spilt upon the ground, which cannot be gathered up.* Who can bring back the departed spirit, or inflate the lungs with a new breath of life? Who can put vitality into the heart and restore the soul from Hades? No one. It cannot be gathered up. The place *shall know it no more* forever (Psalm 103:16).

But here a sweet thought captivates us! This water cannot be lost, but it will descend into the soil to filter through the Rock of Ages, at last to spring up as a pure fountain in heaven – cleansed, purified, and made as clear as crystal. On the other hand, how terrible if it would seep through the black earth of sin and hang in horrid drops in the dark caverns of destruction!

Such is life! Make the best use of it you can, then, because it is fleeting. Look for another life because this life is not a very desirable one; it is so changeable. Trust your life in God's hand because you cannot control its movements. Rest in His arms and rely on His might, for He is able to do for you *exceedingly abundantly above all* that you can ask or think (Ephesians 3:20)!

CHAPTER 29

ON BEING DILIGENT IN BUSINESS

You know those respected city gentlemen. I hope you reverence them as I do since they are the embodiment of wisdom. One of these men said to his son, "William, I am pleased to see you lean toward religion, but take my advice and be reasonable. I have been in business now for forty years, and my advice is to stick to trade and make money, and then attend to religion."

The young man, as young men tend to do, had begun to think for himself. Surprisingly, his thoughts ran in the right way, and therefore he replied, "Father, I am always grateful to you for your good advice, but this time you must excuse me if I differ from you, for the Scripture says, *Seek ye first the kingdom of God, and His righteousness* [Matthew 6:33]. Therefore, I cannot go in for making money first, but I must at once serve God, and I hope I may be no less attentive to business." It is a good rule to begin as you intend to continue. That son was wiser than his counselor. True godliness is as good for this life as for the next. If I had to die like a dog, I would still want to be a Christian.

Place the Christian religion first in the order of time. Begin each week by carefully consecrating the first day to rest and holy worship. Begin each day by giving the dew of the morning to communion with heaven. Begin your married life by seeking the blessing of the great Father and choosing for a partner one who will agree with you in the fear of God. In opening a new business, sanctify the venture with the prayers of godly friends, and in all new enterprises, be guided by the Lord. If we begin, continue, and end with God, our way will be sprinkled with blessings.

Seek also the kingdom of God first in order of preference. If it would ever become a choice between God and the things of the world, never hesitate. If wealth and righteousness run counter to each other, let the gold perish, but hold fast to righteousness. Follow Christ, no matter what it costs you. Blessed is that man who never has to wrestle with such a decision because his mind is made up *rather to suffer affliction with the people of God than to enjoy the pleasures of sin for a season* (Hebrews 11:25). Blessed is the man who knows no course except that of entire consecration to God and righteousness – who is not cautious in answering in this matter, but has his mind decided once for all. This is his motto:

> 'Tis done, the great transaction's done!
> I am my Lord's, and He is mine.[28]

We have lifted our hand unto the Lord, and we cannot go back.

"That is good," someone says, "but, you know, we must live." I am not sure about that. There are occasions when it would be better not to live. An old heraldic motto says, "Better death than false of faith." I am, however, quite clear about another necessity: we must die. We had better take that "must" into consideration, and not quite as often repeat the pretentious phrase, "We must live."

But we will live. We will live without treating the poor badly, or lowering ourselves to questionable financial practices, or lying to the public by a false forecast. We will live without dishonor. Take your ground and keep it. Say, "With God helping me, I will do what I believe is right to do." Any little difficulties that now arise will soon come to an end if you are firmly conscientious. Never be a coward.

> I had as lief not be, as live to be
> In awe of such a thing as I myself.[29]

---

28   These lines are from a hymn by Philip Doddridge (1702-1751) titled "O Happy Day."
29   These lines are from William Shakespeare's play *Julius Caesar*.

Let none of us ever raise a question about whether we will please or displease others by doing right, but let us *seek first the kingdom of God.*

Let godliness be first in intensity. It is to be feared that many people give their strength to their worldly pursuits, and their weakness to their religion. They are "all there" during banking hours, but they are not "all there" at the hour of prayer. They remind me of one whose voice in our assemblies for prayer was exceedingly low and nearly inaudible, but in the shop he could be heard almost too well. Should it be so that self should have our energies and Christ should have our lukewarmness? If ever we grow fervent and enthusiastic, it should be in the noblest of all causes – in the service of the best of Masters. We cannot be too earnest in that work.

We seldom meet with a person who borders upon excess zeal in this matter. We cannot do too much for Him who has redeemed us with His precious blood. Our heart complains that we cannot do enough. Sadly, the comparative sizes of the Bible and the book of our business accounts are frequently symbolic; a neat little Bible is buried under a huge ledger. I claim a different place for things divine. Let that be first which is first. Throw your whole soul into the love and service of the Lord.

A Sunday school teacher asked a child, "Is your father a Christian?" The girl answered, "Yes, I believe that my father is a Christian, but he has not worked much at it lately." No doubt there are many people like that. Their religion has taken a vacation, and they themselves have gone up to a sluggard's bed. Let them be awakened, for *it is high time to awake out of sleep* (Romans 13:11).

Seek the kingdom of God and His righteousness first by giving true Christianity sovereignty over your lives. The helm by which life is steered should be in the hand of God. Our greatest desire should be to glorify God and promote righteousness. This Aaron's rod should swallow up all other rods. Be first a man of God, and after that be a banker, a businessman, or a laborer. I like to see our public men first be Christians, then Englishmen, and then members of their political parties, as their convictions sway them; but in any case, let a man be first a man of God.

I pray to God that our politics, our merchandise, our literature, and our art, were all saturated with this idea: first a Christian. Then the secondary character would rise in excellence and nobility. Science, social laws, trade usages, and domestic life would all be better for coming under the supremacy of a living Christianity. The fear of God should be the foundation and the capstone of the social edifice. "Christ first," and other things in their due order.

Over and above all, let consecration to God shine forth even as the pillar of fire in the wilderness covered and illuminated the entire camp of Israel. Does anyone demand, "What will become of our business if we put godliness first?" The answer is, *All these things shall be added unto you* (Matthew 6:33). Will a young man prosper who is beginning his life, resolving that he will do everything in the fear of God, and that as God helps him, he will do nothing that is contrary to the mind of the Lord Jesus Christ? He will get along as far as this: he will have bread to eat and raiment to put on; all that is necessary for this life *shall be added unto* him.

"Alas!" someone sighs, "I am unemployed and do not know how to provide for myself." Are you sure that this trial has come without your own fault? Then do not be of doubtful mind, for the Lord will provide for you. He has said, *Trust in the LORD, and do good; so shalt thou dwell in the land, and verily thou shalt be fed* (Psalm 37:3). David's experience was, *I have been young and now am old; yet have I not seen the righteous forsaken* (Psalm 37:25). The drunken, the vicious, the lazy, and the dishonest may suffer hunger, and it will be good for them if such discipline helps them; but to the upright, there arises light in the darkness (Psalm 112:4). Those who serve God will not have to complain of His deserting them.

During the reign of Queen Elizabeth, a certain merchant was desired by Her Majesty to go abroad for her upon affairs of state. He pleaded that his own business would suffer. Her Majesty replied, "Sir, if you will mind my business, I will mind your business." You can rest assured that God will care for you if you make His service your delight. *All these things shall be added unto you.*

The blessings of this life come to gracious people in the best shape and form, for they come by divine promise. Suppose that it were now put into the power of each one of us to be rich; I suspect that most of us would be eager to avail ourselves of the opportunity, yet it is doubtful that it would be best for certain of us to have the burden of wealth. It is a question whether some people who behave well where they now are would be half as good, or a tenth as happy, if they were lifted to higher positions. I have seen heroes babble under the influence of luxury. Many people are the creatures of circumstances, and they make poor creatures when their circumstances allow them to engage in self-indulgence. We do not know what is best for us. It is sometimes very much better for us to suffer loss and disappointment than to experience gain and prosperity.

When that eminent servant of God, Mr. Bernard Gilpin, was arrested to be brought up to London to be tried for preaching the gospel, his captors mocked his frequent remark, "Everything is for the best." When he fell from his horse and broke his leg, they were especially amused about it, but the good man quietly remarked, "I have no doubt but that even this painful accident will prove to be a blessing." And so it was, for since he could not travel quickly, the journey was prolonged, and he arrived at London some days later than had been expected. When they reached as far as Highgate, they heard the bells ringing merrily in the city down below. They asked the meaning and were told, "Queen Mary is dead, and there will be no more burnings of Protestants."

"Ah," said Gilpin, "you see it is all for the best." It is a blessing to break your leg if in doing so your life is saved. How often our calamities are our preservatives! A lesser misfortune may prevent a greater. Many people might have soared into the clouds of foolish recklessness if their wings had not been clipped by adversity. It is better to struggle and be honorable than to become wealthy by disgraceful deeds. Agur's prayer, *Give me neither poverty nor riches* (Proverbs 30:8), was a wise one, but our Lord's prayer is even better: *Not as I will, but as Thou wilt* (Matthew 26:39).

All these things shall be added unto you, and the portion of the addition will be arranged by infallible wisdom. Temporal things will come to you in such proportion as you yourself would desire them if you were able to know all things and could perform a judgment according to infinite wisdom. Would you not prefer a portion selected by the Lord to one chosen by yourself? Do you not joyfully sing with the psalmist, *He shall choose our inheritance for us* (Psalm 47:4)?

Does not the promise also imply that necessary things will come to the believer without distressing worry and consuming labor? While others are worrying, you will be singing. While others rise in the morning and cry out, "How will we live through the day?" you will wake to a secure provision, and you will have a happy enjoyment of it. Your place of defense will be the fortress of rocks. Your bread will be given to you, and your waters will be sure.

Contentment with what you have, and confidence in God, will make life peaceful and happy. A dinner of herbs with contentment will yield a flavor of satisfaction unknown to those who eat the fattened ox (Proverbs 15:17). It is better to be happy than to be rich. Happiness lies in the heart rather than in the wallet. It is not what a man has, but what a man is, that will decide his joy or anguish in this life and the next. If God Himself adds to you the things of this life, then while you are serving Him, the lines will fall to you *in pleasant places*, and you will have *a goodly heritage* (Psalm 16:6).

All these things shall be added unto you reminds me that the acquisition of property and possessions often decreases a man rather than adds to him. Have you not seen a man become visibly smaller as his riches grew greater? It is an awful sight that has often pained me. I have distinctly seen a man become "the architect of his own fortune"[30] and the destroyer of himself. He has built up a palatial estate upon the ruins of his own manhood.

It is a pity when a man bricks himself up with his growing gains. Do you see that hole in the wall? The man stands in it and greedily calls for bricks and mortar. He must have golden bricks and silver mortar. They bring him the materials. He calls out eagerly for more. He cannot be content unless he builds himself in. The wall that shuts him out from his fellow men, and from the light of peace and true joy, rises higher and higher month by month and year by year. His sympathies and character are bricked up. Still he thirsts for more metallic material. At last he is built in, buried beneath his own gatherings, lost to all manhood through his accumulations.

---

30   This phrase is thought to have come from the Roman censor Appius Claudius Caecus (c. 312-279 BC).

CHAPTER 30

THE BUSINESSMAN'S GOOD SERVICE

eek ye first the kingdom of God, and His righteousness (Matthew 6:33). I understand this as referring to the practical part of true religion. Seek to have the imputed righteousness of Christ by all means, but seek also to exhibit the infused righteousness that comes by sanctification. Let us aspire after a high degree of holiness. We are called to be saints. Saints are not miraculous beings to be set up in niches and admired, but they are men and women who live, trade, do righteousness, and practice charity in the streets of a city or in the fields of a village. Those who are washed in the blood of the Lamb should not be satisfied with the common cleanliness of morality, but the garment of their lives should be whiter than any laundryman can make it.

Purity suits the disciples of Jesus. In spirit, soul, and body, we should be holiness to the Lord (Exodus 28:36). Our righteousness must exceed that of the scribes and Pharisees (Matthew 5:20). It should be a reproduction of the character of our Lord.

I understand the phrase *His righteousness* to mean that power in the world that is always working in some form or other for that which is good, true, and pure. Everything in this world that is holy, honest, and of good repute may count upon the Christian as its friend, for it is a part of God's righteousness. Does drunkenness destroy the very life of our nation? Do you need men of temperance to battle this evil? The Christian cries, "Write down my name." When the slave had to be freed, the subjects of God's kingdom were at the forefront in that deed of righteousness. Today, if oppression is to be cast down, we dare not refuse our aid. If the people are to be educated and better housed, we applaud the proposal with delight. If the horrible sin of the period is to be denounced and punished, we may not draw back from the loathsome conflict. Let each man in his own position labor after purity, and as God will help us, we may yet sweep the streets of their shame and deliver our youth from corruption.

Every Christian should say of every struggle for better things, "I am in it, cost what it may." Great numbers of people who profess to be Christian forget to seek God's righteousness, and they seem to think that their main business is to save their own souls – poor little souls that they are! Their religion is barely sufficient to fill up the vacuum within their own ribs, where their hearts should be. This selfishness is not the religion of Jesus. The religion of Jesus is unselfish. It enlists a man as a crusader against everything that is unrighteous. We are knights of the red cross, and our bloodless battles are against all things that degrade our fellow men, whether they are social, political, or religious causes. We fight for everything that is good, true, and just.

True Christianity is spread out and extensive in its operations. I see people drawing lines continually and saying, "This much is religious, and this much is secular." What do you mean? This idea is one that fits with the false ideas of sacred places, priests, shrines, and relics. I do not believe in it. Everything is holy to a person who is holy. To the pure, *all things are pure* (Titus 1:15). To a man who seeks first the kingdom of God and His righteousness, his house is a temple, his meals are sacraments, his garments are vestments, every day is a holy day, and he himself is a priest and a king unto God (Revelation 1:6). The sphere of Christianity is coextensive with daily life. I am not to say, "I serve God when I stand in the pulpit," for that might imply that I wanted to serve the devil when my sermon was over. We are not only to be devout at church and pious at prayer meetings, but we should be devout and godly everywhere.

The Christian religion must not be like a fine piece of medieval armor that is merely hung upon the wall or only worn on state occasions. No; it is a garment for the house, for the shop, and for the bank. Your account books and iron safes are to be made by grace *holiness unto the LORD*.

Godliness is for the dining room and the waiting room, the bank and the store. It can neither be put off nor on. It is of the man and in the man if it is real. Righteousness is a quality of the heart. It abides in the nature of the saved man as a fundamental part of his new self. He who is not always righteous is not righteous.

Undefiled religion is a vital matter. It is in the life of the man. I am afraid that the religion of some people is like the shell of the hermit crab. At sea, the dredge brings up innumerable creeping things, and among them are creatures that have their own natural shells to live in. But here comes a fellow who has annexed the shell of a large snail, and he bears it around as if it were his own. He lives in it while it suits him, and he gives up the shell when it becomes inconvenient. The shell is not part of himself.

Avoid such a religion. Beware of a Sunday shell, and a weekday without the shell. The religion that you can part with, you had better part with. If you can get rid of it, get rid of it. If it is not part and parcel of yourself, it is good for nothing. If it does not run right through you like a silver thread through a piece of embroidery, it will not be adequate for your eternal salvation.

I remember a remark of John Newton, who used to be the clergyman at St. Mary Woolnoth Church. He was a thoroughly Calvinistic preacher, but when someone asked him whether he believed in Calvinism, he replied, "I am a Calvinist, but I do not take it as children eat spoonfuls of sugar. I use it to flavor all my preaching, as men use sugar in tea or food." Hypocrites swallow religion in spoonfuls, inviting all to admire the quantity, but sincere seekers after righteousness quietly dissolve their godliness in their lives and sweeten all their common relationships with it. The real saint flavors his ordinary life with grace so that his wife and his children, his servants and his neighbors, are better for it.

Rowland Hill used to say that a man was not a true Christian if his dog and his cat were not better off for it.[31] That witness is true. A man's religion should be to him what perfume is to a rose, or what light is to the sun. It should be the necessary outcome of his existence. If his life is not fragrant with truth and bright with love, the question arises whether he knows the religion of our Lord Jesus. The division between

---

31   A good biography of Rowland Hill is available from Aneko Press.

sacred and secular is most unhappy to both divisions of life. We need them united again.

In the days of Queen Mary, a foolish person dug up the bones of the wife of the German Protestant Reformer Martin Bucer out of spite. Poor woman! She had done nothing wrong, but had simply married a teacher of the gospel. However, she was dragged from her grave to be buried in a dunghill for that supposedly serious offense. When Elizabeth came to the throne, her bones were buried again, but to make the body secure from any future malice of bigots, our prudent forefathers took the relics of a certain Roman Catholic saint, who was enshrined at Oxford, and mixed the remains of the two deceased persons past all chance of separation. In this way, Mrs. Bucer was secured from further disrespect by her unity with the body of one of the canonized. I want the secular things of life to be secured by union with the sacred things to this same degree.

If we could only feel that our ordinary acts are parts of a saintly life, they would not so often be done carelessly. If we lay our poor daily life by itself, it will be disregarded, but if we combine it with our holiest aspirations and activities, it will be preserved. Our religion must be part and parcel of our daily lives, and then the entirety of our lives will be preserved from the Destroyer. Does not Scripture say, *Whether therefore ye eat, or drink, or whatsoever ye do, do all to the glory of God* (1 Corinthians 10:31)?

"But," someone says, "are we not to have amusements?" Yes, you may have such amusements as you can enjoy in the fear of God. Do whatever Jesus would have done. This is liberty enough for one who desires to be like Jesus. There is happiness enough in things that are pure and right; and if not, we will not do evil to find more. We find pleasure enough without hunting for it in the environment of sin. There are joys that are as far above the pleasures of folly as the feasts of kings are above the husks of swine.

At times, our inner life flames up into a blaze of joy, and if it usually burns lower, there is at least a steady fire of peace upon our hearth that makes our life such that we do not envy anyone. It is not slavery that I set before you when I say that we are first of all to seek the kingdom of

God and His righteousness. There is a present wage that justifies the choice. As for the eternal future, it pleads for it with the voice of thunder.

A far more desirable idea is for a person to rise above his possessions, elevating life upon stepping-stones of these barren gains, building with them a pedestal above which the inner manhood rises.

This is what God intends to do in providence to the man who serves Him wholeheartedly. He will add to him the things of this life. These will be thrown in as supplements to the divine heritage. I incur certain small expenses in connection with my study. We need a few matters that may be paid for out of petty cash, but I have never spent, as far as I can remember, a single penny for string and brown paper. That is because as a reader and writer, I buy books, and then the string and brown paper are added to me. My purchase is the books, but the string and brown paper come to me, added as a matter of course. This is the idea. You are to spend your strength on the high and noble purpose of glorifying God, and then the minor matters of *What shall we eat? or What shall we drink? or Wherewithal shall we be clothed?* are thrown in as supplements (Matthew 6:31). Earthly things are only the brown paper and string, and I hope you never think too much of them.

Some people get so much of this brown paper and string that they glory in them and expect us to fall down and worship them. If we refuse this admiration, they are foolish enough to adore themselves. It must not be so among the servants of God. To us, the man is the man, and not the "guinea's stamp."[32]

All these things are small matters to us. The real life of the soul is all in all. Do not slice pieces out of your manhood and then hope to fill up the vacancies with money. He who loses manliness or godliness to gain gold is a great cheater of himself. Keep yourselves complete for God and for His Christ, and let all other matters be additions, not subtractions. Live above the world. Its goods will come to you when you do not bid high for them.

If you hunt the butterfly of wealth too eagerly, you may harm it by the stroke with which you secure it. When earthly things are sought for as the main object, they are degraded into rubbish, and the seeker

---

32   This is a reference from "A Man's a Man for A' That," a poem by Robert Burns (1759-1796). The "guinea's stamp" refers to the image of a man being on a coin rather than being the man himself.

of them has fallen to be a mere man with a rake for picking up waste, turning over a dunghill to find nothing.

Set your heart on nobler things than self! Cry with David, *I will lift up mine eyes to the hills, from whence cometh my help* (Psalm 121:1). Let us so live that it will be safe for God to add to us the blessings of the life that now is. However, that can only be done safely when we have learned to keep the world under our feet.

CHAPTER 31

HOW GOD WOULD WIN THE HEART

A TALK TO CITY MEN

What has God done to win our hearts? If a father has lost the love of his child, our first question would be, "Can he do anything to get it back?" Our God is always doing much to gain man's heart. *He maketh His sun to rise on the evil and on the good*, and He provides the rain from heaven and gives fruitful seasons (Matthew 5:45). We have much happiness, for this world is not, after all, a prison or a penal colony. We have bright days and resilient spirits. We sometimes rejoice with great joy, and are never quite hopeless.

He who gives us our many mercies says, as He gives them, "Will you not love Me, My child, because these things are given to you? Will you not see My hand and believe in My love?" If God has prospered you in business, if God has spared you the wife of your youth, if He has given you children to laugh upon your knee – then love Him for them. These are His tokens of love as He pursues you to love Him.

Yes, and when He changes His hand and gives us trouble, He still has the same intent and purpose. We have our household idols, and He cannot bear these rivals, for He alone is God. He must have our whole heart, and therefore He removes the idols. From some people, He takes away wealth, for when crushed with the fear of poverty, the soul has often sought its wealth in God, and God has been kinder in taking away than in giving. A dear child is taken home whose curly hair had entangled all our affections, and when she has gone among the angels, we also send our hearts to heaven.

Just as a sheep that will not follow the shepherd is compelled to follow him when the shepherd takes its lamb and carries it in his arms, so has it been with many fathers' hearts. Dear children have been evangelists – gospels in flesh and blood – little messengers of mercy to call us back to our great Father. I am certain that people are not without troubles. There is not one among us who has not had his wintry months and his long nights of darkness. To us, then, as in the visions of the night, God speaks, and He says (see Jeremiah 2:13), "Will you not turn away from the broken cisterns that can hold no water, and drink of Me, the ever-lasting fount of joy and love?" Thus, with pleasing words of gentleness and harsher syllables of trial, He calls for our love.

Also, He has put in all of us a conscience that works to the same purpose. Some have tried to numb their conscience, and it goes to be numb until it is quiet. Conscience will become silent by degrees, yet there is a conscience in us that cries every now and then, "This is not right. This is not right. There is no peace in this way of life. There is no future joy to be hoped for in this way." Conscience rings the alarm bell and knocks at our door, like the watchman at night when the house is on fire. Conscience says to us, "Things will be wrong forever unless there is a change. Awake and seek your God!" Do you hear a still, small voice within you calling you to seek your God (1 Kings 19:12)? Listen to it at once, for it is your life.

Best of all, to win our love, God has unveiled Himself in the Book of inspiration and in the person of His dear Son. The face of God is so supremely beautiful that at the sight of it, angels perpetually adore, and when men behold it, though it is only *through a glass, darkly* (1 Corinthians 13:12), love is inevitable. Dr. Watts has well sung:

> His worth if all the nations knew,
> Sure the whole world would love Him too.[33]

You might ask, "How did He unveil His face?" It was in the person of His only begotten Son, who would rather die Himself than see us die, who out of pure, unselfish love left the throne and the royalty of heaven to descend to the manger and to be made like ourselves, to live in poverty

---

33   These lines are from a hymn by Isaac Watts (1674-1748) that begins with "The wondering world inquires to know."

here and at last to die. Behold, on Calvary, where God Himself bears the consequences of sin that we might escape from them; where Jehovah-Jesus bows His head that was wrapped with a crown of thorns, and gives up the ghost in order that, without any violation of justice, God might extend boundless mercy – it was there that He said, "Men, see what I am! I am the God of love! I am just, but even in My stern justice, I am desirous not to unsheathe the sword or to inflict the penalty upon you if you will simply turn to Me. Give Me now your hearts and accept My love in Jesus Christ, trusting My Son with your souls."

Today the God of love declares an act of amnesty and forgiveness for all the past. No matter how little you may have loved, you may now begin to love, for He will cast your transgressions *into the depths of the sea* (Micah 7:19). No matter how far we have gone into the far-off country, He is willing to hold us close to Him and take us back again as if we had never wandered – yes, and even to rejoice over us as the father in the parable rejoiced over the returning prodigal (Luke 15). If we believe in Jesus as the propitiation for sin, He will say concerning our offenses, "I have cast all their sins behind My back. They will not be remembered against them anymore forever."

And then, to show His love, He sets before us a very simple way of salvation. If you go into a dark room and set before yourself the problem, "How can I get this darkness out?" you will be in a great difficulty. You may go around and ask this puzzle to all your philosophers and thinkers: "How can we pump the darkness out of the room?" However, they will not be able to solve the question. But if a little child comes in and opens the window, the darkness is gone.

Now it would be impossible for us to remove all the sin and enmity that is in the human heart, but the gospel says, "Believe in the love of God as it is revealed in Jesus Christ; trust Him, and all will be light." That opens a window, and the darkness flees at once. The soul has light and peace and begins to love God, not because it should, but because it cannot help loving One who has forgiven so willingly and so freely and has given His own Son for our redemption. Yes, He has given that Son to death itself in order that all the past might once for all be obliterated. It is wonderful what effects accompany a childlike faith in Jesus. The transformations that it works are moral miracles.

Many a man would like to be a child again and stand at his mother's knee where he learned his first prayer. He would like to be laid in the cradle again and have the name of Jesus mingled with the hush of a lullaby. He would like to begin life anew with wiser purposes and nobler aims. But, oh, those dark years that have come in between our childhood and today – those years of wandering and sin! But take courage, for you may begin again. Your dream may be in some sense realized. Behold, the Lord suggests to you that you should be born again – that you should be made new creations in Jesus Christ (2 Corinthians 5:17). He tells you that whosoever will come and trust Christ (for that is faith – simply coming and trusting God in Christ Jesus) will find himself reconciled to God by the death of His Son.

Do not fail to remember that the Lord has promised one other great gift that proves His love by a present blessing: He has given us the promise of His Holy Spirit. Inasmuch as our spirit has become weak and rebellious, He gives His own Divine Spirit to come and dwell within us. Young man, that Holy Spirit will dwell in you, will subdue all wayward passion, and will stir up in you all holy desire until you will be God's living and loving servant as long as you live.

Men of middle age – the Holy Spirit will deliver you from wearying care and greed and worldliness, and will give you higher objects of pursuit. Aged men, that Divine Spirit will dwell in you and develop you for the great day of ingathering and for the heaven that is prepared for believers. The Holy Spirit is indispensable to one and all, but it is written, *If ye then, being evil, know how to give good gifts unto your children: how much more shall your heavenly Father give the Holy Spirit to them that ask Him?* (Luke 11:13).

I hear someone make an excuse. Somebody says, "I know these claims, and I intend to think of them sometime, but I have no time right now." Well, your excuse will not help you, because God has given you time. When He made you and appointed your place, He gave you time, yet you have wasted it or have misused it on lesser things. Remember that your time is not yours; you are only a servant, and you are responsible to your Master for every moment of it. If you happen to be a clerk, and your employer says, "That book is not up-to-date; that account was never made out," you do not say, "I could not spare the time." Your time belongs to him whose servant you are. Our time is not our time, but it is God's time, and the first thing a man has to do is to see that it is properly used.

Besides, doing this does not take any time away from needful pursuits. A man will have just as much time for other pursuits when his main pursuit, which sanctifies all, is the glory of God. Do not tell me you have no time. The most industrious businessmen are also very frequently Christian men, and I have seen men who have found time to teach Sunday school, time to be deacons in our churches, and even time to preach – yet these men are nevertheless among the most diligent in business. If they did neglect their business, they would also be failing, I think, in the service of their God, since there is no sharp line of division to be made between business and Christianity. When rightly viewed, our religion becomes our business, and our business is a living part of our religion. It is troublesome to make a gulf in life between one set of actions and another, for life should be all of one piece. *Whether therefore ye eat, or drink, or whatsoever ye do, do all to the glory of God* (1 Corinthians 10:31).

Somebody found fault with us for praying about politics. I do not know any politics that I will not pray about. I know nothing among men that does not come under the broad heavens of my religion. Even if it is something absolutely wrong, I still may pray against it. Christianity should sit as queen over both politics and business. "Oh, but business is business," they say. I know it is, but business has no business to be such business as it often is. The greatest business of a businessman should be to pay his debts to his God and seek to live to His praise. He can do that and still find time enough to pay his debts to man.

Another person replies as if he had given a conclusive answer: "You see that my heart is wrong. I have a heart that will not love God." Yes – that is the trouble with it, but it is your fault, not your excuse. A man who is charged with theft is brought before a judge, and the excuse the man makes is that somehow or other he could never be honest because he always found his heart so much inclined to wickedness. "I was going to give you a month," says the judge, "but I will give you two after that, because by your own confession, you are thief at heart. Your theft was not a chance action. It is evident that you are a bad fellow, and you had better be kept under lock and key."

When someone says, "My heart is so hard; it is set upon evil," that is a confession of a still greater sin. Having made it, do not use it as an excuse, but look upon it as a reason to humble yourself before God and say, *Create in me a clean heart, O God: and renew a right spirit within me* (Psalm 51:10). These excuses evidently do not hold water even now. What will we do when we have to give our final account?

I was once told that the stock exchange was shut because it was settling day. I do not understand the mysteries of that institution, but I do know that there is a settling day coming to us all. You may feast if you will, but you will have to pay the price. You may rejoice in your youth and your manhood, and spend your time and substance as you please, but He who comes in the clouds of heaven will judge us all (Matthew 24:30).

I wish each person would quietly sit down and say, "I will suppose this is where I will be found at the judgment day." Then look up, and with a little imagination, you can picture the great white throne and hear the last decree proclaimed by the archangel's trumpet. What will you say in that day to this question: "Did you love God with all your heart?"

If you have lived a stranger to the ever-blessed God, you will give no answer except your silence – and that silence will seal your doom. May God grant that you may not still owe your debt in that day, but that you will now be led by the Holy Spirit to repentance of past faults, and to a simple, earnest trust in Jesus – and then you will meet the last summons without a bit of fear!

CHAPTER 32

THE NEED OF A CITY MAN

A philosopher has remarked that if a man knew that he had thirty years of life before him, it would not be an unwise thing to spend twenty of those years in mapping out a plan of living and putting himself under rule, for he would do more with the ten well-arranged years than with the whole thirty if he spent them at random. There is much truth in that saying. A man will not do much by firing off his gun if he has not learned to take aim.

I am possibly addressing some people who have so far lived haphazardly. If so, I invite them to a more hopeful method of living. To have a great many ambitions and intentions is much the same thing as having no aim at all, for if a man shoots at many things, he will hit none, or none worth hitting. It is a great thing to know what we are living for, and to live for a worthy purpose with the undivided energy of our being. When the end comes, will we have made a success of life? Has our purpose been a right one, and has it been rightly pursued? Are the results of our conduct such as we will wish them to have been when the conflict of this mortal life is over? These questions deserve consideration at once.

Another question arises out of them: What place should religion occupy in reference to a person's life? That is a question that naturally arises in the arranging of life, for whatever we choose to think of it, there is such a thing as religion in the world, and there is within us some yearning after spiritual things. We cannot help feeling that we need somewhat more than this visible world can offer us. Many of us find our greatest joy in the cultivation of that feeling, for to us it is the sign of our spiritual nature and the prophecy of immortality. To us this life is mainly worth living because it promises to be the introduction to a better life.

> Alas for love, if thou wert all,
> And nought beyond, O earth![34]

It would be sad if this life were all, and there were not a higher and better state of existence! No ringing of the church bells would be more mournful than that which signified the death of man's hope of immortality.

What position should religion occupy in your life and mine? The answer must depend very much upon another question: What is religion, and what does religion itself demand? What are the requirements of the great God, and of the soul, and of eternity? *Seek ye first the kingdom of God, and His righteousness; and all these things shall be added unto you* (Matthew 6:33).

Needless and excessive anxiety is very common among city men, and it is not rare anywhere. Certain of us are nervous, timid, doubtful, and prone to fear. There are plenty of pessimists around, although they will hardly recognize themselves by that title. To them, something bad is always just ahead. We are about to take a leap in the dark. All their birds are owls or ravens. All their swans are black. If it rains today, it will rain tomorrow, and the next day, and the next, and in all probability there will be a flood. Or if it is fine today, it will be dry tomorrow, and so on for months, and the earth and all the meadows will perish with drought. As for the sun, they observe with pleasing despair that it has spots. They hardly notice its light, but they dwell upon its spots with thoughtful horror. Minds of this sort "find poisons in trees, deaths in the running brooks, dirges in stones, and ill in everything."[35]

I suppose they cannot help it, yet Christian men must help it, for the Lord's command is plain and binding: "Be not therefore anxious" (Matthew 6:25-34).

Fretful anxiety is forbidden to the Christian. It is needless. *Behold*

---

34 These lines are from "The Graves of a Household," a poem by Felicia Hemans (1793-1835).
35 This seems to be based upon a couple lines from William Shakespeare's play *As You Like It* that say, "Finds tongues in trees, books in the running brooks, sermons in stones, and good in everything."

the fowls of the air, said Christ, *for they sow not, neither do they reap, nor gather into barns; yet your heavenly Father feedeth them. Are ye not much better than they?* (Matthew 6:26). If you have a Father in heaven to care for you, are you not put to shame by every little bird that sits upon the branch and sings, even though it does not have two grains of barley in all the world? God takes charge of the fowls of the air, and thus they live free from care. Why do not we?

Our Lord also taught that such anxiety is useless as well as needless, for with all our care, we cannot add a cubit to our stature (Matthew 6:27). Can we do anything else by fretful concern? What if the farmer laments that there is no rain? Do his fears unstop the bottles of heaven? Or if the merchant moans because the wind detains the ship from bringing his merchandise, will his complaining turn the gale to a different direction? We do not better ourselves a bit by all our worry and anger. It would be infinitely wiser to do our best, and then cast our care upon our God (1 Peter 5:7). Prudence is wisdom, for it adapts means to ends, but anxiety is folly, for it groans and worries and accomplishes nothing.

Besides, according to our Savior, anxiety about worldly things is what the unbelievers do: *After all these things do the Gentiles seek* (Matthew 6:32). They have no God and no providence, and therefore they try to be a providence to themselves. As for the man of God who can say, "God's providence is my inheritance," why should he despair because of trouble? Let the heir of heaven act a nobler part than the mere man of the world who has his portion in this life and who lives without God and without hope.

Our distrust of God is childish and dishonoring. I was going through the streets one day, driven by a friend in a four-wheeled coach, and he, being a good driver, needed to drive into narrow places, where it seemed to me that we would be crushed by the wagons and other large vehicles. I hesitated in my timidity and expressed my unwise alarms quite freely. With a smile, he placed the reins in my hand and said, "If you cannot trust me, would you like to drive yourself?" I was entirely free from that ambition, and I assured him that he could drive as he liked rather than make me the driver.

Certainly our great God could well put the same proposal to those who are complaining of His providence. If we cannot trust Him, could we manage better ourselves? If we are men in Christ, let us believe in our God. Let us leave the governance of the great world outdoors, and of the little world within our own gates, to the Lord God, our heavenly Father, who will surely cause all things to work together for good to those who love Him (Romans 8:28).

It is clear that within us there is a propensity to be anxious. Can we not utilize it? Can we not put it to use for us? I think so. Some people are naturally thoughtful and careful; can they not transform this tendency into a benefit? We have a tendency to be anxious. Very well, then, let us be anxious – but let our anxiety run in the right direction. This is a mental excitement; let us apply it to some useful purpose. *Seek ye first the kingdom of God, and His righteousness.* Seek that with all your care. Seek that with all your energy. Be anxious about that. Let your whole mind run in that direction with eagerness and thought. You cannot be too careful or too energetic when God and righteousness are concerned.

True religion: what is it? Without using a single unnecessary theological term, I can answer that true religion is *the kingdom of God.* I may say that the great God has always had a kingdom in this world. In previous times, He set up a kingdom among His people Israel, to whom He gave laws and statutes, but now the Lord is King over all the world: *The God of the whole earth shall He be called* (Isaiah 54:5). *The earth is the Lord's, and the fulness thereof; the world, and they that dwell therein* (Psalm 24:1).

God has a kingdom in this world, but it is too much neglected and forgotten by men. The first thing to be done by us is to enter that kingdom. Blessed is that man who has the Lord God to be his King, and has learned to arrange his life according to divine law. The highest liberty comes from wearing the yoke of God. The servant of men who dares not call his soul his own is a servant to be pitied, but the servant of God, who fears nothing but sin, is a man of princely character. We must bow before God so that we may conquer among men. If we determine to surrender ourselves entirely to the Lord, we will become influential among our fellow men.

We can only enter into this kingdom of God by being born again of His Spirit, for *except a man be born again, he cannot see the kingdom of God* (John 3:3). In that new birth, we learn to submit ourselves to the Lord Jesus Christ and to find eternal life in Him. God has appointed the Lord

Jesus *heir of all things*; by Him also He *made the worlds* (Hebrews 1:2). He says of Him, *Kiss the Son, lest He be angry, and ye perish from the way, when His wrath is kindled but a little* (Psalm 2:12). Faith in Christ casts our sins at the foot of His cross and brings us an inward life unto holiness. We must believe in Jesus and trust in His great atonement for sin, for apart from His full atonement, there is no salvation and no true service of God. This faith puts us into the kingdom of God, for to *as many as received Him, to them gave He power to become the sons of God, even to them that believe on His name* (John 1:12). The first concern of every person should be to be a loyal subject of the kingdom of God.

When we feel that we are reconciled to God and are under His supreme control, our next goal should be to continue there and to become more and more completely obedient to divine rule so that we may more fully enjoy every privilege of the kingdom. In the kingdom of God, every man is a king and a priest (Revelation 1:6; 5:10). He who serves God reigns. He who serves God is the possessor of all things. All things are ours when we are Christ's.

> This world is ours, and worlds to come:
> Earth is our lodge, and heaven our home.[36]

Let the Christian seek to know to the fullest what is the heritage of the saints in Christ Jesus.

Our next business should be to spread that kingdom – to try to bring others under the dominion of Christ. It should be the lifework of each person to bring others to confess the sovereignty of the Lord Jesus. What opportunities most of you possess! Your position, your education, and your wealth all give you advantages for serving the Lord. Are you using them?

It is a great joy to the Christian minister to have people around him who are missionaries in their daily lives. With great joy I have listened to some poor girl who has confessed her faith in Christ, and then has added very timidly, "There is another girl waiting outside who would like to speak to you. She works with me in a warehouse in the city,

---

36   These lines come from a hymn by Isaac Watts (1674-1748) that begins with "How vast the treasure we possess!"

and I spoke to her. She sought Jesus, and I believe she is converted."
I am afraid that many people who run a business are less diligent in
winning souls than the poor workers they employ. Should it be so? He
lives most and lives best who is the means of imparting spiritual life
to others. May not some of you eventually come to a lonely end from
lack of usefulness?

Not long ago, we heard of the shipwreck from which a mother
was washed on shore, but all her children were found drowned.[37] She
telegraphed to her husband two words. The first was very pleasing to
his eye: "Saved." The next was full of misery: "alone." Would you or I
like to have it so – "Saved alone"? God forbid. When we reach heaven's
gate, may we be able to say, "Here am I, and the children that You have
given me" (Isaiah 8:18).

This is the meaning of seeking the kingdom of God. The reign of
our Lord is to be our main objective if we desire to lead a well-ordered,
useful, happy, and honored life.

---

37   This telegraph in 1873 was from Anna Spafford to Horatio Spafford, the author of the hymn
     "It Is Well with My Soul." The children who drowned were all daughters – aged twelve,
     seven, four, and eighteen months.

CHAPTER 33

BLESS THE LADS

And he blessed Joseph, and said, God, before whom my fathers Abraham and Isaac did walk, the God which fed me all my life long unto this day, the Angel which redeemed me from all evil, bless the lads; and let my name be named on them, and the name of my fathers Abraham and Isaac; and let them grow into a multitude in the midst of the earth.
(Genesis 48:15-16)

Joseph was one by himself. In Jacob's family, he was like a swan in a duck's nest. He seemed to be of a different type from the rest, even from his childhood. He was the son of old age, the son of the elders; that is, he was a child who was mature in thoughtfulness and devotion when he was young. He reached an early ripeness that did not end in early decay.

In consequence of this, Joseph was one by himself in the nature of his trials. Through his brothers' hatred of him, he was made to suffer greatly, and at last he was sold into slavery and underwent trials in Egypt of the severest kind. *The archers have sorely grieved him, and shot at him, and hated him* (Genesis 49:23). Notice the recompense, though, for he had blessings that were entirely his own. *His bow abode in strength, and the arms of his hands were made strong by the hands of the mighty God of Jacob* (Genesis 49:24). He was as distinguished by the favor of God as by the disfavor of his brethren.

When Jacob was old and about to die, Joseph gave him a blessing all to himself, in addition to that which he received with his brothers. In the forty-ninth chapter of Genesis, we read, *Gather yourselves together, and hear, ye sons of Jacob; and hearken unto Israel your father* (Genesis 49:2). They did so, and they received as a family such blessings as their father's prophetic eye foresaw. Before this, however, *by faith Jacob, when he was dying, blessed both the sons of Joseph* (Hebrews 11:21) at a private meeting granted specifically to them (Genesis 48:15-22).

If his adversity had not so abounded, his consolations would not have so abounded. Do you seem yourself to be marked out for special sorrows? Do the arrows of affliction make your life their target, and are you disciplined above all other people? Do not be regretful, for the arrows are sent by covenant love, which intends by their wounds to prepare you for a special work that will lead up to a special blessing from your Father who is in heaven.

Jacob blessed Joseph, and we understand that he blessed him through blessing his children. Joseph is doubly blessed by seeing Ephraim and Manasseh blessed. Dear young people, your fathers can say, "We have no greater joy than that our children walk in the truth" (3 John 1:4). If any of you who are unconverted knew your parents' deep searching of heart about you, I do not think that you would be careless and indifferent about divine things very long. If you could imagine the flashes of heavenly joy that would light up your parents' hearts if they saw you saved in the Lord, it would help persuade you to consider your ways and turn unto the Lord with full purpose of heart. Next to giving to His chosen the covenant of grace, God Himself can do no greater earthly kindness to them than to call their children by His grace into the same covenant. Will you not think of this?

Young men and women usually feel great interest in their father's life story (if it is a worthy one), and what they hear from them about their personal experience of the goodness of God will stay with them. We all read biographies, and we value the results of experience that we find there, but the biographies of our own relatives are especially treasured. When these biographies are not read, but spoken, what wonderful force they have!

I remember in my younger days hearing a minister, blind with age, speak at the communion table. He bore witness to us young people who had just joined the church that it was good for us that we had come to put our trust in a faithful God. As the good man, with great feebleness, yet with great earnestness, told us that he had never regretted having given his heart to Christ as a boy, I felt my heart leap within me with delight that I had such a God to be my God. His testimony was one that a younger man could not have given. He might have spoken more fluently, but the weight of those eighty years behind it made the old man eloquent to my young heart.

We who are growing gray in our Master's service should not be hesitant to speak well of His name. You will not be able to do as much good in heaven as you can on earth, for they all know about it up there; but people here need our witness to the God whom we have tested and proved. Let us make opportunities to speak well of the Lord, even the God who has fed us our entire lives and has redeemed us from all evil. This is one of the best ways in which to bless the children. The benediction of Jacob was intertwined with his biography. The blessing that he had himself enjoyed, he wanted for them, and as he invoked it, he helped to secure it by his personal testimony.

One more thing I want you to see is that Jacob, in desiring to bless his grandsons, introduced them to God. He speaks of *God, before whom my fathers Abraham and Isaac did walk, the God which fed me all my life long unto this day* (Genesis 48:15). This is the great distinction between man and man. There are two types of people: he who fears God, and he who does not fear Him.

The religion of this present age, such as it is, has a wrong direction in its course. It seeks after what is called "the enthusiasm of humanity," but what we need far more is enthusiasm for God. We will never go right unless God is first, middle, and last. I despair for benevolence when it is not based upon devotion. We will not long have love for others if we do not first and primarily develop love to God.

What boys need in starting out in life is God. If we have nothing else to give them, they have enough if they have God. What girls need in leaving the nurture of home is God's love in their hearts, and then it is a small matter whether they have fortunes or not. The essence of true human life lies in fellowship with God. Life in God, life by the knowledge of the Most High, life through the Redeeming Angel – this is life indeed.

Jacob died as one who had been delivered from all evil – even the evil of old age. His eyes were dim, but that did not matter, for his faith was clear. I love to think that we are going where our vision of God will not be through the eye, but through the spiritual understanding. These were brighter in Jacob in his old age than ever before. His faith and love, which are the earthly forms of those perceptions, were discerning God in a more powerful manner than ever, and it therefore signified little that the eyes that he would need no longer were failing him.

We cannot say that he was in decay, after all, for he was losing what he only needed in this world of shadows, and was getting ready for the higher state. His spiritual perception grew as his bodily capabilities declined, and therefore he felt that his life was ending in a fullness of blessing such as he desired for the children of his dearest son. How earnestly I desire a similar blessing for all young people! May the Lord God Almighty bless you! When your earthly abilities fail, may heavenly graces more than supply their place!

God, before whom my fathers Abraham and Isaac did walk (Genesis 48:15). As with a pencil, he sketches the lives of Abraham and Isaac. He does not fill it in with coloring, but the outline is perfect; you see the two men in their entire career in those few words. They were men who recognized God and worshipped Him beyond all others of their age. God was a real existence to them. They spoke with God, and God spoke with them. They were friends of God, and enjoyed close acquaintance with Him. No agnosticism blinded their understandings and deadened their hearts. They were worshippers of the one living and true God. They are happy children who have such fathers, and even happier children who are like those fathers!

They not only recognized God, but they acknowledged Him in daily life. I take the expression, *God, before whom my fathers Abraham and Isaac did walk*, to mean that He was their God in everyday life. They not only knelt before God when they prayed, but they walked before Him in everything. When they went forth from their tents and when they returned from their flocks, they walked before God. They were never away from His service or without His presence. He was their dwelling place. Whether they stopped under an oak tree or stayed by a well, whether they entertained strangers or walked in the field to meditate, they lived and moved in God.

This is the kind of life for you and for me. Whether we live in a huge house or in a poor cottage, if we walk before God, we will live a happy and a noble life, whether that life is public or unknown. Oh, that our young people would strongly believe this!

They walked before God. That is, they obeyed His commands. They heard His call and they followed His commands. Abraham left his country and kindred to go to an unknown land that God would show him. Even more, he took his son, whom he greatly loved, and stood prepared to sacrifice him at God's command. Isaac also yielded himself up to be slain if Jehovah so willed. To them, the will of the Lord was most important. He was law and life to them, for they loved and feared Him. They were quick to hear the words of God, and they rose up early to obey them. They lived as if they were always in the immediate presence of the All-seeing.

They trusted Him completely. In this sense, they always saw Him. We talk about following Him. We cannot follow Him except as we trust Him. Because they trusted Him, they followed Him. Notwithstanding all the danger and difficulty of their pilgrim state, they lived in perfect security in an enemy's land, for the Lord had said, *Touch not Mine anointed, and do My prophets no harm* (Psalm 105:15). They were calm and restful because they walked before God, knowing Him to be their friend (2 Chronicles 20:7; Isaiah 41:8; James 2:23) and knowing that He was their shield and their *exceeding great reward* (Genesis 15:1). They had no anxiety in regard to material things, for they depended upon the All-sufficient God. Therefore, these two men, Abraham and Isaac, though much tested and tried, led peaceful lives. They conversed with heaven while they sojourned on earth.

They enjoyed the favor of God, for this also is intended by walking before Him. His face was toward them. They sunned themselves in His smile. God's love was their true treasure. We read that God had blessed Abraham in all things, and of Isaac we hear even the Philistines say, *We saw certainly that the LORD was with thee* (Genesis 26:28). God was their wealth, their strength, and their exceeding joy. I say again, they are happy sons who have such ancestors, and they are happier still if they follow in their path!

Jacob spoke of Abraham and Isaac, and some of us can speak of those who went before us. Those of us who can look back upon godly ancestors who are now in heaven must feel that many ties bind us to follow the same course of life. If they had transgressed against the Lord, our duty would have caused us to quit the ways of the family, even as Abraham left his kindred who dwelt on the other side of the flood; but since their way was right, we are doubly called to follow it because it is the good old way and it is the way our godly fathers walked.

There is a charm about those things that were prized by our fathers. Heirlooms are treasured, and the best heirloom in a family is the knowledge of God. When I spoke the other day with a Christian brother, he seemed very happy to tell me that he came from a family that came from Holland during the persecution of the Duke of Alva, and I felt a brotherhood with him in claiming a similar descent. I dare to say that our fathers were poor weavers, but I would much rather be descended from someone who suffered for the faith than have the blood of all the emperors within my veins. There should be a sacredness to young people in the faith for which their ancestors suffered.

Do not choose the society of Egypt with its wealth and honors, but keep to the line of Israel and claim the inheritance of Jacob, as Ephraim and Manasseh did. Do not let it be said that as your family increased in riches, it departed from the living God. Will the goodness of God be twisted into a reason for apostasy?

The way of holiness in which your fathers went is a good way for you, and it is right that you maintain the godly traditions of your house. In the old times, they expected sons to follow the secular calling of their fathers, and although that may be regarded as an old-world mistake, yet it is good when sons and daughters receive the same spiritual call as their parents. Grace is not tied to families, but still the Lord delights to bless *to a thousand generations* (Deuteronomy 7:9).

We are very far from believing that the new birth is of blood, or of the will of the flesh, or of the will of man. The will of God reigns here supreme and absolute, yet there is a sweet appropriateness in passing on the holy loyalty from grandfather to father and from father to son. I like to feel that I serve God *from my forefathers* (2 Timothy 1:3). If our fathers were wrong, we should boldly dissent from them and *obey God rather than men* (Acts 5:29). However, where they are right, we are obligated to follow them.

I stood in a sort of dream as I gazed upon my much-beloved grandfather's grave. I was encouraged by seeing the record of his fifty-four years of service in the midst of one church and people. I rejoiced that if he could rise from the dead, he would find his grandson preaching that very same old-fashioned and much despised Calvinistic doctrine of the grace of God, which was his joy in life and his comfort in death.

A godly ancestry casts responsibility upon young people. These Ephraims and Manassehs recognize that their fathers knew the Lord, and the question arises why they should not know Him. Beloved young friends, the God of your fathers desires to be found by you and wants to be your God. The prayers of your fathers have gone before you. Let them be followed by your own. Be hopeful of being heard at that mercy seat where they found grace to help in every time of need (Hebrews 4:16). They died in the hope that you would fill their places. Will not that hope become fact?

Do I speak to some who have godly parents in heaven, yet who are themselves pursuing the ways of sin or of worldliness? Registered upon that file are your mother's prayers. I trust they will yet be heard. Even now they stand like a hedge around you, making it hard work for you to go to hell. Will you force your way to the lake of fire over your father's grave? Will you, by a desperate effort, push aside your pleading mother's figure and pursue your dreadful road to ruin? If so, you will involve yourselves in tremendous guilt and regret. I plead with you to hear the tender voice of love that now invites you to be blessed!

A godly ancestry should fill a person's situation with great hopefulness. He can argue, "If God blessed my ancestors, why should He not bless me? If they sought mercy and found it, why should not I? My father and my mother were not perfect any more than I am, but they had faith in God, and He accepted them and helped them. If I have faith in God, He will accept me and will be faithful to me. They were saved as sinners trusting in the blood of Jesus, and why should not I?" I beg you to put this argument to the test, and you will find it to hold true.

CHAPTER 34

JACOB, A YOUNG WORKING MAN

Jacob had been a shepherd, and therefore he knew what shepherding included. The illustration is full of meaning. There had been a good deal of Jacob about Jacob, and he had tried to shepherd himself. Poor sheep that he was, while under his own guidance he had been caught in many thorns and had wandered in many wildernesses. Because he so much wanted to be a shepherd to himself, he had put much effort into it. But overall, despite his obstinance, the shepherding of the covenant God had been exercised toward him, and he acknowledged it.

Our version rightly says that the Lord had fed Jacob all his life long: *God, before whom my fathers Abraham and Isaac did walk, the God which fed me all my life long unto this day* (Genesis 48:15). Take that sense of it, and you who have a daily struggle for your daily bread will see much beauty in it. Jacob had a large family, yet they were fed. Some of you say, "It is all very well of you who only have a few people to provide for to talk of God's providence." I answer that it is better still to talk of God's providence where a large household requires large provision.

Remember that Jacob had thirteen children, yet his God provided them bread to eat and clothing to put on. None of that large company were left to starve. You might think that Jacob was a man of much wealth. He was not so when he began life. He was only a working man, a shepherd. When he left his father's house, he did not have any attendants with camels and tents. I suppose he carried his little bit of provision in a handkerchief, and when he laid down that night to sleep, with a stone for his pillow, the hedges for curtains, the heavens for his canopy, and the ground for his bed, he had no fear of being robbed. God was with him. Apart from this, he had nothing to begin life with except his own hands. Whatever he later received from his father Isaac, he first had to fight his own way. However, he knew no lack either at the beginning or at the end, for he could speak of the great Elohim as *the God which fed me all my life long.*

Hundreds of us can say the same thing. I remember one man who came to be wealthy who used to show me with great pleasure the axle of the cart that he previously used to wheel his goods through the streets when he began in business. I liked to see him aware of his beginnings. Do not go out and say, "See how I have been successful by my own talents and hard work!" Do not talk so proudly, but say, "God has fed me." Mercies are all the sweeter when they are seen as coming from the hand of God.

Besides being fed, Jacob had been led, even as sheep are guided by the shepherd who goes before them. His journeys for that period had been unusually long, perilous, and frequent. He had fled from home to Padanaram. After many years, he had returned to Canaan and had met with his brother Esau. After that, in his old age, he had journeyed into Egypt. To go to California or New Zealand in these times is nothing at all compared to those journeys in Jacob's day, but he says, "God has shepherded me all my life long." He means that the great changes of life had been wisely ordered. At home and in exile, in Canaan and in Goshen, God had been a shepherd to him. He sees the good hand of God upon him in all his wanderings, and he now finds himself sitting up on his bed and blessing Joseph through his sons. I am glad that he went into detail with these young men, for they needed to be confirmed in their commitment to God. They were in a perilous condition, for they had been introduced to the abundance and culture of Egypt, and were tempted to forsake the poor family of the Hebrews.

Some young fellows begin where their fathers left off. Having the means of self-indulgence, they are inclined to follow the ways and light-heartedness of the period. Oh, that the Holy Spirit would make you feel that you need God with wealth as much as your fathers needed God without wealth! You may still come to poverty with all your inheritance if you cast off the fear of the Lord and fall into sin. You who begin life with nothing but your own brains and hands, trusting in your father's God, will yet have to sing as your fathers sang, *the God which fed me all my life long*.

Young men and young women beginning life, I urge you to seek first *the kingdom of God and His righteousness*! It is not life to live without God. You miss the heart, the cream, the crown of life if you miss the presence of God. Without God, life is only a bubble that is filled with toil and trouble. Life ends in broken hope if you do not have hope in God. With God, though, you are as a sheep with a shepherd. You are cared for, guided, guarded, fed, and led, and your end will be peace without end.

Bear with me while I follow Jacob in his word about redeeming mercies: *The Angel which redeemed me from all evil* (Genesis 48:16). There was a mysterious Person who was God, and yet was the Angel or messenger of God. He puts this Angel in harmony with the Elohim, for this Angel was God – yet He was his Redeemer. He saw Him performing the role of the next of kin. Although He was God, He was also Jacob's *goel*, or redeemer, and as His kinsman, He brought about redemption for him.

Like Job, Jacob's faith enabled him to know that his Redeemer lives (Job 19:25). He saw that this covenant messenger had redeemed him from all evil, and he magnified the name of the Lord who revealed Himself in this Angel. When he was in his most distressing difficulties, this redeeming Angel always interposed. Jacob fell into a bad situation through the influence of his mother, and he did Esau serious wrong. He fled for his life, and at that time there was a great gulf between him and God. Then that Angel came in and bridged the gulf with a ladder by which he might rise to God (Genesis 28). The kinsman, God, came in, and showed him how the abyss could be crossed so that he could return to his God. When he was away in Padanaram, he began to sink very low while negotiating with harsh Laban. Then again the Angel came and said, *Get thee out from this land, and return unto the land of thy kindred* (Genesis 31:13).

The Redeeming Angel held back wrathful Laban, and when Esau came to meet him in fierce anger, the Angel specifically appeared to Jacob. The Angel wrestled, as a Man, with Jacob to get Jacob out of Jacob, and to raise him into Israel (Genesis 32). How marvelous was the redemption that was worked for him that night at Jabbok! Jacob came forth from the conflict limping, but he walked before the Lord far better than before. With the promise that He would go down with him, that same mysterious Person had told him to go down into Egypt. It was the presence of the Angel of God who held His shield over Jacob and preserved him from all evil.

Jacob has spoken of ancestral mercies, personal mercies, and redeeming mercies, and now he deals with future mercies as he cries, *Bless the lads* (Genesis 48:16). He began by blessing Joseph, and he finished by blessing Joseph's sons. Dear friends, if God has blessed you, I know you will want Him to bless others. There is the stream of mercy that is deep, broad, and clear. You have drunk of it, and you are refreshed, but it is as full as ever. It will flow on, will it not? You do not suppose that you and I have dammed up the stream so as to keep it to ourselves, do you? No, it is too strong and too full of a stream for that. It will flow on from age to age. God will bless others as He has blessed us.

Unbelief whispers that the true church will die out. Do not believe it. Christ will live, and His church will live with Him until the heavens are no more. Has He not said, *Because I live, ye shall live also* (John 14:19)? "Oh," you say, "but we will not see such holy men in the next generation as in past ages." Why not? I hope the next age will see far better men than any of those who are with us at this time. Pray that it may be so. Instead of the fathers, may there be the children, and may these be princes before the Lord!

The stream of divine grace will flow on. Oh, that it may take sons and daughters in its path! *Bless the lads.* Sunday-school teachers, is not that a good prayer for you? Ask the Lord to bless the boys and the girls because He has blessed you.

We do not need to say in what precise form or way the blessing will come. Let us leave it in all its breadth of inconceivable blessing. May the Lord bless our youth as only He can, and if He causes them to fear and trust Him, He will be blessing all of us, as well as blessing ages to come. The work of the Lord will depend upon these Ephraims and Manassehs in the years to come! Therefore, we pray with emphasis, *Bless the lads.* As for us, we are content to continue working, saying, *Let Thy work appear unto Thy servants*, but our fervent desire is that our children may reap the result of our labors; therefore we add, *and Thy glory unto their children* (Psalm 90:16).

In Essex, I took the opportunity to visit the place where my grandfather preached so long, and where I spent my earliest days. I walked like a man in a dream. Everybody seemed bound to recall some event or other of my childhood. What a story of divine love and mercy it brought before my mind! Among other things, I sat down in a place that will always be sacred to me. There stood in my grandfather's parsonage garden two arbors made of yew trees, cut into sugarloaf fashion. Although the old parsonage has given way to a new one, and the old chapel has gone also, the yew trees still flourish as before. I sat down in the right-hand arbor and reminisced about what had happened there many years ago.

When I was staying with my grandfather, Mr. Knill came to preach in the village. He had been a missionary in St. Petersburg and was a mighty preacher of the gospel. He came to preach for the London Missionary Society, and he arrived on Saturday at the parsonage. He was a great soul winner, and he soon noticed the boy. He said to me, "Where do you sleep, for I want to wake you up in the morning and talk with you."

I showed him my little room. At six o'clock, he called for me to get up, and we went into that arbor. There, in the sweetest way, he told me of the love of Jesus and of the blessedness of trusting in Him and loving Him in our childhood. With many stories, he preached Christ to me, and he told me how good God had been to him. Then he prayed that I might know the Lord and serve Him. He knelt down in that arbor and prayed for me with his arm around my neck. He did not seem content unless I was with him in the interval between the services, and he heard my childish talk with patient love.

On Monday morning, he did as he had done on Sunday, and again on Tuesday. Three times he taught me and prayed with me. Before he had to leave, my grandfather had come back from the place where he had gone to preach, and all the family members were gathered for morning prayer. Then, in the presence of them all, Mr. Knill took me on his knee and said, "This child will one day preach the gospel, and he will preach it to great multitudes. I am persuaded that he will preach in the chapel of Rowland Hill, where (I think he said) I am now the minister."

He spoke very solemnly, and he called upon all present to witness what he said. Then he gave me a coin as a reward if I would learn the hymn:

> God moves in a mysterious way
> His wonders to perform.[38]

I was made to promise that when I preached in Rowland Hill's chapel, that hymn would be sung. Think of that as a promise from a child! Would it ever be other than an empty dream? Years flew by. After I had begun to preach in London for a little while, Dr. Alexander Fletcher was to give the annual sermon to children in Surrey Chapel, but he got sick, and I was asked without much notice to preach to the children. "Yes," I said. "I will if the children will sing 'God Moves in a Mysterious Way.' I made a promise long ago that the song would be sung."

And so it was. I preached in Rowland Hill's chapel, and the hymn was sung. I cannot describe my emotions on that occasion. Still, that was not the chapel that Mr. Knill intended. Without me seeking the opportunity, the minister at Wotton-under-Edge, which was Mr. Hill's summer residence, invited me to preach there. I went on the condition that the congregation would sing "God Moves in a Mysterious Way," and this was also done. After that I went to preach for Mr. Knill himself, who was then at Chester. What a meeting we had! Notice this – he was preaching in a theater, and his preaching in a theater took away from me all fear about preaching in secular buildings – it set me free for the campaigns in Exeter Hall and the Surrey Music Hall. This was significant in me overcoming my fear of then speaking in even more theater services.

> God moves in a mysterious way
> His wonders to perform.

After more than forty years of the Lord's loving-kindness, I sat again in that arbor! No doubt it is not as impressive for outsiders to hear, but to me it was an overwhelming moment. The current minister of Stambourne Meetinghouse, along with the members of his family,

---

38   These are the opening lines from a hymn by William Cowper (1731-1800).

including his son and his grandchildren, were in the garden, and I could not help calling them together around that arbor while I praised the Lord for His goodness.

An irresistible impulse was upon me to ask God to bless those boys who stood around me. Do you not see how the memory prompted the prayer? When they grow up, I want them to remember my testimony of God's goodness to me, and for that same reason I tell it to young people. God has blessed me all my life long and has redeemed me from all evil, and I pray that He may be your God!

I would especially address you who have godly parents. I urge you to follow in their footsteps so that you may one day speak of the Lord as they were able to do in their day. Remember that special promise: *I love them that love Me; and those that seek Me early shall find Me* (Proverbs 8:17).

May the Holy Spirit lead you to seek Him, and you will live to praise His name as Jacob did!

CHARLES H. SPURGEON - A BRIEF BIOGRAPHY

Charles Haddon Spurgeon was born on June 19, 1834, in Kelvedon, Essex, England. He was one of seventeen children in his family (nine of whom died in infancy). His father and grandfather were Nonconformist ministers in England. Due to economic difficulties, eighteen-month-old Charles was sent to live with his grandfather, who helped teach Charles the ways of God. Later in life, Charles remembered looking at the pictures in *Pilgrim's Progress* and in *Foxe's Book of Martyrs* as a young boy.

Charles did not have much of a formal education and never went to college. He read much throughout his life though, especially books by Puritan authors.

Even with godly parents and grandparents, young Charles resisted giving in to God. It was not until he was fifteen years old that he was born again. He was on his way to his usual church, but when a heavy snowstorm prevented him from getting there, he turned in at a little Primitive Methodist chapel. Though there were only about fifteen people in attendance, the preacher spoke from Isaiah 45:22: *Look unto me, and be ye saved, all the ends of the earth.* Charles Spurgeon's eyes were opened and the Lord converted his soul.

He began attending a Baptist church and teaching Sunday school. He soon preached his first sermon, and then when he was sixteen years old, he became the pastor of a small Baptist church in Cambridge. The church soon grew to over four hundred people, and Charles Spurgeon, at the age of nineteen, moved on to become the pastor of the New Park Street Church in London. The church grew from a few hundred attenders to a few thousand. They built an addition to the church, but still needed more room to accommodate the congregation. The Metropolitan Tabernacle was built in London in 1861, seating more than 5,000 people. Pastor Spurgeon preached the simple message of the cross, and thereby attracted many people who wanted to hear God's Word preached in the power of the Holy Spirit.

On January 9, 1856, Charles married Susannah Thompson. They had twin boys, Charles and Thomas. Charles and Susannah loved each other deeply, even amidst the difficulties and troubles that they faced in life, including health problems. They helped each other spiritually, and often together read the writings of Jonathan Edwards, Richard Baxter, and other Puritan writers.

Charles Spurgeon was a friend of all Christians, but he stood firmly on the Scriptures, and it didn't please all who heard him. Spurgeon believed in and preached on the sovereignty of God, heaven and hell, repentance, revival, holiness, salvation through Jesus Christ alone, and the infallibility and necessity of the Word of God. He spoke against worldliness and hypocrisy among Christians, and against Roman Catholicism, ritualism, and modernism.

One of the biggest controversies in his life was known as the "Down-Grade Controversy." Charles Spurgeon believed that some pastors of his time were "down-grading" the faith by compromising with the world or the new ideas of the age. He said that some pastors were denying the inspiration of the Bible, salvation by faith alone, and the truth of the Bible in other areas, such as creation. Many pastors who believed what Spurgeon condemned were not happy about this, and Spurgeon eventually resigned from the Baptist Union.

Despite some difficulties, Spurgeon became known as the "Prince of Preachers." He opposed slavery, started a pastors' college, opened an orphanage, led in helping feed and clothe the poor, had a book fund for pastors who could not afford books, and more.

Charles Spurgeon remains one of the most published preachers in history. His sermons were printed each week (even in the newspapers), and then the sermons for the year were re-issued as a book at the end of the year. The first six volumes, from 1855-1860, are known as *The Park Street Pulpit*, while the next fifty-seven volumes, from 1861-1917 (his sermons continued to be published long after his death), are known as *The Metropolitan Tabernacle Pulpit*. He also oversaw a monthly magazine-type publication called *The Sword and the Trowel,* and Spurgeon wrote many books, including *Lectures to My Students, All of Grace, Around the Wicket Gate, Advice for Seekers, John Ploughman's Talks, The Soul Winner, Words of Counsel for Christian Workers, Cheque Book of the Bank of Faith, Morning and Evening*, his autobiography, and more, including some commentaries, such as his twenty-year study on the Psalms – *The Treasury of David*.

Charles Spurgeon often preached ten times a week, preaching to an estimated ten million people during his lifetime. He usually preached from only one page of notes, and often from just an outline. He read about six books each week. During his lifetime, he had read *The Pilgrim's Progress* through more than one hundred times. When he died, his personal library consisted of more than 12,000 books. However, the Bible always remained the most important book to him.

Spurgeon was able to do what he did in the power of God's Holy Spirit because he followed his own advice – he met with God every morning before meeting with others, and he continued in communion with God throughout the day.

Charles Spurgeon suffered from gout, rheumatism, and some depression, among other health problems. He often went to Menton, France, to recuperate and rest. He preached his final sermon at the Metropolitan Tabernacle on June 7, 1891, and died in France on January 31, 1892, at the age of fifty-seven. He was buried in Norwood Cemetery in London.

Charles Haddon Spurgeon lived a life devoted to God. His sermons and writings continue to influence Christians all over the world.

OTHER SIMILAR TITLES

WORDS OF WARNING,
BY CHARLES H. SPURGEON

This book, *Words of Warning*, is an analysis of people and the gospel of Christ. Under inspiration of the Holy Spirit, Charles H. Spurgeon sheds light on the many ways people may refuse to come to Christ, but he also shines a brilliant light on how we can be saved. Unsaved or wavering individuals will be convicted, and if they allow it, they will be led to Christ. Sincere Christians will be happy and blessed as they consider the great salvation with which they have been saved.

Available where books are sold.

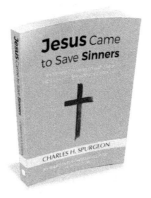

JESUS CAME TO SAVE SINNERS, BY CHARLES H. SPURGEON

This is a heart-level conversation with you, the reader. Every excuse, reason, and roadblock for not coming to Christ is examined and duly dealt with. If you think you may be too bad, or if perhaps you really are bad and you sin either openly or behind closed doors, you will discover that life in Christ is for you too. You can reject the message of salvation by faith, or you can choose to live a life of sin after professing faith in Christ, but you cannot change the truth as it is, either for yourself or for others. As such, it behooves you and your family to embrace truth, claim it for your own, and be genuinely set free for now and eternity. Come and embrace this free gift of God, and live a victorious life for Him.

Available where books are sold.

ACCORDING TO PROMISE,
BY CHARLES H. SPURGEON

The first part of this book is meant to be a sieve to separate the chaff from the wheat. Use it on your own soul. It may be the most profitable and beneficial work you have ever done. He who looked into his accounts and found that his business was losing money was saved from bankruptcy.

The second part of this book examines God's promises to His children. The promises of God not only exceed all precedent, but they also exceed all imitation. No one has been able to compete with God in the language of liberality. The promises of God are as much above all other promises as the heavens are above the earth.

Available where books are sold.

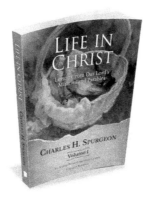

LIFE IN CHRIST (VOL. 1), BY CHARLES H. SPURGEON

Men who were led by the hand or groped their way along the wall to reach Jesus were touched by his finger and went home without a guide, rejoicing that Jesus Christ had opened their eyes. Jesus is still able to perform such miracles. And, with the power of the Holy Spirit, his Word will be expounded and we'll watch for the signs to follow, expecting to see them at once. Why shouldn't those who read this be blessed with the light of heaven? This is my heart's inmost desire.

– Charles H. Spurgeon

Available where books are sold.

HONEST FAITH, BY CHARLES H. SPURGEON

The paragraphs of this little book are not supposed to be an argument. It was not my aim to convince an opponent but to assist a friend. How I have personally threaded the labyrinth of life thus far may be of helpful interest to some other soul who is in a maze. I hope that these pages will assist some true heart to say "he fought his doubts and gather'd strength." Let no man's heart fail him, for the prevalent skepticisms of today are but "spectres of the mind." Face them, and they fly.

Available where books are sold.

FOLLOWING CHRIST, BY CHARLES H. SPURGEON

You cannot have Christ if you will not serve Him. If you take Christ, you must take Him in all His qualities. You must not simply take Him as a Friend, but you must also take Him as your Master. If you are to become His disciple, you must also become His servant. God-forbid that anyone fights against that truth. It is certainly one of our greatest delights on earth to serve our Lord, and this is to be our joyful vocation even in heaven itself: *His servants shall serve Him: and they shall see His face* (Revelation 22:3-4).

Available where books are sold.

CPSIA information can be obtained
at www.ICGtesting.com
Printed in the USA
BVHW050120080223
658118BV00012B/404